BIRDS

Reader's Digest
Wild**Britain**

BIRDS

PUBLISHED BY
THE READER'S DIGEST ASSOCIATION LIMITED
LONDON ■ NEW YORK ■ SYDNEY ■ MONTREAL

CONTENTS

HOW TO USE THIS BOOK

The birds described in this book are arranged in their family groups, starting with the more primitive families and ending with the most advanced species – the passerines, or perching birds. Becoming familiar with the family groups will narrow the search to decide which species you have seen. In 'How birds are grouped' (pp. 18-29), all the major families are listed and described, and one or more birds from each group are illustrated. These are the first pages to turn to when you spot an unfamiliar bird. Check through the descriptions and illustrations, to establish in which group the bird belongs. Then turn to the relevant pages in the main part of the book to complete the identification.

For beginners to birdwatching, 'How to identify birds' (pp. 8-17) explains the basic techniques of bird identification. By looking at these pages you can quickly train your eye to spot the essential characteristics of different species.

Sometimes there are marked differences between the plumages of males and females of the same species, or between their winter and summer or adult and juvenile plumages. All the main plumage variations which occur during a bird's stay in Britain are illustrated on the page dealing with that species in the main part of the book.

How to read the maps

Distribution maps in the main part of the book show when and where you are most likely to see each species. The time of year when you see a bird, or the part of Britain where you see it, can be useful clues to its identity.

● **RED DOTS** show the sites of breeding colonies
PURPLE shows the usual breeding range of summer visitors
GREEN shows the areas where a resident species breeds and remains all year round
BLUE shows the areas where a species is found in winter
GREY indicates where passage migrants occur

The winter range of birds and the range of passage migrants are less precise than the breeding range of resident birds or summer visitors because they depend on factors such as the severity of the weather. All birds, particularly passage migrants, may sometimes be seen outside their usual range.

How birds are classified

The modern system of classification groups birds according to their evolutionary relationship with one another, and gives each of them a set of scientific names.

SPECIES The basic unit of the modern system is the species, an interbreeding group of individuals.

GENUS The next, larger division is the genus, a group of closely related species of birds, usually showing obvious similarities. The black-headed gull, for instance, is one of many species belonging to the main gull genus, *Larus* (the name is a Latinised version of the Greek word meaning a rapacious sea-bird, probably a gull). A bird's scientific name always states the genus first, then the species. The black-headed gull is called *Larus ridibundus* – translated literally, the name means 'Gull, laughing'. Genus and species names are always written in italics, but families, orders and other groups are not.

FAMILIES When one genus closely resembles another, they are grouped together to make a family. Gulls are similar in many ways to terns, and both belong to the family Laridae, named after the Greek word for a gull. Their closest relatives are the terns in the family Sternidae. All bird families are grouped into about 30 different orders. The family of gulls and terns belong, together with a great variety of other sea and shore birds, in a number of different families of the order Charadriiformes, named after the Greek for 'plover'.

CLASS All the orders together make up the zoological class *Aves* – 'Birds'.

HOW TO IDENTIFY BIRDS

Knowing what to look for is the key to success in identifying birds. The size, shape and colouring of a bird are the first and most obvious clues to its identity. But how it stands or moves, how it swims or flies, how it sings, feeds or approaches its mate – these and other aspects of its behaviour may be just as distinctive as its plumage. The time of year, and the place where the bird is seen, are also identification points. Some birds only visit Britain at particular times of the year, coming from breeding or wintering grounds that may be thousands of miles away. Other birds are so well adapted to life in a particular habitat that they are only rarely encountered outside it.

MALLARD (FEMALE)

Wing coverts
Primaries
Secondaries
Scapulars
Tertials
Alula (or bastard wing)
Speculum (contrasting patch of glossy secondary feathers in many ducks)

Supercilium
Eye-ring
Moustachial stripe

REED BUNTING (FEMALE)

OYSTERCATCHER

Wing-bar
Rump
Terminal band

HOUSE SPARROW (MALE)

Crown
Forehead
Ear coverts
Bill
Nape
Chin
Back
Throat
Rump
Breast
Upper tail coverts
Belly
Flanks
Tail
Hind claw
Tarsus
Under tail coverts
Toes

Naming the parts

Putting the right name to the feather areas, back and legs of a bird is almost as important as naming the bird itself. For it provides a language in which to discuss birds with other birdwatchers, and it makes for quick and straight-forward note-taking in the field.

Size and shape

When an unfamiliar bird is seen, the first point to note is its size. This can be deceptive so the easiest way to fix this is by comparing it with a bird that is known. A bird can look a different size under different light conditions such as mist or a heat haze. A more distant bird will look proportionately bigger than it really should compared to a nearer one when viewed through binoculars. The shape of a bird can also be very distinctive, but the shape can change according to the conditions; a robin looks much slimmer when alert in warm weather than when resting on a cold winter's day, when it fluffs up its feathers to trap an insulating layer of air and looks much plumper. A long-eared owl when relaxed is relatively plump but when alarmed, it adopts a very tall, thin posture.

HOUSE SPARROW
14.5cm | Heavily built, with thick bill

BLACKBIRD
25cm | Sturdy, adult male's bill yellow

PIED WAGTAIL
18cm | Long and slender with long slim tail

BLACK-HEADED GULL
38cm | Long, pointed wings

WOOD PIGEON
40cm | Heavy-bodied; broad wings

MALLARD
58cm | Stout-bodied; long wings

MUTE SWAN
152cm | Huge bulk, long neck, curved when not in flight

HOW DOES IT BEHAVE?

Some birds run, some walk, some hop, some shuffle.
Some perch high in trees, some stay close to the ground,
some cling to tree-trunks or climb straight up them.
There are birds which are only ever seen singly or in
pairs, and others which invariably feed, roost or travel
in large flocks. Observing a bird's behaviour and
habits may give important clues to its identity.

HOUSE SPARROW *Moves on the ground
by short hops, feeding in noisy groups and
frequently taking dust baths.*

STARLING *Usually seen in flocks
feeding on the ground –
walking, running, probing
for grubs and squabbling.*

DIPPER *Plunges or wades
into the water in search of
food, often becoming
entirely submerged.*

NUTHATCH *Moves in
quick jerks, up, sideways
or, uniquely down on
tree-trunks. Woodpeckers
and treecreepers, by
contrast, only climb
upwards.*

DUNNOCK *Shuffles or creeps
like a mouse along the ground,
with body held almost horizontal
and legs almost hidden.*

LITTLE GREBE *Sometimes jumps with a splash before diving, or hides in the water by lowering its body until only its head still shows.*

GANNET *Dives seawards with wings half closed, then closes them completely just before hitting the water.*

MALLARD *Flies up almost vertically from the surface when alarmed; occasionally dives for food but more often simply dabbles and up-ends.*

Sandwich tern

ARCTIC SKUA *Skuas often feed piratically, chasing other seabirds such as terns or gulls until they drop or disgorge their food.*

MOORHEN *Swims high in the water and patters along the surface before taking off. In water, constantly flicks is tail, showing white tail patch.*

BIRDS IN FLIGHT

To identify a bird in the air, observe whether its flight is fast and direct, or slow and laboured; whether it zigzags or climbs and falls in an undulating pattern; whether it flaps, glides, soars or hovers. The angle at which it holds its wings, and the wings' shape and size, are also important. Other points to look for include whether the bird shows any distinctive wing or tail markings, and how it holds its head and legs.

SWIFT *Very fast flight with rapid beats of long, scimitar-shaped wings; frequently twists and turns in the air, and alternates between flapping and gliding.*

ROOK *Direct and regular flight, with occasional gliding, often in loose, straggling flocks; wings are broad with deeply slotted tips.*

KESTREL *Hovers with tail fanned out and long, pointed wings holding it motionless against the wind; then dives on its prey.*

SWALLOW *Swoops and wheels in the air with easy, flowing wing-beats, often low over ground, catching insects on the wing.*

HERON *Flies slowly on down-curved wings, with head drawn well back, chest bulging and legs trailing behind.*

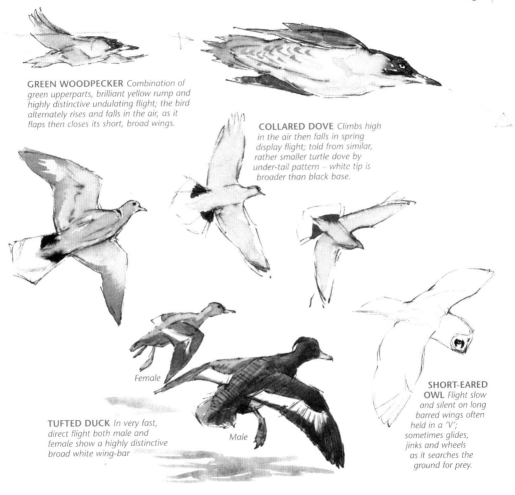

GREEN WOODPECKER *Combination of green upperparts, brilliant yellow rump and highly distinctive undulating flight; the bird alternately rises and falls in the air, as it flaps then closes its short, broad wings.*

COLLARED DOVE *Climbs high in the air then falls in spring display flight; told from similar, rather smaller turtle dove by under-tail pattern – white tip is broader than black base.*

Female

TUFTED DUCK *In very fast, direct flight both male and female show a highly distinctive broad white wing-bar*

Male

SHORT-EARED OWL *Flight slow and silent on long barred wings often held in a 'V'; sometimes glides, jinks and wheels as it searches the ground for prey.*

FIELDMARKS AND OTHER FEATURES

The shape of a bird's tail is often a useful recognition feature, and its tail, like its wings, head, neck and rump, may show distinctive patches of colour; these are what ornithologists call the bird's field marks or field characters. Wing markings may take the form of stripes, bars or patches. The tail may be deeply forked, notched, lyre-shaped, wedge-shaped, rounded or square; and it may have white outer feathers, a white base, bars across it, or a terminal band. The length of a bird's legs and the shape of its bill may also help identification, and give information about how the bird feeds.

House martin

Swallow

Sand martin

SWALLOWS AND MARTINS *In flight one of the swallow's most distinctive identification features is its deeply forked tail. The house martin can be distinguished from the sand martin by its white rump.*

Whinchat

Wheatear

WHINCHAT AND WHEATEAR *Its pure white rump and base of tail with a T-shaped black pattern at the end of the tail make the wheatear easy to identify. Equally distinctive are the white patches on the whinchat's wings and tail.*

REDSTART *The constantly quivering, vivid orange tail instantly identifies a redstart. The male's black mask contrasts with the female's paler face.*

Male

Female

PIED WAGTAIL *The slim, delicate body and long, wagging tail are typical of all wagtails. It is the only black-and-white wagtail in the British Isles.*

Little ringed plover

Ringed plover

RINGED PLOVERS *Little ringed plovers have a prominent yellow eye-ring, the white band above the eye extending above the black of the crown and a narrower black breastband and a white line running across the crown. The legs and bill of the two species are also different in colour.*

SPARROWHAWK *Its strong hooked bill is designed for tearing apart the flesh of its prey. The long legs, armed with razor-sharp talons are for seizing and gripping.*

REED WARBLER *These rather plain brown acrobats of the reed-beds are rarely seen out in the open. The long, thin bill is typical of insect-eaters.*

TREECREEPER *No other small British bird has a long, slim down-curved bill – an adaptation for picking insects from behind bark.*

AVOCET *The slender upcurved bill is adapted for skimming insects from mud or shallow water. The bird's long leaden-blue legs are suitable for wading at the water's edge.*

Juvenile

SHELDUCK *The bill is adapted for sieving marine organisms from the water, or for shearing grass. The webbed feet are adapted for swimming. Young birds (above) are much smaller than the adults.*

Male

BULLFINCH *The stout bill and the male's grey, pink, black and white plumage are unmistakeable. The white rump indentifies the bird in flight. The bill is adapted for cracking seeds.*

THE VARIETY OF PLUMAGES

In many species males are more brightly coloured than females; the females need camouflage when nesting, and males have to defend territory and attract a mate. Young birds may have several colourings before acquiring adult plumage. Adults of many species have colourful breeding plumage and more subdued winter plumage.

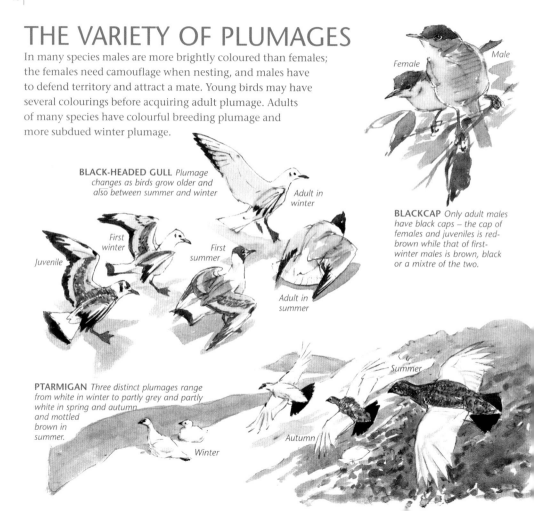

Female

Male

BLACK-HEADED GULL *Plumage changes as birds grow older and also between summer and winter*

Adult in winter

Juvenile

First winter

First summer

Adult in summer

BLACKCAP *Only adult males have black caps – the cap of females and juveniles is red-brown while that of first-winter males is brown, black or a mixtre of the two.*

PTARMIGAN *Three distinct plumages range from white in winter to partly grey and partly white in spring and autumn and mottled brown in summer.*

Winter

Summer

Autumn

IDENTIFYING BIRDS BY SONG

Some birds which look almost identical turn out, when they sing, to be quite different species. Even professional ornithologists find it hard to distinguish between a chiffchaff and a willow warbler, for instance, except by listening to their songs. Song is a bird's way of advertising its presence and identity, whether to attract a mate, to defend its territory, or for some other reason. For the birdwatcher it gives the opportunity to identify birds without even seeing them.

LAPWING *Males deliver their spring song in a twisting, tumbling display flight, mostly between March and May.*

SKYLARK *Song, usually delivered high in the air, may last uninterrupted for five minutes or more.*

TIME OF SIGHTING

Some birds visit Britain in the summer to breed, then fly south to Africa or the Mediterranean before the winter comes. At the same time as the summer visitors are leaving, millions of other birds are flying out of their nesting grounds in the far north, from the Arctic to Siberia, and coming south to Britain to take advantage of the relatively mild winter weather. There are other birds which pass through Britain on migration, on their way between their breeding and wintering grounds. So the time when a bird is seen may be a clue to its identity. The distribution maps in the main part of this book indicate by their colouring whether birds are resident in Britain, summer visitors, winter visitors or passage migrants.

WHITE-FRONTED GEESE *Huge flocks of birds, often flying in formation, arrive in Britain in October and stay until April.*

HOW BIRDS ARE GROUPED

Shape and size are the first clues to a bird's identity, whether you catch only a quick glimpse of the bird, or have time to study it in detail. Even if you cannot instantly put a name to the bird, its general appearance may at least suggest the family group to which it belongs. In this identification key, all the major families of British birds are described, and one or more species from each family are illustrated. Deciding to which family a bird belongs is a great aid to working out which species it is, since this narrows down the choice – often to relatively few birds. With some families, such as gulls, waders and warblers, there are more possibilities – though here, the families are usually comprised of various well defined subgroups – such as plovers, sandpipers, shanks and other waders. The information given about each family includes the habitat where the birds are most likely to be seen, and the size range of the species in each family. To complete an identification, refer to the main descriptions of birds on the pages indicated in the key.

Wildfowl

Swans are the largest of the wildfowl, graceful in the water and powerful in the air. Geese are also large full bodied birds with long necks and short legs. In almost all species of ducks, males are more boldly coloured than females. All wildfowl fly fast and powerfully, frequently maintaining formation.
SEE PAGES: *31-68*

Gamebirds

Heavy-bodied land birds, with stout, short bills, stubby, rounded wings, strong legs and feet adapted for scratching the ground for food. Gamebirds often run in preference to flying. Flight is usually fast and aboured, bursts of very rapid wing beats alternating with brief glides.
SEE PAGES: *69-79*

Swans
Anatidae
120-152cm
Marshes, lakes, rivers

Grouse
Tetraonidae
36-86cm
Mountains, moors, woods

Male

Black grouse *page 72*

Bean goose *page 34*

Partridges and quail
Phasianidae
18-34cm
Farmland, heaths

Mute swan *page 31*

Male

Red-legged partridge *page 74*

Ducks
Anatidae
36-66cm
Coastal and inland water such as ponds and lakes; marshes

Mallard *page 46*

Geese
Anatidae
55-100cm
Marshes, crops

Male

Pheasants
Phasianidae
53-89cm
Fields, woods

Pheasants *page 78*

Divers and grebes

Divers are large, streamlined swimming and diving birds, with stout necks, very short tails and sharply pointed bills. Grebes are smaller, with longer, thinner necks, Both families are clumsy on land, but expert in water. Flight is fast and direct.
SEE PAGES: *80-87*

Tubenoses

Shearwaters and fulmar-petrels are ocean-going birds with long, narrow wings. They are superb flyers that flap and glide on long narrow, stiffly-held wings. Storm petrels are also birds of the open ocean, sometimes seen inland after gales. They flutter over the water, searching for plankton and small marine organisms.
SEE PAGES: *88-90*

Gannets and cormorants

Gannets are large seabirds, often seen diving from the air for fish. On migration, they frequently fly in line, low over the water. Cormorants dive from the surface, chasing fish under water. They often stand with their wings half open, drying out their feathers.
SEE PAGES: *91-93*

Divers
Gaviidae
53-84cm
Coastal and
inland water

Red-throated diver
page 81

Grebes
Podicipedidae
25-48cm
Coastal and
inland water

Great
crested
grebe
page 84

Shearwaters
Procellariidae
36cm
Offshore

Manx shearwater
page 89

Fulmars
Procellariidae
15-47cm
Offshore

Fulmar
page 88

Gannets
Sulidae
90cm
Offshore

Gannet
page 91

Cormorants
and shags
Phalacrocoracidae
76-90cm
Offshore

Cormorant
page 92

Herons

Large wading birds with long necks and legs and long, sharp pointed bills. Their wings are broad and rounded. Flight is slow, with neck kinked and legs trailing behind.
SEE PAGES: *94-97*

Birds of prey

All birds of prey have sharp, hooked bills for tearing meat and strong feet armed with talons for killing and carrying prey. They are masters of flight, some soar, some hover, some stoop or dive on their prey, some fly their prey down. In most species, females are larger than males.
SEE PAGES: *98-121*

Bitterns, herons and egrets
Ardeidae
36-90cm
Marshes, tidal flats

Grey heron
page 95

Bittern
page 97

Kites
Accipitridae
55-60cm
Wooded valleys

Red kite
page 98

Harriers
Accipitridae
40-50cm
Marshes, heaths, fields

Marsh harrier
page 99

Hawks
Accipitridae
30-60cm
Woods, heaths, hedgerows

Goshawk
page 106

Buzzards
Accipitridae
50-58cm
Woods, marshes, fields

Buzzard
page 108

Eagles
Accipitridae
70-90cm
Mountains, moors

Golden eagle
page 111

Kestrel
page 114

Falcons
Falconidae
27-48cm
Woods, mountains, fields, urban areas

Crakes and rails

Medium sized or small long-legged birds, usually living on or near water, they prefer running or swimming to flying. Flight is usually laboured, with legs trailing behind. Crakes and rails are very secretive.
SEE PAGES: *122-127*

Crakes and rails
Rallidae
27-28cm
Swamps, fields

Water rail
page 122

Moorhens and coots
Rallidae
33-38cm
Swamps, freshwater lakes, rivers

Coot
page 127

Waders

Generally plump shore birds, with long legs and bills and pointed wings. In most species male and females are alike. Flight is strong and swift. Most waders are highly migratory, travelling together in huge flocks, sometimes many thousands strong.
SEE PAGES: *128-171*

Oystercatchers
Haematopodidae
43cm
Rocky shores, mud-flats, marshes, fields

Oystercatcher
page 129

Plovers
Charadriidae
19-28cm
Shores, mud-flats, marshes, fields, mountains

Ringed plover
page 141

Sandpipers
Scolopacidae
13-25cm
Shores, mud-flats, marshes, streams, moors

Curlew sandpiper
page 147

Snipe and woodcock
Scolopacidae
27-34cm
Marshes, woods

Snipe
page 156

Godwits
Scolopacidae
38-40cm
Estuaries, marshes, mud-flats

Black-tailed godwit
page 158

Curlews
Scolopacidae
40-55cm
Marshes, mud-flats, moors

Curlew
page 160

Shanks
Scolopacidae
23-30cm
Marshes,
mud-flats

Greenshank
page 163

Phalaropes
Scolopacidae
20cm
Offshore, coasts,
a few on inland
waters

Grey
phalarope
page 171

Skuas
Closely related to gulls and
terns, skuas have white flashes
on slender, dark wings, webbed
feet and often long central tail
feathers. Flight is powerful and
rapid. They are often seen
chasing other seabirds and
robbing them of food.
SEE PAGES: *172-174*

Skuas
Stercorariidae
45-58cm
Offshore, coasts,
moors.

Arctic skua
page 172

Gulls
Very common seabirds, often
found scavenging inland, with
webbed feet and pointed
wings. Plumage is usually grey,
white and black. Males and
females are alike; young birds
are flecked with brown.
SEE PAGES: *175-185*

Kittiwake
page 177

Gulls
Laridae
28-79cm
Coasts, inland,
water, open spaces

Herring gull
page 179

Terns
Graceful seabirds with narrow
wings and forked tails. Bodies
slimmer and bills longer, more
slender and pointed than those
of gulls. Plumage is usually
pale grey or black and white;
caps black in summer. They fly
buoyantly over water, often
hovering before diving for fish.
SEE PAGES: *186-194*

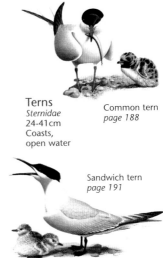

Terns
Sternidae
24-41cm
Coasts,
open water

Common tern
page 188

Sandwich tern
page 191

Auks

Stout, black and white seabirds, with short tails and short, pointed wings. On land, their stance is upright; in the water they are expert swimmers and divers, chasing fish under water. Flight is rapid, with fast wing-beats.
SEE PAGES: *195-197*

Auks
Alcidae
30-42cm
Offshore,
sea cliffs

Guillemot, *page 196*

Pigeons

Stout, rather heavy birds, with small heads and broad, pointed wings, angled at wrist. They often feed in flocks on the ground. Flight is rapid and powerful. with occasional gliding. SEE PAGES: *198-201*

Pigeons and doves
Columbidae
28-40cm
Cliffs, quarries, woods,
farmland, urban areas

Wood pigeon *page 198*

Owls

Mainly night-hunting birds of prey, with round heads, half-hidden hooked beaks and large eyes. They fly silently, hunting for prey and are most often seen at dusk.
SEE PAGES:
202-207

Barn owl
*page
202*

Owls
Tytonidae, Strigidae
22-38cm
Buildings,
marshes, woods

Cuckoos

Our cuckoo is a long-tailed bird with long, pointed wings. Two toes point forwards, two backwards. In flight it can easily be mistaken for a small bird of prey. SEE PAGES: *208-209*

Cuckoo
Cuculidae
33cm
Heaths,
woodland
edges, scrub

Cuckoo *page 208*

Nightjars

Our nightjar is a nocturnal insect-eater, with long wings and tail, short bill but very wide gape and large, flat head. Flight is silent, smooth, wheeling.
SEE PAGES: *210-211*

Nightjar
Caprimulgidae
27cm
Heaths,
woods

Nightjar *page 210*

Kingfishers and relatives

Brilliantly coloured little bird with large head, short tail and long, sharp bill used to catch fish. Dives from perch, or hovers over water before it dive. Flight is fast and direct.
SEE PAGES:
212-214

Kingfisher
Alcedinidae
16.5cm
Streams, rivers,
lakes, ponds

Kingfisher
page 212

Woodpeckers

Colourful, broad-winged birds, with strong, sharp bills adapted for chipping and boring into tree trunks. Short, stiff tail is used for support when climbing trees. Flight is undulating.
SEE PAGES: *215-219*

Woodpeckers
Picidae
14.5-32cm
Woods, hedgerows

Green woodpecker
page 216

Swifts

Dark bird with long, curved wings, almost entirely aerial, flying fast to catch insects. Swifts are often seen in flocks, alternately flapping wings and gliding. SEE PAGE: *220*

Swift
Apodidae
16.5cm
Open spaces, urban areas

Swift
page 220

Larks

Streaky, brown birds of open country, which nest and feed on the ground. Songs are usually delivered in flight. They often gather in flocks when the breeding season is over.
SEE PAGES: *221-223*

Larks
Alaudidae
15-18cm
Coasts, marshes, heaths, fields

Skylark
page 222

Swallows and martins

Highly aerial small birds with long, pointed wings, forked tails, short legs and small feet. They are fast and graceful in flight, and use their wide mouths to catch insects in the air. Plumage is dark above and pale below. SEE PAGES: *224-227*

Swallows and martins
Hirundinidae
12-19cm
Open spaces, sand pits, buildings

Swallow *page 224*

Pipits and wagtails

Small, delicate, slender, long-tailed birds, with fine pointed bills adapted for catching insects. They feed mostly on the ground, running or walking. Flight is undulating.
SEE PAGES: *228-233*

Pipits and wagtails
Motacillidae
14.5-18cm
Open spaces, shorelines, rivers, mountains

Pied wagtail
page 231

Dippers

Our species is plump and short-tailed with white throat and breast. Perches on rocks in streams, walking and diving into the water to catch insects.
SEE PAGE: *234*

Dipper
Cinclidae
18cm
Mainly upland streams, and rivers; a few may visit coast in hard winters

Dipper *page 234*

Wren

Tiny, active bird with short, barred brown tail held cocked upwards. Flight is rapid and direct, whirring on short, rounded wings.
SEE PAGE: *235*

Wren
Troglodytidae
9.5cm
Ubiquitous; woods, gardens, moors, islands

Wren
page 235

Accentor

Streaked, grey and brown bird, with sharp, thin insect-eater's bill. It usually feeds on the ground, moving with a mouselike shuffle, singing from an exposed perch.
SEE PAGE: *236*

Accentor
Prunellidae
14.5cm
Gardens, woods

Dunnock *page 236*

Thrushes

A diverse group of birds, ranging from small, warbler-like birds such as the chats, to the plump, long-legged thrushes. They feed mainly on the ground, eating insects, worms and fruit.
SEE PAGES: *237-250*

Chats and redstarts
Turdidae
14-16.5cm
Heaths, woods

Whinchat
page 242

Wheatear
Turdidae
15cm
Open spaces

Wheatear
page 241

Thrushes
Turdidae
21-27cm
Moors, mountains, woods, marshes, urban areas

Blackbird *page 247*

Old world warblers

All warblers are slim, active, insect-eating birds, mostly with rather dull, brown plumage. Many species are shy and secretive, more likely to be heard than seen. A wide variety of songs helps to distinguish different species.
SEE PAGES: *251-263*

Reed warblers
Sylviidae
12.5-14cm
Reed-beds, thickets

Reed warbler
page 253

Scrub warblers
Sylviidae
12.5-14cm
Heaths, woods, hedgerows

Whitethroat *page 256*

Leaf warblers, goldcrests
Sylviidae
11.5-12.5cm
Woods, hedgerows, gardens

Chiffchaff
page 261

Old World flycatchers
Small birds with rather flat,
pointed bills, adapted for
catching insects in the air.
They perch very upright
watching for insects, then
dart to catch them.
SEE PAGES: *264-265*

Flycatchers
Muscicapidae
12.5-14cm
Woods

Pied flycatcher
page 265

Long-tailed tits
A tiny, very long-tailed
songbird, closely related to
true tits. It is often found
feeding in mixed flocks.
SEE PAGES:
266-267

Long-
tailed tits
Agithalidae
14cm
Woodlands, bushy
commons, waste-
land, gardens

Long-tailed tit
page 267

True tits
Small, very lively and acrobatic
birds, many of them brightly-
coloured. In winter they often
feed in mixed flocks.
SEE PAGES: *268-274*

True tits
Paridae
11.5-16.5cm
Woods,
hedgerows,
gardens,
reedbeds

Great tit
page 269

Crested tit
page 270

Blue tit
page 268

Nuthatch
A bird with a long, sharp bill
for picking insects from the
bark of trees. It can run down
tree trunks as well as up them.
SEE PAGE: *275*

Nuthatch
Sittidae
14cm
Woods and
gardens

Nuthatch
page 275

Treecreepers

Ours is small, brown-backed, with a fine down-curved bill. It climbs spirally up tree trunks, probing the bark for insects, and is usually seen singly.
SEE PAGE: *276*

Treecreeper
Certhiidae
12.5cm
Woods

Treecreeper *page 276*

Crows

Largest of the perching birds, with broad wings and strong bills, legs and feet. Plumage of most is black. Often found in flocks, they walk or hop on the ground.
SEE PAGES:
277-285

Crows
Corvidae
34-64cm
Cliffs, woods, fields, marshes, urban areas

Chough *page 280*

Magpie
page 278

Jay
page 277

Carrion crow
page 283

Old World oriole

Thrush-sized, colourful fruit-eating birds that are very secretive, keeping mainly to tree-tops.
SEE PAGE: *286*

Orioles
Oriolidae
24cm
Wooded areas

Golden oriole
page 286

Shrikes

Medium-sized perching birds with hooked bills adapted for catching small birds, rodents and large insects. Tails are long and rounded, wings broad. Flight is undulating.
SEE PAGE: *287*

Shrikes
Laniidae
17-24cm
Heaths, downland

Red-backed shrike
page 287

Waxwings

Short-tailed, fruit-eating bird with highly distinctive crest on head. They are usually seen in flocks. Flight is fast and direct, similar to the flight of starlings.
SEE PAGE: *288-289*

Waxwing
Bombycillidae
18cm
Hedgerows, woods, gardens with berry-bearing trees

Waxwing *page 288*

Starlings

Our species is a common, medium-sized bird, with speckled, dark plumage, sharp bill and short tail. Flight is rapid and direct. Flies, roosts and feeds in large flocks.
SEE PAGES: *290-291*

Starling
Sturnidae
22cm
Urban areas, woods, grassland

Starling
page 290

Sparrows

Small, sturdy perching birds, with stout, strong bills for cracking seeds. They hop along the ground when feeding, and are highly gregarious.
SEE PAGES: *292-294*

Sparrows
Plocidae
14-14.5cm
Heaths, woods, fields, urban areas

House sparrow
page 292

Finches

Mostly small seed-eating birds with stout, heavy bills. Males are usually more brightly coloured than females. Often flock outside breeding season.
SEE PAGES: *296-306*

Finches
Fringillidae
11.5-18cm
Woods, fields, gardens

Chaffinch
page 296

Siskin
page 299

Crossbill
page 303

Buntings

Similar to finches, with strong, stout bills; but feed mainly on ground instead of in trees. Males are usually more brightly coloured than females.
SEE PAGES: *307-311*

Buntings
Emberizidae
15-18cm
Coasts, swamps, heaths, fields

Snow bunting
page 307

Corn bunting
page 309

Cirl bunting
page 311

Birds

MUTE SWAN

In powerful flight, mute swans present a graceful spectacle and make an exciting, unmistakable sound – a throbbing 'wing music'. Britain's only resident swans, they are quieter than the migrant species but not entirely mute: they hiss and snort when angry, and can even honk weakly. The mute swan is the world's second heaviest flying bird – only slightly behind the Kori bustard of Africa – and can weigh 18kg. A serene appearance belies its aggressiveness when breeding.

Neck outstretched

Wings produce throbbing 'hum'

Orange bill with black knob at base

Curved neck

Mute swan

Cygnus olor

152cm

| J | F | M | A | M | J |
| J | A | S | O | N | D |

Widespread in Britain and Ireland, except extreme north.

BEWICK'S SWAN

Loud honking sounds are heard as V-shaped skeins of Bewick's swans wing across Britain's winter skies. These migrants from Siberia appear on marshland pools, where they feed on seeds and water plants. Bewick's swan is rather goose-like, with a relatively short neck and rounded head. These features, together with the smaller yellow bill patch, help to distinguish it from the larger whooper swan. Its bill patches, like human fingerprints, are peculiar to individuals.

Neck shorter than in other swans

Rounded head

Small, rounded or square yellow patch

Grey-brown

Juvenile

Bewick's swan

Cygnus columbianus bewickii

120cm

J F **M** A M J
J A **S O N D**

Wet meadows mainly in eastern and western Britain and Ireland.

Adult

WHOOPER SWAN

Unlike the mute swan, the whooper is particularly noisy, producing the loud trumpeting call which accounts for its name. On the other hand, the wing-beats of whoopers are quiet, making only a subdued hissing or swishing sound. Although the odd pair may nest in Scotland, they are mainly winter visitors from Iceland. The long thin neck and relatively smaller head plus long wedge-shaped bill (giving a more elongated, sloping profile) distinguish whoopers from smaller Bewick's swans.

Large angular yellow patch

Long thin neck

Family groups graze in fields in winter

Slow, silent wing-beats

Whooper swan

Cygnus cygnus

152cm

J **F** **M** **A** M J
J **A** S **O** **N** **D**

Open waters and farmland in Ireland and Britain; occasionally breeds in Scotland.

Juvenile often paler brown than Bewick's swan

BEAN GOOSE

On marshy grassland in East Anglia or south-west Scotland in winter, a scattered flock of large geese may sometimes appear. At first they resemble greyish-brown farmyard geese, but closer inspection may reveal the darker, browner plumage, long necks and black and orange-yellow bills of bean geese, scarce visitors from northern Scandinavia and Russia. It is unique among our geese in often nesting among the birch and pine trees of northern Europe instead of in open country. The nest is concealed under the trees. Almost all the birds appear in two areas, the Yare Valley, Norfolk and the Slamanna Plateau, Falkirk.

Flocks forage in fields

Juvenile bird has duller legs

Black and orange-yellow bill

Dark head and neck

Long dark head and neck visible in flight

Orange-yellow legs and feet

Bean goose

Anser fabalis

70-89cm

J	F	M	A	M	J
J	A	S	O	N	D

Wet meadows in eastern England and south-west Scotland.

PINK-FOOTED GOOSE

To the wildfowl enthusiast, the sound of an approaching flock of wild and wary pink-footed geese is thrilling music. The calls of individuals vary widely in pitch between 'ang-ang' and 'wink-wink', producing a chorus that has led some experts to call them the most musical of grey geese. Numbers visiting Britain have increased in recent decades, probably because of a reduction in shooting and better protection of their roosts. The visitors to Britain come from Greenland and Iceland.

Often fly in large, noisy flocks

Pale forewing visible in flight

Pink on bill

Grey back

Juvenile browner, with duller legs and feet

Flocks pick over stubble after harvest

Pink legs and feet

Pink-footed goose

Anser brachyrhynchus

60-76cm

J F M A M J
J A S O N D

Farmland in Scotland and England, close to secure estuarine or open water roosts.

WHITE-FRONTED GOOSE

A white blaze on the forehead, black bars across the belly, and orange legs and feet make the white-fronted goose the most distinctive of the grey geese. Young birds, however, lack these characteristic body markings and can be confused with other species. White-fronted geese flock in from their Arctic breeding grounds in Russia and Greenland in late September or early October to winter on the marshlands of Britain and Ireland.

Flocks may also feed at night

Dark fore-wing visible in flight

Greenland race has orange bill (Russian race's bill is pink)

White forehead

Juvenile bird lacks white forehead

Black bars (heavier on Greenland race)

Orange legs

White-fronted goose

Anser albifrons

66-76cm

J **F M A** M J
J A **S O N D**

Marshes and meadows, mainly on western and eastern coasts.

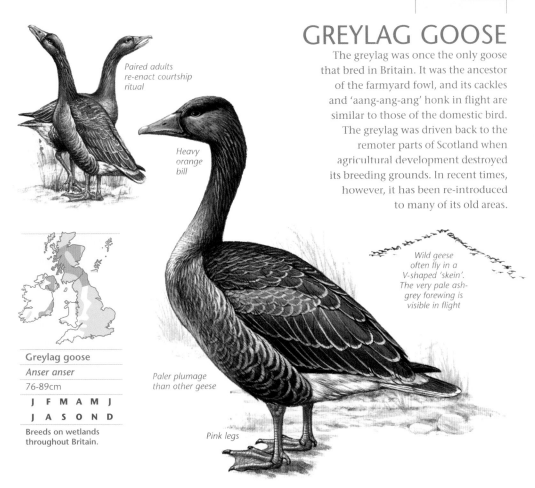

GREYLAG GOOSE

The greylag was once the only goose that bred in Britain. It was the ancestor of the farmyard fowl, and its cackles and 'aang-ang-ang' honk in flight are similar to those of the domestic bird. The greylag was driven back to the remoter parts of Scotland when agricultural development destroyed its breeding grounds. In recent times, however, it has been re-introduced to many of its old areas.

Paired adults re-enact courtship ritual

Heavy orange bill

Wild geese often fly in a V-shaped 'skein'. The very pale ash-grey forewing is visible in flight

Paler plumage than other geese

Pink legs

Greylag goose

Anser anser

76-89cm

J F M A M J
J A S O N D

Breeds on wetlands throughout Britain.

CANADA GOOSE

The first specimens of this very large goose were brought to Britain from Canada in the 17th century as decorative birds for parkland lakes. Later, attempts were made to increase their numbers as game birds; but the Canada goose is too tame and flies too low to make a sporting target. It has now spread out of its parkland homes, and its numbers are still increasing. The nest consists of plant material placed close to water, and is defended aggressively.

Long neck and deep wing-beats

Head lowered nearly to ground level in aggressive display when threatened

Birds stay in safe waters after breeding

Canada goose

Branta canadensis

90-100cm

J	F	M	A	M	J
J	A	S	O	N	D

Grassland by lakes, mainly in England.

White chin-patch

Black head
and neck

Juvenile bird has
duller chin patch
and more mottled
upper parts

BARNACLE GOOSE

In the air or on the ground, family groups of barnacle geese bicker among themselves with a noisy dog-like yapping. Rarely silent for long, they produce the loudest clamour of all when taking flight. Coastal grass is their favourite food, but they will also graze on pasture land. Wintering flocks come to Britain from Spitzbergen or Greenland. Introduced birds now nest locally in England.

White face

Black neck

Wings flicked alternately in mating display

Grey back with white-edged black bars

Grey-barred flanks and white belly

Barnacle goose

Branta leucopsis

58-68cm

| J | F | M | A | M | J |
| J | A | S | O | N | D |

Coastal marshes, mainly in western Scotland and Ireland.

BRENT GOOSE

Small dark Brent geese begin to arrive in eastern and southern England in large numbers during October from their breeding grounds in the Arctic tundra. The young fly south with their parents, often when only three months old. The almost black plumage is broken only by a small, white neck-patch and striking white undertail coverts. In flight Brent geese form long wavering lines, usually low above water or ground.

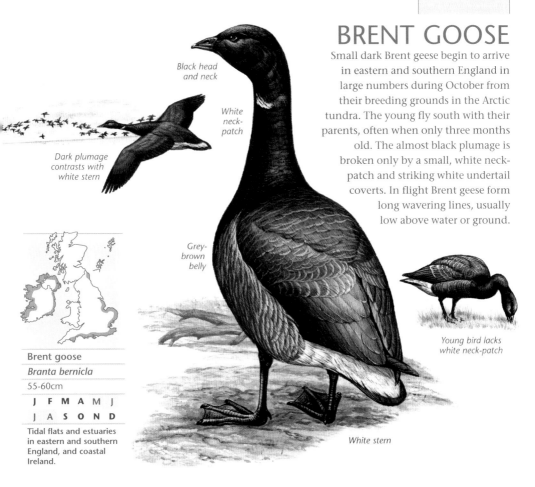

Black head and neck

White neck-patch

Dark plumage contrasts with white stern

Grey-brown belly

Young bird lacks white neck-patch

White stern

Brent goose

Branta bernicla

55-60cm

J F M A M J
J A S O N D

Tidal flats and estuaries in eastern and southern England, and coastal Ireland.

SHELDUCK

Large numbers of these colourful wildfowl leave Britain each summer after breeding to moult in the tidal estuaries of the Heligoland Bight off the north German coast. They return in autumn, and after three to six months their duller eclipse plumage gives way to handsome breeding dress. The nest is often placed in a rabbit hole or similar location. On hatching, the young are led to water and form crèches under the eye of a few resident non-breeding adults.

Dark green head

Chestnut breast-band

Red, knobbed bill

Female similar, lacks bill knob

Head-up 'salute' between pair intending to take flight

Black stripe down centre of belly

Male in breeding plumage

Shelduck

Tadorna tadorna

60cm

| J | F | M | A | M | J |
| J | A | S | O | N | D |

Estuaries all around coast; sometimes inland.

Male

Female

Green wing-patches

MANDARIN DUCK

This wonderfully plumaged little duck is not a native of Europe, for it is an introduced species of 'perching duck' from eastern Asia that has managed to escape from captivity and establish itself as a breeding species. In this country mandarin ducks are to be found on large parkland lakes with well vegetated islands, and undisturbed tree-lined river banks. The nest is placed in holes in trees, or in nest-boxes. The male is unmistakable with his golden ruff and erectile, chestnut-orange wing-fans. Females are drab greyish-brown with whitish 'spectacles'.

White streak on head

White 'spectacles'

Golden ruff

Female

Chestnut-orange wing-fans

Male

Mandarin duck

Aix galericulata

43cm

J F M A M J
J A S O N D

Breeds on lakes and rivers near trees, mainly in southern England.

WIGEON

Although they feed in water and occasionally 'up-end' in typical duck fashion, wigeon are unusual in that they also often graze on grass like geese. They may be seen flying in long irregular lines as they pass by on migration or to winter feeding grounds, when the loud, whistling 'whee-ooo' calls of the drakes can be heard. The majority of birds wintering in Britain are migrants from northern Europe.

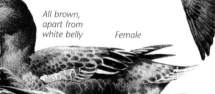

Male

Female

Large white forewing patches

All brown, apart from white belly

Female

Immature male

Male

Chestnut head, pale crown

Wigeon

Anas penelope

45cm

J	F	M	A	M	J
J	A	S	O	N	D

Freshwater pools and estuaries; breeds in north.

RED-BREASTED MERGANSER   GOOSANDER   PINTAIL   SHOVELER   MANDARIN

MALLARD   GADWALL   TEAL   GARGANEY   WIGEON

EIDER   TUFTED DUCK   POCHARD   COMMON SCOTER   SHELDUCK

Identifying ducklings

The easiest way of identifying chicks is by identifying the parent birds, which are usually close by. Most birds whose young leave the nest soon after hatching have their nests on the ground – although mallards sometimes nest in trees and mandarins always do. So how do their chicks, which leave the nest before they can fly, get safely to the ground? As mallard chicks have been seen clinging to their mother's feathers in the water or climbing on to her back in moments of danger, it has been suggested that they may ride to the ground in a similar way. But the correct explanation is that the chicks of such tree-nesting birds, when they scramble out of the nest and drop, fluttering, to the ground, are saved from injury by their extreme lightness.

MALLARD

In town and country, this is the most familiar duck in the British Isles. It is as much at home on a park lake or city canal as it is on a quiet country backwater or remote reservoir. Mallards in towns are very tame, but those in rural areas are wary, for they are much sought after by wildfowlers. Mallards are typical of dabbling ducks in that they feed on the water surface, or by up-ending, and spring straight up into the air from the water.

Males

Moulting male resembles female but bill yellow

Violet-blue wing-patch

Orange-yellow bill

Female

Mallard

Anas platyrhynchos

58cm

| J | F | M | A | M | J |
| J | A | S | O | N | D |

Resident near water in all areas.

Green head

White collar

Yellow bill

Dark maroon-brown breast

Female

Pale belly

Males pull back necks and flick water with bills in courtship displays

GADWALL

Before 1850 this duck was known only as a winter immigrant from parts of its wide breeding range, in north-west Russia and eastern Europe. Today, a few breed in Scotland, Ireland and South Wales and, after a major increase, many hundreds of pairs now nest in England, mostly in East Anglia. Eggs are laid in May in a ground hollow. As with all ducks, the nest is lined with down feathers pulled by the female from her breast.

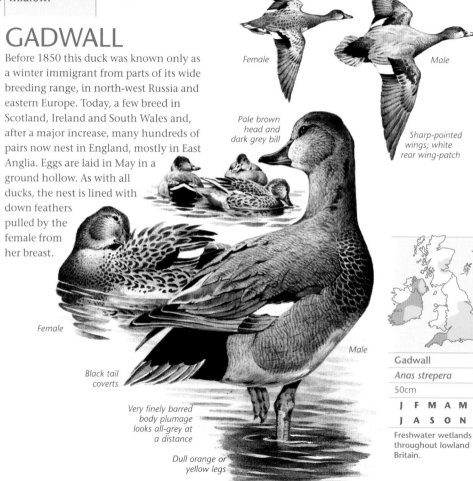

Female

Male

Pale brown head and dark grey bill

Sharp-pointed wings; white rear wing-patch

Female

Male

Black tail coverts

Very finely barred body plumage looks all-grey at a distance

Dull orange or yellow legs

Gadwall

Anas strepera

50cm

J F M A M J
J A S O N D

Freshwater wetlands throughout lowland Britain.

PINTAIL

Both on the ground and in the air, the pintail is the most elegant of the British ducks. Its long slender neck and wings and its long central tail feathers, which can add an extra 10cm to the male's length, make it easy to recognise and attractive to watch. Most pintails spend only winter in Britain and Ireland, and the breeding population is no more than 50 pairs, mainly in scattered sites in Scotland and eastern England. Their nests are less camouflaged than those of other ducks.

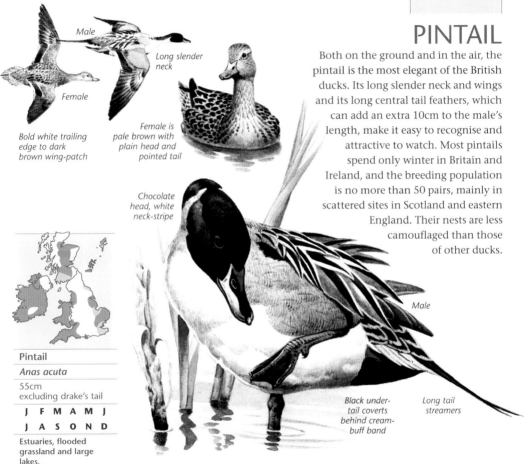

Male

Female

Long slender neck

Bold white trailing edge to dark brown wing-patch

Female is pale brown with plain head and pointed tail

Chocolate head, white neck-stripe

Male

Black under-tail coverts behind cream-buff band

Long tail streamers

Pintail

Anas acuta

55cm
excluding drake's tail

J F M A M J
J A S O N D

Estuaries, flooded grassland and large lakes.

TEAL

With their variegated colouring, male teal are attractive little ducks, but because they are a favourite quarry of wildfowlers they are often too wary to allow close views. Teal fly fast, and spring vertically into the air when alarmed. They are found on small ponds, marshland drains and mud-flats, where they dabble in the shallows for plants and small animals. Only about 3,000 pairs breed in the British Isles, but winter migrants increase the numbers greatly, by up to a quarter of a million birds.

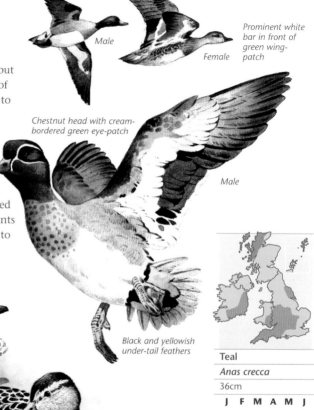

Male

Female

Prominent white bar in front of green wing-patch

Chestnut head with cream-bordered green eye-patch

Male

Black and yellowish under-tail feathers

Female dark brown, with green wing-patch

Male in eclipse

Teal					
Anas crecca					
36cm					
J	F	M	A	M	J
J	A	S	O	N	D

Ponds and marshes; far commoner in winter.

GARGANEY

As they are particularly timid birds, the most frequent sighting of garganey may be of a pair springing from a pool in alarm, the drake showing a blue-grey forewing. The male has a distinctive dry, rattling display call. They are the only British ducks that are summer visitors, migrating to spend winter in Africa. Like other dabbling ducks, in their post-breeding 'eclipse' plumage, drakes resemble ducks with their mottled brown colouring.

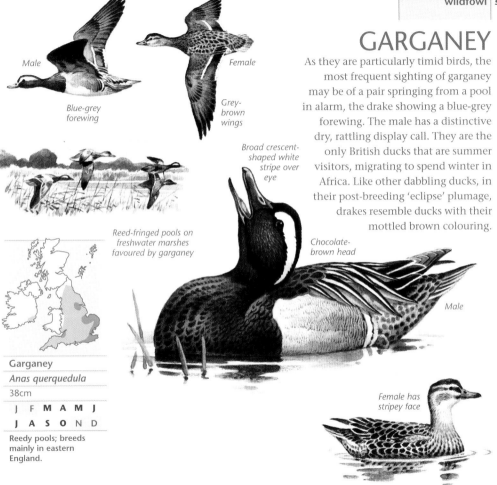

Male

Blue-grey forewing

Female

Grey-brown wings

Broad crescent-shaped white stripe over eye

Reed-fringed pools on freshwater marshes favoured by garganey

Chocolate-brown head

Male

Female has stripey face

Garganey

Anas querquedula

38cm

J **F M A M J
J A S O** N D

Reedy pools; breeds mainly in eastern England.

SHOVELER

The huge shovel-like bill that gives this species its name is used, in the typical manner of dabbling ducks, for sifting large volumes of water to filter out small aquatic plants and animals. The shoveler's patchy distribution is governed partly by the availability of marshy areas with muddy shallows rich in food. The ducklings start to develop the large bill when very young.

Brown head and body with dark brown belly; blue-grey forewing

Female

Male

Blue-grey forewing

Green head can look black at long range

Shovel-shaped bill

White breast; chestnut sides

Shoveler

Anas clypeata

50cm

J F M A M J
J A S O N D

Shallow, richly vegetated waters in most lowland parts of Britain and Ireland.

POCHARD

The brick-red head, black breast and two-tone black-and-grey beak of the pochard drake are distinctive; the female is a dowdy greyish-brown with lighter streaks. Pochards nest in reed-beds and other vegetation bordering fresh water. In winter, sites such as gravel pits and reservoirs are favoured; there the birds dive for molluscs, other animals and plants. The nest may be on the ground, but sometimes a platform is made of water plants built up from the bottom in shallow water. The equally striking red-crested pochard, when seen wild in Britain, is probably an escape from a wildfowl collection.

Red-crested pochard
Netta rufina

Female

Brick-red head

Male

Male

Black breast and rear

Light and dark grey back and wings

Female dull brown, with diffuse pale patches behind bill

Pochard

Aythya ferina

45cm

J F M A M J
J A S O N D

Lowland waters, mostly in eastern Britain and lowland Scotland; winter visitors widespread.

TUFTED DUCK

A stranger to Britain before about 1840, the tufted duck is now the country's most common diving duck. These birds, which have become very tame, have been helped by the development of lakes from disused gravel pits and by the spread of reservoirs. The introduction of the zebra mussel, a favourite source of food, from Russia in the last century also encouraged their spread. Tufted ducks also eat small fish and insects. Males look black and white with a drooping crest; females are brown, with pale sides. In after-breeding plumage drakes become browner. Both sexes show a broad white wing-bar in flight.

Male strikes 'bill down' pose after mating

Short, pointed wings

White sides

White wing-bar

Purple-black head and tuft

Male

Female

Tufted duck

Aythya fuligula

43cm

J F M A M J
J A S O N D

Widespread on fresh water; many immigrants in winter.

SCAUP

This duck's name may have come from its habit of feeding on broken shells, called scaup (probably derived from an old Scottish word, 'scalp' for a mussel bed; its diet is largely made up of mussels, which it obtains by diving under water. In winter it is mainly a visitor from northern Europe, gathering in bays and estuaries; but rivers and lakes are preferred by the very few that have bred in Britain. Wintering birds are usually in flocks; large ones may contain hundreds or even thousands of birds.

Male

Dark green-black head, no crest

White wing-bars

Female

Male

Pale grey back

White patch at base of bill

Female has brown head and upper parts

Scaup

Aythya marila

48cm

J F M A M J J A S O N D

Estuaries and coasts, rarely breeds.

Scaup rest on sand-banks

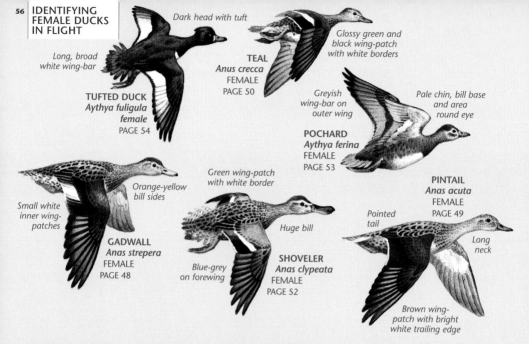

Dark head with tuft

Long, broad white wing-bar

TUFTED DUCK
***Aythya fuligula
female***
PAGE 54

TEAL
Anus crecca
FEMALE
PAGE 50

Glossy green and black wing-patch with white borders

Greyish wing-bar on outer wing

Pale chin, bill base and area round eye

POCHARD
Aythya ferina
FEMALE
PAGE 53

Orange-yellow bill sides

Small white inner wing-patches

Green wing-patch with white border

PINTAIL
Anas acuta
FEMALE
PAGE 49

Pointed tail

Long neck

GADWALL
Anas strepera
FEMALE
PAGE 48

Huge bill

SHOVELER
Anas clypeata
FEMALE
PAGE 52

Blue-grey on forewing

Brown wing-patch with bright white trailing edge

Identifying female ducks in flight

Most male ducks advertise their presence with bold plumage patterns in the breeding season. Females do not need to advertise to attract a mate, and when incubating eggs they must be inconspicuous to avoid predators. In general they have dull brown, streaky plumage, making them difficult to tell apart. The best means of identification is often the speculum – a bright patch on the secondary feathers on the trailing edge of the wing, which usually differs in colour from one species to another. Most ducks fly fast and silently, making identification in flight still harder. Head shape may give a clue, and behaviour may help, as in the almost vertical take-off of the teal and the straggling lines of eiders low over the sea.

Short bill

Green and black
wing-patch with
white border

WIGEON
Anas penelope
FEMALE
PAGE 44

White
belly

MALLARD
Anas platyrhynchos
FEMALE
PAGE 46

Dark,
unmarked
wings

Pale face-patch
and brown cap

COMMON SCOTER
Melanitta nigra
FEMALE
PAGE 60

Large white
wing-patch

Chocolate-
brown head,
white collar

GOLDENEYE
Bucephala clangula
FEMALE
PAGE 62

Large purple-blue
wing-patch with
white borders

Narrow white
wing-bar

Flattened
head profile

Heavy body

EIDER
*Somateria
mollissima*
FEMALE
PAGE 58

Red-brown head
contrasts sharply
with white chin
and foreneck

White inner
wing-patches

Red-brown head
lacks clear-cut division from
white chin and foreneck

White inner
wing-patches

GOOSANDER
Mergus merganser
FEMALE
PAGE 65

RED-BREASTED MERGANSER
Mergus serrator
FEMALE
PAGE 64

EIDER

The soft breast feathers of the eider duck have long been prized by man as a filling for the warm bedcover to which they have given their name – the eiderdown. In nature, the duck plucks the down from her breast to line her nest and protect the clutch of three to ten eggs. In Iceland, the down is still collected from the nests, in strictly controlled quantities, for commercial use. The nest is on the ground, often in an exposed site where the duck's drab colouring acts as camouflage. The male, by contrast, has striking black and white plumage, with tints of pink and green. It has a very distinctive display call, a deep, cooing 'ahr-hoo'. Eiders feed mainly on crabs and molluscs.

Black cap

Green on neck

Male in after-breeding moult, blackish brown and white

Sloping head

Female mottled brown

Black belly

Male

Eider

Somateria mollissima

58cm

| J | F | M | A | M | J |
| J | A | S | O | N | D |

Rocky coasts, breeding in Scotland, northern Ireland, north-west England and the Farne and Coquet Islands, Northumberland.

Female

Black rump

Male

Bill-tossing and neck-jerking are features of the males's courtship display

LONG-TAILED DUCK

The period from the end of September to the end of October sees the arrival in British waters of the wintering population of long-tailed ducks from their northern breeding grounds. The voice of the male is melodious, resonant and far-carrying, and the sound of several males uttering their yodelling 'z-zhulee' calls together has been likened to the distant skirl of bagpipes.

The nest, a mere scrape in the ground, sparsely lined with plant material and down, is usually sited in thick vegetation not far from water. The elongated central tail feathers extending to 12.5cm, which give this duck its name, are borne only by the male.

Female, winter

Plain brown wings

Shallow upstrokes and deep downbeats

Male, winter

Very long tail streamers

Dark cheek-patch

Brown ear-patch

Female

Male, winter

Brown breast-band

Long-tailed duck

Clangula hyemalis

40cm
excluding drake's tail

J F M A M J
J A S O N D

Winters off coasts of northern Ireland, Scotland and eastern England.

COMMON SCOTER

In contrast to having the multi-coloured finery of many drakes, the male common scoter is almost black, with only an orange-yellow patch on its bill. Females are all brown, with a pale face. The 200 or so British and Irish breeding pairs select lochs in mountainous or moorland country, building a nest in a ground hollow near the shore. In winter, when they move to coastal waters, where they dive for molluscs, they are joined by birds that breed in Arctic and sub-Arctic regions. Large flocks are restless, forming long, straggling lines of dark birds flying over the water.

Female

Male

Female

Pale face, dark cap

Female

Yellow patch on bill

Male

All-dark wings

Male

When uneasy, male swims low in water

Common scoter

Melanitta nigra

48cm

J F M A M J
J A S O N D

Around the coast, breeding inland in Ireland and Scotland.

White wing-patches

Female

Male

Red legs show in flight

Orange-yellow bill sides

White wing-patch

VELVET SCOTER

If a few of the birds in a flock of scoters look slightly larger than the rest, and have white patches on their faces and wings, then some velvet scoters have mingled with common scoters. They usually only winter in Britain, around northern and eastern coasts, far from their Arctic and sub-Arctic breeding grounds. Flocks do not usually number more than 12-20 birds. Molluscs such as mussels form the bulk of the velvet scoter's food, which it obtains by diving to the bottom – which may be 6m or more down. Feeding birds usually remain submerged for 20-40 seconds.

Velvet scoter

Melanitta fusca

55cm

J F M A M J
J A S O N D

Mainly a winter coastal visitor. Very rarely seen inland.

Wings slightly open under water. Mussels are a favourite food

Female has two pale face patches and darker face than male

GOLDENEYE

This striking bird is normally a winter visitor from northern Scandinavia and Asia, but 200 or so pairs nest in Scotland, usually in tree holes close to water. The male has black and white plumage and a large angular head with a green sheen; there is a white spot on each cheek. The female is mainly grey except for a chocolate head, white collar and white wing patch. In winter, goldeneyes inhabit sheltered bays and estuaries and inland waters, diving for water animals such as insect larvae, mussels and crabs. Their wings make a loud whistling noise.

Nests in holes in trees or in nestboxes. The provision of special nestboxes has encouraged dramatic growth of the Scottish breeding population.

Courting birds splash and raise bills

White spot on cheek

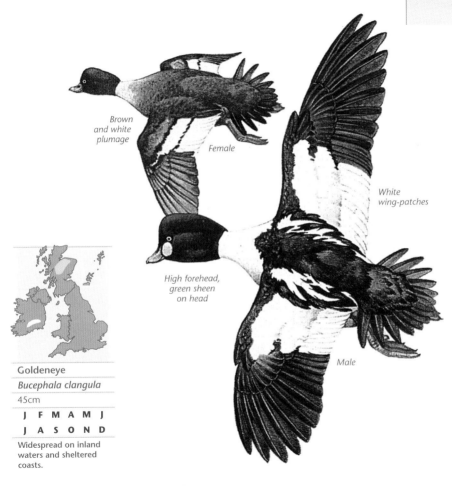

Brown
and white
plumage

Female

White
wing-patches

High forehead,
green sheen
on head

Male

Goldeneye

Bucephala clangula

45cm

J F M A M J
J A S O N D

Widespread on inland
waters and sheltered
coasts.

RED-BREASTED MERGANSER

These ducks are unpopular among fishermen because of their taste for trout and salmon fry. But conservationists point out that they take as many predatory coarse fish, thus helping the game fish to survive. Like the goosander and smew, the red-breasted merganser belongs to a well-defined group of ducks called the sawbills. It has tooth-like projections on its bill, which help it to grasp slippery prey. Since about 1950, it has spread from Scotland into northern England and Wales as a breeding species. It nests by rivers, on the ground in crevices or dense vegetation.

Male

Female

SIngle black line on white wing-patch

Two black lines on white wing-patch

Wispy double crest

Dark green head

Long, thin red bill

Male

Ginger head and short spiky crest

Female

White chin and throat lacks sharp division from brownish head

Black-spotted red-brown breast bordered by black-and-white area

Duckling

Red-breasted merganser

Mergus serrator

58cm

| J | F | M | A | M | J |
| J | A | S | O | N | D |

Breeds by fresh water and on sheltered bays and estuaries, usually in coastal waters in winter.

GOOSANDER

Although the goosander suffers persecution by man because of its liking for small salmon and trout, it has managed to spread from Scotland into England, Wales and Ireland. Goosanders nest in holes in trees, or nest-boxes; also on the ground in rock crevices or under buildings. When breeding they stay close to rivers, but in winter they move to larger stretches of water, mainly inland. The female has a brown foreneck, unlike the similar female merganser.

Male

Female

Large pure white wing-patch

Smaller pure white wing-patch

Dark chestnut head with bulbous or shaggy crest

Dark green head bulges at rear

White chin, sharply demarcated from dark head and neck

Female

Male

Pinkish-white body

Nests in hollow tree or rock crevice

Goosander

Mergus merganser

66cm

J F M A M J
J A S O N D

Upland rivers, wintering also on lowland lakes.

SMEW

From breeding areas in Russia and
northern Scandinavia these small
handsome ducks are scarce winter
visitors to our south-eastern estuaries
and freshwater lakes. Although striking
in appearance, they are not easily or
often seen, for they are scarce as well as
being shy and elusive birds that fly fast.
Their main food is fish, molluscs and
crustaceans, which they catch under
water with the aid of a saw-edged bill.
Recent declines have unknown causes.
Usually only about 100 individuals
winter in the British Isles.

Female

White wing-flashes stand out

Male

Dense flocks fish together

Courting male uses head gestures

Black line at back of head

White crest

Female

Mottled greyish body

Black eye-patches

Chestnut cap; white cheeks

Black centre to back

Black lines on breast

Male

Smew

Mergellus albellus

40cm

J **F** **M** A M J
J A S O **N** **D**

Lakes and reservoirs in eastern and southern England, quite often on smaller waters; sometimes on sheltered estuaries and coasts.

RUDDY DUCK

This species is a member of the stiff-tailed duck family, so called because of their habit of holding the tail erect. A native of North America, it was introduced into ornamental wildfowl collections and subsequently escaped into the wild. So successful were these escapees that ruddy ducks are well established as a British breeding species, and still spreading. They inhabit ponds, lakes and reservoirs, especially those with reedy edges and other vegetation. Nests are woven platforms of vegetation, attached to reeds or other plants.

Male

Plain wings

Brown cap

Stripe on face

Female

Black cap and very bright blue bill; chestnut body and white face

Male

i

A controversial cull is currently under way, aimed at killing all ruddy ducks in the UK. The justification for the cull is that the ruddy duck is spreading to continental Europe where it could threaten the survival of the small, endangered western European population of the scarce white-headed duck by interbreeding and swamping its genes.

Ruddy duck

Oxyura jamaicensis

40cm

| J | F | M | A | M | J |
| J | A | S | O | N | D |

Breeds on vegetation-fringed lakes chiefly in central and southern England.

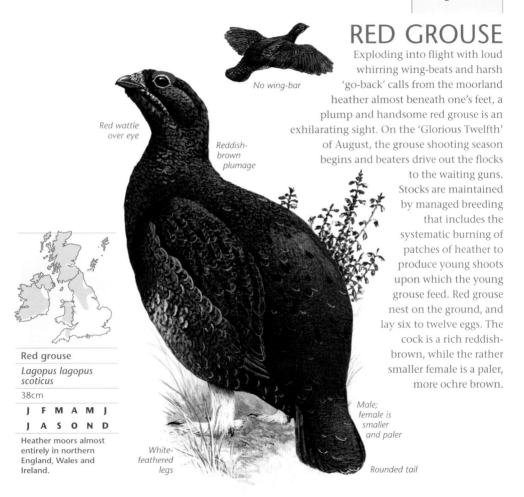

RED GROUSE

Exploding into flight with loud whirring wing-beats and harsh 'go-back' calls from the moorland heather almost beneath one's feet, a plump and handsome red grouse is an exhilarating sight. On the 'Glorious Twelfth' of August, the grouse shooting season begins and beaters drive out the flocks to the waiting guns. Stocks are maintained by managed breeding that includes the systematic burning of patches of heather to produce young shoots upon which the young grouse feed. Red grouse nest on the ground, and lay six to twelve eggs. The cock is a rich reddish-brown, while the rather smaller female is a paler, more ochre brown.

No wing-bar

Red wattle over eye

Reddish-brown plumage

Male; female is smaller and paler

White-feathered legs

Rounded tail

Red grouse

Lagopus lagopus scoticus

38cm

J F M A M J
J A S O N D

Heather moors almost entirely in northern England, Wales and Ireland.

PTARMIGAN

The ptarmigan is the only British bird that changes colour with the seasons to camouflage itself against predators. It changes from greyish-brown and white in summer to almost pure white in winter. A bird of northern climes, this grouse inhabits the high rocky tops and slopes of Scottish mountains, where bilberry, crowberry and heather provide food. The melting snow in May and June sees the start of the breeding season and skirmishes between cocks.

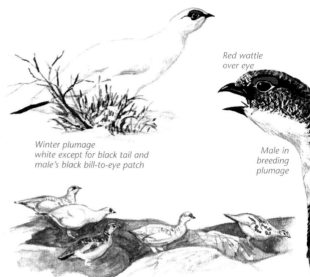

Winter plumage
white except for black tail and male's black bill-to-eye patch

Red wattle over eye

Male in breeding plumage

Moulting birds show a variety of intermediate plumages in autumn

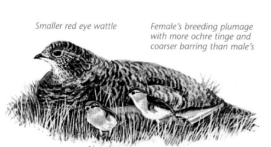

Smaller red eye wattle

Female's breeding plumage with more ochre tinge and coarser barring than male's

Ptarmigan
Lagopus muta
36cm
J F M A M J
J A S O N D
Scottish mountain-tops.

Female in winter lacks black face-patch

Black tail

Summer birds have brown bodies contrasting with white wings

Greyish-brown body looks dark grey at a distance

Ptarmigan feed on sparse tundra vegetation on mountain-tops

White belly and wings

Uses well-feathered feet to dig in snow for buried food

BLACK GROUSE

In the mating season, black grouse gather at a communal courtship display site at dawn and dusk known as a 'lek'. Each male stands with tail fanned and erect, wings spread and drooped. He faces a rival male and utters a prolonged bubbling sound which is sometimes interrupted by a loud, scraping 'tcheway'. Fights take place, with the victorious bird taking on another rival. Females strut nonchalently between the combatants before selecting their mates from the victors. The nest is a shallow scrape in the ground well hidden among grass or heather.

Male

Distinctive lyre-shaped tail; white wing-bar

Female

Notched tail

Female has grey-brown, barred plumage

Glossy black plumage

Male

Lyre-shaped tail

Large red wattle over eye

Black grouse

Lyrurus tetrao

53cm

J F M A M J
J A S O N D

Moorland fringes in northern Britain and Wales often near forests or young plantations.

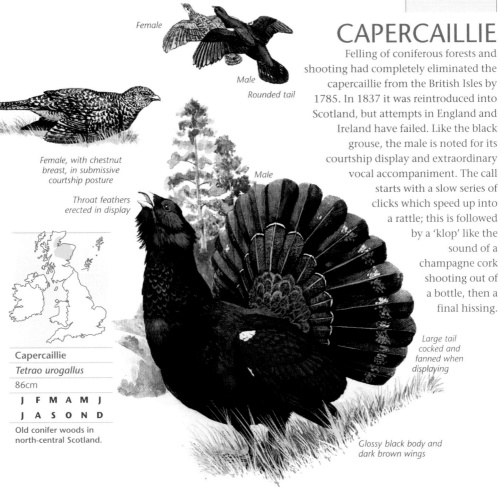

CAPERCAILLIE

Felling of coniferous forests and shooting had completely eliminated the capercaillie from the British Isles by 1785. In 1837 it was reintroduced into Scotland, but attempts in England and Ireland have failed. Like the black grouse, the male is noted for its courtship display and extraordinary vocal accompaniment. The call starts with a slow series of clicks which speed up into a rattle; this is followed by a 'klop' like the sound of a champagne cork shooting out of a bottle, then a final hissing.

Female

Male
Rounded tail

Female, with chestnut breast, in submissive courtship posture

Throat feathers erected in display

Male

Large tail cocked and fanned when displaying

Glossy black body and dark brown wings

Capercaillie

Tetrao urogallus

86cm

J F M A M J
J A S O N D

Old conifer woods in north-central Scotland.

RED-LEGGED PARTRIDGE

This game bird was first introduced deliberately into Britain in 1673, but the birds died out. Successful introductions date from 1770 when many eggs were brought in from France. Further imports occurred in the 19th and 20th centuries, and today the red-legged partridge greatly outnumbers native species. Although introduced for shooting purposes, the red-leg is not a particular favourite of hunters because of its reluctance to fly and preference to remain in cover, where its plumage helps it avoid detection. The nest is placed in vegetation on the ground. If two clutches of eggs are laid, the second just a few days after the first, the male has to care for one of the nests.

White cheeks

Red tail-sides with greyish rump and tail centre

Red bill

Black throat band and shawl-like streaks

Bright red legs

Birds prefer to seek safety in cover, not flight

Red-legged partridge

Alectoris rufa

34cm

J F M A M J
J A S O N D

Heaths and farmland in central and southern England.

Red-brown tail-sides

Coveys fly low and fast, with glides

GREY PARTRIDGE

One of Britain's most popular game birds, the partridge has suffered a huge decline of almost 80 percent in the past 25 years or so in the British Isles, due to agricultural intensification. Shoots take place in early September, when the birds have gathered together in family groups called coveys. By February the surviving birds have paired and taken up territories which the cocks defend vigorously. Courtship often takes the form of a running chase, the cock and hen taking turns to pursue each other. The nest is on the ground. Occasionally two hens, or sometimes a single female will lay in one nest clutches as many as 24-29 eggs.

Male

Orange-brown face

Grey neck and breast

Female has duller markings

Grey partridge

Perdix perdix

30cm

J F M A M J
J A S O N D

Farmland in lowland Britain and Ireland; declining very rapidly.

Brown horseshoe mark

Pinkish-grey legs

PHEASANT · GREY PARTRIDGE · RED-LEGGED PARTRIDGE · QUAIL

CAPERCAILLIE · BLACK GROUSE · RED GROUSE · PTARMIGAN

Identifying game-bird chicks

To human eyes many groups of chicks look alike – mere fluffy bundles of feathers on what seem oversized, stilt-like legs. Closer inspection will show that there are marked differences between the chicks of different species, with the plumage of the adult bird often foreshadowed in the down of the young one. If you want to identify a chick, see if you can spot the parent – which is bound to be nearby. Not surprisingly, most birds whose young leave the nest soon after hatching have their nests on the ground, and the parents of many species, including most of these game birds have evolved distraction displays when danger threatens – feigning a broken wing or some other injury to draw predators away from their young (see pages 342–43).

Longer-winged than other game birds; flies fast with few glides, often dropping quickly into cover, except for migrants

QUAIL

The distinctive liquid 'whit-whit-whit' call of the quail rises from southern cornfields and hayfields in spring and early summer. The bird resembles a tiny partridge; unlike the partridge, it is not a resident but a scarce long-distance migrant from Africa that breeds in small numbers in Britain. In some years it is found scattered over much of Britain in larger numbers than usual, but a typical count of calling males in recent years is about 300 in the UK and less than 30 in Ireland. Its nest, on the ground, is hidden among tall vegetation. The male bird sometimes has more than one mate, sharing a single nest.

Black centre to throat

Cream and brown stripes on head

Streaked back

Paler sandy-brown beneath

Female is drabber, with less distinct head markings, a pale throat centre and a spotted breast

Quail

Coturnix coturnix

18cm

| J | F | M | A | **M** | **J** |
| **J** | **A** | **S** | **O** | N | D |

Lowland farmland throughout the British Isles; numbers fluctuate.

PHEASANT

Though it is Britain's most widespread game bird the pheasant is not a native, for it was introduced from Asia in the Middle Ages. The rearing of pheasants for shooting has encouraged estate owners to maintain wooded habitats, so bringing benefit to other forms of wildlife. However, many foxes, crows and birds of prey have been killed to protect the pheasant from predators. The colourful and handsome males are distinctive with their very long tail, iridescent blackish-green and violet head and metallic coppery sheen on their body, which is marked with dark crescents on breast and flanks.

Red face

Dark green head

Male

Female smaller, shorter-tailed and duller brown

Pheasant

Phasianus colchicus

53-89cm

J F M A M J
J A S O N D

Woods and farms throughout Britain and Ireland, except far north-west Scotland.

Bird can rise steeply in alarm with loud wing-beats and hoarse 'ku-tuk-ku-tuk . . .' alarm calls

Very long, pointed, dark-barred tail

Usually seen on the ground by day, pheasants prefer to roost at night in trees

Some males dark green; some have white neck-ring

RED-THROATED DIVER

In summer dress, the smallest and commonest of our divers sports a blood-red throat patch and a pearl-grey head, which make it unmistakable. Identification in winter is complicated by the fact that the face and red throat are moulted to white, making confusion with other divers a possibility. At this time, however, it may be distinguished by the distinctly upturned bill, the greater area of white on the head and neck, including a little white in front of the eyes, and the white speckled back. During the breeding season the red-throated diver inhabits small, shallow lochs in the Scottish Highlands.

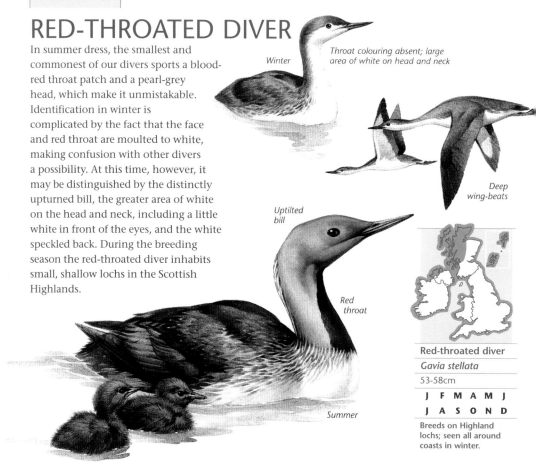

Winter

Throat colouring absent; large area of white on head and neck

Deep wing-beats

Uptilted bill

Red throat

Summer

Red-throated diver

Gavia stellata

53-58cm

| J | F | M | A | M | J |
| J | A | S | O | N | D |

Breeds on Highland lochs; seen all around coasts in winter.

GREAT NORTHERN DIVER

Heavy, straight bill, held horizontally

Winter

Paler, uptilted yellowish-white bill

Great Northern diver
Gavia immer

Slow, powerful wing-beats

White-billed diver
Gavia adamsii

Many cinemagoers will have heard the wailing call of this species, for it is so eerie that recordings are often dubbed into scenes in thrillers to heighten suspense. In Britain this breeding call is unlikely to be encountered in the wild, for the species is mainly a winter visitor from Iceland. The striking greenish and black and white plumage of the breeding season is lost in winter, but the bird is still identifiable by its large size, bulky dagger-like bill and steep forehead. The white-billed diver, a rare vagrant from arctic Russia, is even larger, with paler colouring.

Neck patches

Summer

Large whie-chequered patches above

White spots on back and sides

Great northern diver

Gavia immer

76-84cm

J **F** **M** **A** **M** J

J **A** **S** **O** **N** **D**

Coasts of north-west Britain and western Ireland.

BLACK-THROATED DIVER

One of the most haunting sounds to be heard in the Highlands of north-western Scotland is the wailing cry of the black-throated diver as it asserts ownership of its territory. Unlike the slightly smaller red-throated diver it prefers bigger stretches of water on which to breed, but, like it, moves to the coast in the winter. In summer the adults have large white patches on the black back, and a black throat. After breeding, however, this plumage is lost, leaving only the straighter bill, and sharper demarcation between the dark and light areas of the head and neck, to distinguish this species from its red-throated cousin.

White on lower head and breast less extensive than in red-throated diver

Rather shallow wing-beats

Winter

Darker than red-throated diver, with sharper demarcation between dark and light areas

Black and white neck and back

Summer

Black-throated diver

Gavia arctica

58-68cm

J F M A M J
J A S O N D

Breeds in Highlands; on most coasts in winter.

LITTLE GREBE

During its busy search for small fish or water insects on reedy lakes and rivers, the little grebe resembles a small fluffy ball, diving frequently and bobbing up again. It is often called the dabchick, and is not much larger than a duckling. Its nest is a floating platform of water plants, often close to the bank.

Alarmed bird submerges body

Little grebe

Tachybaptus ruficollis

25-30cm

J F M A M J
J A S O N D

Widespread on lowland fresh water.

Like other grebes, looks tail-less

Summer

Pale patch near base of bill

Chestnut throat

Winter

Dull brown above

Buffish below

No wing-patches

Reluctant to fly, but when it does, patters weakly over low water.

GREAT CRESTED GREBE

In winter plumage white face and neck are conspicuous

Juvenile has white head and neck with black-brown streaks

Before the breeding season, the adults of both sexes acquire conspicuous dark head plumes which they erect during their elaborate courtship display. This involves head-shaking, diving, fluffing out the plumes and presenting each other with water plants while rising from the water breast to breast. During the autumn the plumes are lost, but the bird can still be distinguished by its very white face and neck.

The red-necked grebe ventures to Britain's eastern and southern coasts chiefly when in its drab winter garb. It is smaller and duskier than the great crested grebe.

Courting birds present vegetation and shake heads breast to breast

Great crested grebe

Podiceps cristatus

48cm

| J | F | M | A | M | J |
| J | A | S | O | N | D |

Large lakes, except in far north; also on coasts in winter.

Double crest

Ruff

Chicks carried on back

Winter

White wing-patches fore and aft

White extends over eye

No white above eye

Dusky neck

Red-necked grebe
Podiceps grisegena

BLACK-NECKED GREBE

For breeding, this beautiful small grebe prefers shallow lakes with a rich growth of fringing water plants and plentiful food. It is a rare breeder in Britain. Outside the breeding season immigrants from central and northern Europe join local breeders at estuaries and sea channels as well as larger inland lakes. It is a capable diver and eats small fish and water snails, but in summer prefers insects, grubs and other food taken from the surface or from vegetation. Springtime courtship involves pairs in a variety of displays, including a water dance similar to that of the great crested grebe.

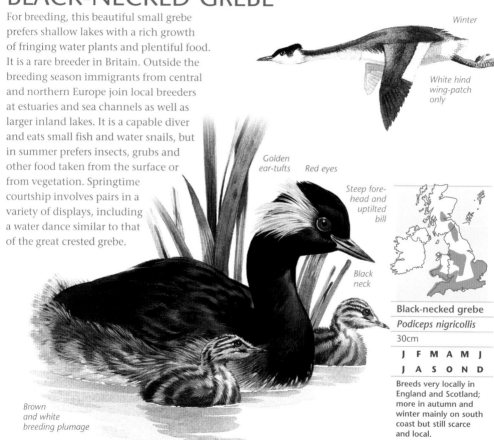

Winter

White hind wing-patch only

Golden ear-tufts

Red eyes

Steep forehead and uptilted bill

Black neck

Brown and white breeding plumage

Black-necked grebe

Podiceps nigricollis

30cm

J F M A M J
J A S O N D

Breeds very locally in England and Scotland; more in autumn and winter mainly on south coast but still scarce and local.

SLAVONIAN GREBE

Straight bill

In winter plumage, cheeks are whiter and head flatter than black-necked grebe

Slavonian grebe

Podiceps auritus

33cm

J F M A M J
J A S O N D

Mainly winter visitor to coasts, but nowhere common.

Horn-shaped golden tufts

As with other grebes, chicks often ride on parent's back

Red eyes

Chestnut neck and flanks

Small white patch on front of wing as well as hind wing-patch.

Small numbers of Slavonian grebes breed on the remoter inland lochs of the Scottish Highlands. After wintering on coastal waters, paired birds return to their breeding grounds and take part in an elaborate ritual of display ceremonies before they mate. The bird's lovely summer plumage is chestnut and black with long golden ear-tufts; in winter, the flatter head, straight bill and white neck distinguish it from the black-necked grebe. Slavonian grebes' main food is water insects and their larvae in summer and small fish in winter.

FULMAR

The population of this superficially gull-like seabird in Britain and Ireland has increased astonishingly since the first pioneers arrived in the Shetlands in 1878. There are now over 500,000 breeding pairs around our coastlines. This expansion was probably aided by the growth of the fishing industry, and the large quantities of offal discarded by fishermen after cleaning their catch. Fulmars spray intruders into their nesting areas with a stinking oil if they approach too close to the rocky ledge where a bird has laid its single egg. This fluid comes from the bird's stomach and is shot out through its nostrils to a distance of up to 2.7m.

Long narrow wings, held stiffly outstretched

Dark smudge in front of eye

Grey back

Heavy bill with tube-shaped nostrils

White head

White underparts catch light as birds bank and turn

Birds with dark-coloured heads and underparts breed in Arctic waters

Courting pairs squat on cliff ledges

Fulmar

Fulmarus glacialis

47cm

J F M A M J
J A S O N D

On most cliffbound coasts; some nest on coastal buildings. More widespread offshore in winter.

MANX SHEARWATER

Using powerful wing-beats, interspersed with long glides in which its wings appear to 'shear' the waves, the Manx shearwater is one of nature's longest and most accomplished travellers. One bird ringed on the Welsh island of Skokholm reached Australia during its oceanic wanderings, while another taken to Massachusetts, 3000 miles across the Atlantic, returned to its chick in just 12½ days. Usually seen in flight, or sitting buoyantly on the sea, the birds come to land only during the breeding season, and then only during darkness to avoid predators, especially large gulls.

White underparts

Huge flocks gather near colonies at dusk

Manx shearwater

Puffinus puffinus

36cm

J F M A M J
J A S O N D

Ninety per cent of the total world population breeds in the British Isles on isolated islands.

Black upper parts

Sits high in water

Long, narrow, stiff wings

The chick has dense down; it does not leave its burrow until it flies, at about ten weeks old.

STORM PETREL

Mariners once believed that the sight of storm petrels following a ship was a warning of an impending storm. In fact the birds were feeding on the marine life disturbed by the ship's wake. The storm petrel spends most of its life on the open sea and has the habit of pattering – apparently 'walking' – on the surface of the water. When breeding, it comes ashore at night, to remote islands off western Britain and Ireland. Colonies vary in size from a few pairs to many thousands. The favourite nesting sites are on beaches, but stone walls are also used as shelter for the single egg.

The larger Leach's petrel is brownish-black with a v-shaped, divided white rump and a forked tail. The underwings are all-dark.

White patches under wings

Sooty-brown plumage

White rump; square tail

Pale wing-bar

Brownish-black plumage

Paler brown diagonal band on inner wing

Leach's petrel
Oceanodroma leucorhoa

Forked tail

Storm petrel

Hydrobates pelagicus

15cm

J F M A M J
J A S O N D

Breeds on remote islands off western Britain and on coast of Ireland.

GANNET

Our largest seabirds, gannets nest in densely packed, noisy, smelly colonies, mostly on islands, on sea-cliffs or adjacent slopes. Over 70 per cent of the world population breeds in the British Isles. Flying out to sea, gannets plummet into the water from as high as 30m to catch their herring-sized prey.

Immature, second year in flight

Yellowish-buff head

Dagger-like bill

Gannet

Morus bassanus

90cm

J F M A M J
J A S O N D

Coastal; breeds mainly on islands (a few at coastal sites) in north and west.

Adult

Cigar-shaped body, head and tail

Third-year bird

Black wingtips

Long narrow wings, spanning almost 2m swept back when diving

CORMORANT

This very big, reptilian-looking waterbird has increasingly been breeding by inland waters as well as on coasts in recent years. Here it has come into conflict with anglers, who accuse it of seriously depleting fish stocks. In reality, there is no hard evidence that it causes long-term damage to fish stocks. Cormorants nest in colonies which sometimes number hundreds of pairs. They build large nests on cliff tops and rocky islets along coasts, and inland in trees beside lakes.

Long, gently sloping forehead

White cheeks

Adult, breeding plumage

Bluish gloss to black body plumage

Bronze gloss on wing feathers, edged black to form scaly pattern

White thigh-patch

Wings held outstretched to dry when perched (like shag)

Cormorant

Phalacrocorax carbo

90cm

| J | F | M | A | M | J |
| J | A | S | O | N | D |

On coasts, and inland on lakes and rivers.

SHAG

Steeper forehead

Short, upcurved crest

Slimmer bill

Juvenile dull brown with little pale feathering below, unlike young cormorant

Adult, breeding plumage

Black all over, with oily greenish gloss

Over the last hundred years the shag has generally increased around British coasts, and it is still doing so in some areas. In summer, the shag's glossy, greenish-black plumage, short crest on the front of the head and smaller size distinguish it from the related cormorant. Its bulky nest of sticks and seaweed, lined with grass, is placed on inaccessible rocky ledges and in sea caves.

Shag

Phalacrocorax aristotelis

76cm

J F M A M J
J A S O N D

Rocky coasts, breeding mainly in west and north; rare inland.

GREY HERON

Its very large size, long legs, and long sinuous neck make the grey heron unmistakable. Walking very slowly or poised alert and motionless in or beside shallow water, this watchful bird waits patiently for a fish, frog or small mammal to come within range of its long, dagger-like bill. Then it stabs the prey and swallows it whole. Herons nest in colonies, usually in tall trees, but sometimes on cliffs and in reed-beds and bushes.

The purple heron is a rare visitor from mainland Europe to reedbeds and other wetlands in southern England. The little egret (page 96) is distinguished by its long head plumes, black legs and yellow feet. It is increasingly colonising south-coast estuaries.

Huge broad wings flap slowly

Long legs trail behind tail

Neck drawn back and chest bulging in flight

Adult early in breeding season; bills and legs brighter, with reddish tinges

Duller, greyer plumage overall including dusky neck

Immature bird

White crown

Black sides to crown end in long, wispy crest

Long, sharp yellow bill

Black streaked neck

Grey heron

Ardea cinerea

90cm

J F M A M J
J A S O N D

Widespread on rivers, lakes, estuaries and seashores.

Long, yellowish-brown legs

Black crown

Black line down very thin ginger neck

Rich purplish-brown on fore-wing

Purple heron
Ardea purpurea

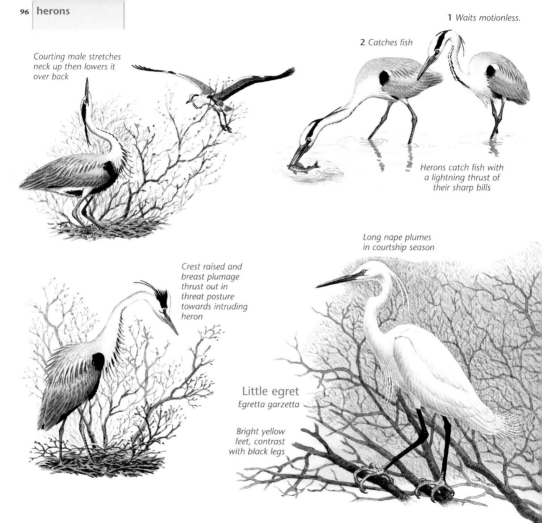

Courting male stretches neck up then lowers it over back

1 *Waits motionless.*

2 *Catches fish*

Herons catch fish with a lightning thrust of their sharp bills

Crest raised and breast plumage thrust out in threat posture towards intruding heron

Long nape plumes in courtship season

Little egret
Egretta garzetta

Bright yellow feet, contrast with black legs

BITTERN

The bittern was exterminated as a British breeding species in 1868 by hunting and habitat destruction. Forty years later migrants from Europe managed to recolonise in Britain, but after a peak in the 1950s they again declined with the drainage of many reed-beds. Bitterns rarely take to the air, preferring to skulk among the reeds where their barred and streaked brown and black plumage makes them extremely difficult to see. Males have a resonant booming 'song' in the breeding season, like the sound made by blowing over the top of a bottle; this can carry up to 5km.

Compact and owl-like in flight

Birds climb reeds by grasping them in clumps

Plumage golden-brown with black markings

Stockier build than heron with shorter, thicker neck and bill

Greenish legs

Bittern

Botaurus stellaris

76cm

J F M A M J
J A S O N D

Breeds in large reed-beds, mainly in eastern England; in winter visits smaller reedbeds, marshes and even ditches.

RED KITE

The child's toy kite was named after this bird because of its habit of soaring and swooping overhead. By the early 1900s gamekeepers – wrongly believing them to be a threat to their birds – had shot and poisoned them to the verge of extinction in Britain. Although strictly protected since 1903 their recovery was slow, and birds were confined as breeders to central Wales. Aided by reintroductions since 1989 in England and Scotland, numbers have now soared to more than 600 pairs. Apart from carrion, the kite eats small mammals, birds and insects.

Pale, finely-streaked head

Long, reddish, forked tail

Male; female is slightly duller

Long wings, often held angled; white patches near tips

Red kite

Milvus milvus

60cm

| J | F | M | A | M | J |
| J | A | S | O | N | D |

Wooded hills in Wales, Scotland and central England; hunts over moorland, in winter over bogs and other open country

Cream shoulders and head

Female

Birds sail along with wings in a shallow 'V'

Juvenile

Chocolate body

MARSH HARRIER

Reduced to a single pair by 1971, this powerful hunter has staged a remarkable recovery. Helped by protection, about 360 females now nest in Britain, chiefly in eastern England. Most migrate, but a few remain near their breeding grounds in winter. At the approach of spring they somersault and dive in mid-air in a courtship display, the male often dropping food to the female, who deftly catches it in her talons. Some males mate with one female, but many are bigamous. Marsh harriers feed on small mammals such as water voles and birds such as moorhens and ducks and their young.

Brown upper parts

Male

Paler head

Grey tail

Streaked reddish and buff underparts

Female is largest of all British harriers

Marsh harrier

Circus aeruginosus

50–58cm

J F M A M J
J A S O N D

Reed-beds and marshes, some also breeding in nearby arable fields mainly in eastern England; on migration in drier, open habitats.

HEN HARRIER

Almost any creature up to the size of a hare or duck is game for the powerful talons of this moorland marauder though much of its prey consists of songbirds and voles. Centuries ago, when the bird was more widespread, it preyed on poultry, and so obtained its name and was persecuted by farmers as well as by gamekeepers who resented its taking of grouse. By the end of the 19th century hen harriers had virtually ceased to breed on the mainland; but thanks to protection some have today recolonised old haunt, though it still faces illegal shooting and poisoning.

Black wing-tips

Male

Pale grey above, white below

White rump

Female rolls over to catch prey dropped by male

Streaked below and barred on wings and tail

Female brown

Female shows white rump in flight

Holds wings in shallow 'V'

Hen harrier

Circus cyaneus

43-50cm

J F M A M J J A S O N D

Breeds on moors and young conifer plantations; widespread in winter, visiting heaths, farmland and marshes.

MONTAGU'S HARRIER

Reduced to from 50-odd pairs in the 1950s to none by 1974, Montagu's harrier now breed in very small numbers. Unlike its close relative the hen harrier, it is only a summer visitor, arriving in April from its wintering grounds in Africa to breed in southern England before returning south in September. The harriers nest on the ground formerly on marshes, heaths and moors and dunes. but now among crops on farms. Their flight is particularly buoyant and graceful.

Wings raised in shallow 'V'

Female

Black wingtips

Grey plumage, narrow black wing-bars (single above, double below)

Male

Rusty streaks on whitish underparts; rump grey, not white

Outer tail feathers barred rust-brown

Female brown with streaks

White rump-patch narrower and more U-shaped than hen harriers

Montagu's harrier

Circus pygargus

40–45cm

J F M **A M J**

J A S O N D

Breeds mainly in fields of barley, wheat and oilseed rape.

Pale patch near
end of wing

BUZZARD
Buteo buteo
DARK FORM:
wing-span 114-140cm
PAGE 108

Holds wings
in shallow 'V'
when soaring

Shorter,
broader
wings than
golden eagle

Short
broad
head

BUZZARD
Buteo buteo
RARER PALE FORM:
wing-span 114-140cm
PAGE 108

Medium-
length tail
often fanned

Finely
barred
tail

Dark 'wrist'
patch

Underparts
variable in
colour

Large birds of prey in flight

If any group of birds warrants the description 'majestic' it is the larger birds of prey, such as the eagles, buzzards, kites, larger hawks and osprey. Though they vary considerably in their size, shape and hunting techniques, all are masters of the air, and a sight of any of them adds excitement to a birdwatcher's day. Birds of prey feed mostly on animals, and they have powerful feet and talons with which to seize their prey and carry it off to their nests or other feeding places. There they use their powerful, hooked bills to tear the flesh apart. The forward-looking eyes of a bird of prey give it binocular vision like a human's, enabling it to judge distance accurately and pinpoint its prey exactly. Its vision is in many ways greatly superior to that of

More deeply 'fingered' wingtip feathers than buzzard's

White on base of tail

GOLDEN EAGLE
Aquila chrysaetos
IMMATURE
PAGE 111

GOLDEN EAGLE
Aquila chrysaetos
ADULT: wing-span
190-230cm
PAGE 112

Head pointed and prominent with powerful bill

Longish tail

White wing-patches

White wing-patches

Entirely dark below

Long wings

ours, enabling it to spot distant fine detail or movement. Long, relatively broad, wings are characteristic of the larger birds of prey. The flight feathers at the tips of the wings are 'slotted', or spread like fingers. This permits low-speed soaring without the danger of stalling; the feathers are tapered to produce the slotted effect.

Wings flat when soaring; smoothly downcurved when gliding

Long wings, often held angled at 'wrist' joint

RED KITE
Milvus milvus
Wing-span 140-152cm
PAGE 98

Plumage varies from pale to dark

Reddish plumage, bold white wing-patches

Long, forked tail, often angled and twisted

Slim, protruding head

Prominent black wrist-patches on wings

Crows often mob birds of prey

Long tail, double bar at base

Long wings, narrow at base and tips, broad at centre

Very pale underparts

HONEY BUZZARD
Pernis apivorus
Wing-span 119-127cm
Rare breeder, migrant
PAGE 109

ROUGH-LEGGED BUZZARD
Buteo lagopus
Wing-span 127-152cm
Rare winter visitor
PAGE 108

Tail whitish contrasting with big dark band at tip

CONTRASTS IN SIZE, SHAPE AND COLOUR

Often, larger birds of prey are seen only as they soar overhead at a great height, borne up by thermals, or rising currents of hot air. Circling in a column of air the bird can gain height rapidly until it becomes little more than a speck in the sky. When it decides to move off it simply closes its wings and tail and goes into a shallow dive.

In this way a bird of prey can cover vast distances with little expenditure of energy. Because they so often soar high above the ground, the most practical way of distinguishing one species from another is from the features visible from below. These include its overall silhouette; the length, breadth and shape of its wings and tail and their relative proportions; the

Very long wings, often angled at 'wrist' joint

GOSHAWK
Accipiter gentilis
JUVENILE
PAGE 106

White eye-stripe and dark cheek patch

Hovers before diving for fish

Deep chest

Streaked underparts

Dusky breast-band

Barred underparts

Long and prominent white undertail coverts, tail round-ended

Short, broad, rounded wings, like adult

Mainly white under-parts including head

GOSHAWK
Accipiter gentilis
ADULT:
Wing-span 99-119cm
PAGE 106

OSPREY
Pandio haliaetus
Wing-span 147-163cm
PAGE 112

size of its head and the extent to which head and neck project in front of the wings. If the bird is lower and near enough to see plumage details, look for the number and thickness of any bars of dark and light colouring on the tail; barring across or streaking along the body; and the pattern of dark and light on the wings. Apart from its overall shape and colour, each species has characteristics of flight and behaviour which help to distinguish it from other species. Its flight may be easy and buoyant, or heavy and laboured. When gliding or soaring, it may hold out its wings above, horizontal with or below the level of the body. It may catch its prey by a high-speed chase, by a rapid pounce or by plunging into the water.

GOSHAWK

This big dashing hawk is a very efficient killer. Swift but controlled, it swoops through the trees to take its prey completely unaware with its powerful talons. The goshawk is much larger than the commoner and similarly plumaged sparrowhawk, and can take wood-pigeons, crows, game birds, rats and hares. Until the 1950s the goshawk was a rare breeding species in Britain, but since then its numbers have increased considerably, aided by escapes from falconry training and by deliberate introductions. The nest of sticks is made high in a tree.

White stripe above eye prominent

Broad, rounded wings

Tail has rounded tip

Long tail, white under-tail coverts

Barred underparts

Juveniles have buff, dark-streaked (not barred) underparts

Goshawk

Accipiter gentilis

50-60cm

| J | F | M | A | M | J |
| J | A | S | O | N | D |

Well-wooded areas in various parts of Britain; also hunts in open habitats.

SPARROWHAWK

A watcher must be alert to spot the quick flurry and chorus of frantic alarm calls as this yellow-eyed predator darts down a woodland ride or along a hedgerow, scattering terrified birds. Although most prey is captured with the advantage of surprise, the sparrowhawk is capable of overtaking a quarry by its sheer speed and agility. The nest is a flattened bulky platform of sticks, sometimes based on an old nest of another species. Males are much smaller than the females.

Female larger and duller, with brown upper parts

Broad, rounded wings

Tail longer than goshawk's, square-ended

Long yellow legs

Male has blue-grey upper parts

Barred, reddish-brown underparts

Sparrowhawk

Accipiter nisus

30–38cm

| J | F | M | A | M | J |
| J | A | S | O | N | D |

Nests in woodland, hunts along woodland edges and hedges.

BUZZARD

A familiar sound in hilly country in western and northern Britain is the loud mewing 'kiew' of a buzzard as it soars, apparently without effort, or hovers over a wooded hillside. This keen-sighted bird scans the ground for small mammals, especially rabbits and voles. Buzzards prefer open hillsides with wooded valleys and tall trees or cliffs on which to breed. They build a large nest of sticks which is decorated with greenery.

The bigger rough-legged buzzard, an occasional visitor to eastern Britain from Scandinavia, is larger, longer-winged, with an almost white tail with at its end 1-4 dark bands (the last one broad). It hovers far more often than the buzzard.

Wings held in shallow 'V'

Wing-tip feathers separated like fingers when soaring

Wings pointed when gliding

Broad, rounded wings, typically pale below with brown on forewings and trailing edge

Fan-like tail, with many narrow bars

Short neck and broad head

Pale underparts

Rough-legged buzzard
Buteo lagopus

White tail, black band at tip

Buzzard

Buteo buteo

50-55cm

J F M A M J
J A S O N D

Hills and wooded valleys in western and northern Britain, now spreading into central and eastern England.

EUROPEAN HONEY BUZZARD

Head held forward on slim neck

Long tail

Male has mainly grey head

Narrow head

The main diet of this species is unusual for a bird of prey, consisting mainly of wild bees and their honey, and other insects. It may, however, be supplemented by small mammals, nestling birds, lizards and frogs. The honey buzzard is one of our rarest breeders, for no more than 50 or so pairs nest each year, scattered throughout Britain. Despite its similarity to the buzzard, it is not a true buzzard, being more closely related to the kites.

Distinct bars on tail, broad band near tip

Honey buzzard

Pernis apivorus

50-58cm

| J | F | M | A | M | J |
| J | A | S | O | N | D |

Summer visitor to woodlands, especially with conifers, in various parts of Britain.

WHITE-TAILED EAGLE

In 1907 these huge birds ceased to breed in the British Isles, after long years of persecution and disturbance by man. Until recently, the only sightings were of the odd birds that strayed from their breeding grounds in Scandinavia. A reintroduction programme has now resulted in more than 30 breeding pairs becoming established in Scotland. Nests are massive stick constructions on a sea-cliff or tree. The white-tailed eagle is more of a scavenger than the golden eagle and takes rotting fish stranded on the shore as well as live prey. It is not closely related to the golden eagle but is instead a member of the sea eagle family.

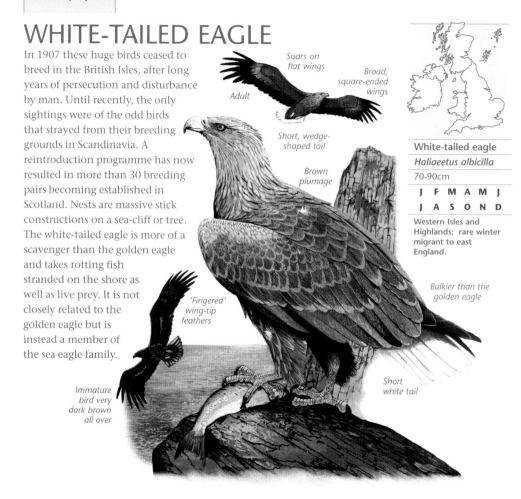

Soars on flat wings

Adult

Broad, square-ended wings

Short, wedge-shaped tail

Brown plumage

'Fingered' wing-tip feathers

Immature bird very dark brown all over

Bulkier than the golden eagle

Short white tail

White-tailed eagle

Haliaeetus albicilla

70-90cm

J F M A M J J A S O N D

Western Isles and Highlands; rare winter migrant to east England.

GOLDEN EAGLE

In flight the 'king of birds' gives the impression of unequalled power and control, with its broad wings spanning up to 2.3m and the wingtip feathers spread as though feeling for the currents of rising air which will bear it up to its mountain-top stronghold. It kills prey such as grouse, seabirds, hares and foxes, and also eats carrion. Formerly more widespread, the golden eagle is now restricted mainly to remote mountain areas in Scotland. Pairs build a large stick nest on a rocky ledge or isolated tree; two eggs are laid, but normally only the first-hatched eaglet survives.

Golden feathers on back of head and nape

Body dark-brown; pake panel on inner wings

Golden eagle

Aquila chrysaetos

76-89cm

J F M A M J
J A S O N D

Mountains and islands in Scotland, apart from a pair that has bred in Cumbria and reintroduced birds in north-west Ireland

Tail base slightly paler with dark bars

Long wings

White patches on wings and tail

Immature

Soars with wings in a narrow 'V'

Adult

Entirely dark below

OSPREY

An osprey making a kill is a spectacular sight. Fish make up almost its entire diet, and a hunting bird flies over water at a considerable height, with alternate spells of flapping and gliding, until it spots a fish near the surface. It pauses, sometimes hovering briefly, before turning and plunging feet first with partly closed wings. In the 1950s a pair of ospreys bred near Loch Garten in Scotland after an absence of 50 years. Since then their numbers have increased to more than 160 pairs. They build bulky stick nests in tall trees, close to large expanses of water.

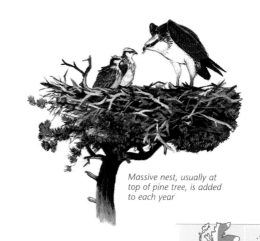

Massive nest, usually at top of pine tree, is added to each year

Long wings sharply angled at wrist joint in flight; can look rather gull-like

Osprey hovers about 30m above water, then plunges on prey

Osprey

Pandion haliaetus

50-58cm

J	F	M	**A**	**M**	**J**
J	**A**	S	**O**	N	D

By lakes and rivers in Scotland; now spreading to England and Wales.

Dark brown upper parts

Paler edged feathers on upper parts

Juvenile

Dark mark through eye

Variable breast-band of brown streaks, usually more prominent in female

Tiny spikes on soles of toes give grip on slippery fish

White crown and underparts

KESTREL

A medium-sized, brownish falcon hovering above a roadside verge often catches the eye of the passing motorist – and usually means death for a vole or some other some small mammal below. Lift-like, the bird drops by stages, finally pouncing and grasping with its talons. Kestrels, along with sparrowhawks, are Britain's most widespread birds of prey. They favour open country, but also flourish in urban areas with parks as well as motorway verges. They nest in holes in trees, tall buildings or nest-boxes. The adult male sports a russet back and wings, offset by a dove-grey crown and tail. Females are brown with dark spots.

Pairs sometimes breed in nest-boxes

Chestnut back

Long, usually pointed wings

Grey head

Male

Grey tail with black band at tip

Female is brown, heavily spotted above, with mainly rusty-brown tail

Young male has barred grey tail

Kestrel

Falco tinnunculus

34cm

| J | F | M | A | M | J |
| J | A | S | O | N | D |

All types of open country including urban areas; most numerous in rough grassland.

MERLIN

Flying low and fast with quick, shallow wing-beats, the male merlin, little larger than a mistle thrush, quarters the moors in search of its prey – mainly small birds such as meadow pipits, skylarks and stonechats. On sighting a quarry, the merlin rises above it, then drops to sink its talons into its victim. Unfortunately, this beautiful small falcon has declined considerably over the past two centuries.

Broad-based, pointed wings

Male

Shorter tail than kestrel

Female dull brown above, buff-white streaked dark below

Male

Blue-grey upper parts

Male

Merlin often takes prey in level flight

Streaked, reddish-brown underparts

Black tail-band

Male stonechat

Merlin

Falco columbarius

27-33cm

J F M A M J
J A S O N D

Breeds on moorlands and coasts; winters in lowlands, mainly on coastal salt marshes and farmland.

Short, broad, blunt-ended wings

SPARROWHAWK
Accipiter nisus
ADULT MALE:
wing-span 60-68cm
PAGE 107

SPARROWHAWK
Accipiter nisus
ADULT FEMALE:
wing-span 70-79cm
PAGE 107

Long square-ended tail

Much smaller than female

Chest less deep than goshawk

Brownish-grey barred underparts

Red-brown barred underparts

Smaller birds of prey in flight

Although the smaller birds of prey lack the sheer bulk and power of the larger species, they share the same features of a sharp, hooked bill, long needle-sharp claws on powerful toes, and fierce-looking eyes that face forward to give binocular vision. Their dominance over other bird species gives them an air of majesty which has encouraged royalty and noblemen through the ages, to pursue the sport of falconry. The birds' imperious qualities were appropriate to their owners' position in life, and lent rulers added nobility in the eyes of their subjects.

The smaller birds of prey fall into two distinct groups or families, the hawks and the falcons. The hawks are members of the same family as the larger birds of prey - the eagles, buzzards and

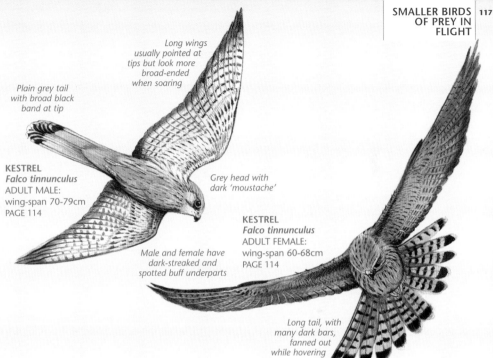

Long wings
usually pointed at
tips but look more
broad-ended
when soaring

Plain grey tail
with broad black
band at tip

KESTREL
Falco tinnunculus
ADULT MALE:
wing-span 70-79cm
PAGE 114

Grey head with
dark 'moustache'

KESTREL
Falco tinnunculus
ADULT FEMALE:
wing-span 60-68cm
PAGE 114

Male and female have
dark-streaked and
spotted buff underparts

Long tail, with
many dark bars,
fanned out
while hovering

their relatives - but the falcons are grouped in a family of their own. Hawks have short, rounded wings, quite different from the falcons' longer, tapered, sharply pointed wings.

WINGS SHAPED FOR DIFFERENT HABITATS
Difference in wing shape is linked to the habitats in which the birds live and to their modes of hunting. Hawks such as the sparrowhawk are birds of woodland or countryside with scattered trees; here, long wings would be a disadvantage when darting and manoeuvring between tree trunks and interlacing branches. Within the hawk family, the goshawk can be half as big again as the sparrowhawk and the female is larger than the male, but it is not always easy to

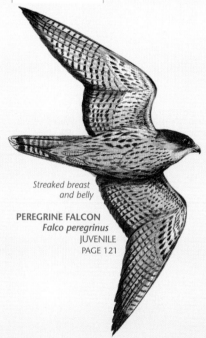

Streaked breast and belly

PEREGRINE FALCON
Falco peregrinus
JUVENILE
PAGE 121

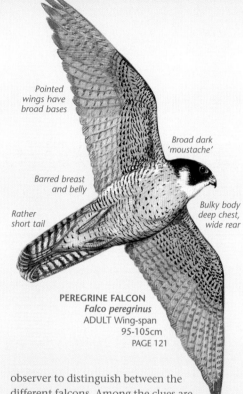

Pointed wings have broad bases

Broad dark 'moustache'

Barred breast and belly

Rather short tail

Bulky body deep chest, wide rear

PEREGRINE FALCON
Falco peregrinus
ADULT Wing-span
95-105cm
PAGE 121

judge size at a distance. Features such as dark barring of plumage and relative length of tail may then be clues.

Falcons are mainly birds of open country, with long wings designed for high-speed flight and quick acceleration, though some also have the manoeuvrability of the hawks. Habitat, hunting technique and silhouette all help the observer to distinguish between the different falcons. Among the clues are the kestrel's persistent hovering; the little merlin's moorland habitat and dashing low-level flight; the hobby's swift-like silhouette, speed and agility; and the peregrine's size, heavy build, short tail and rarely witnessed, breathtaking 'stoop' or dive on to its prey. Colour and pattern

*Relatively
short, broad-
based wings*

*Female is bigger,
grey-brown above, with
dark-streaked buff breast
and tail with several
broad, dark bars*

*Long, sickle-
shaped wings*

*Boldy streaked
breast and
belly*

*Fast, direct
flight*

*Reddish
thighs*

*Medium-
length tail*

*Black
'moustache'*

*Medium-
length square-
ended tail*

MERLIN
Falco columbarius
ADULT MALE:
Wing-span 60-68cm
PAGE 115

HOBBY
Falco subbuteo
ADULT:
Wing-span 73-84cm
PAGE 120

*The hobby's speed enables it to catch
agile, fast-flying swallows on the wing.
As well as small birds it often catches
dragonflies, eating these while flying*

of plumage may also be visible, though
immature birds and females often have less
striking plumages than adult males. The
adult male kestrel is the only British species
with a rich reddish-brown back and wings
and a slate-grey tail with a single dark bar
near its tip; while the adult hobby has
reddish thighs and a streaked breast.

HOBBY

For speed, grace and agility in flight the hobby has few rivals, even among its fellow falcons. Whether delicately picking a dragonfly out of the sky, or swooping down to seize a swallow in full flight, it presents a breathtaking spectacle. Hobbies are great travellers, for they spend the winter in Africa before migrating north to breed in Britain. They lay their eggs in the old tree nest of a crow or large bird. The hobby's plumage is striking, and in flight its long wings, angled back, give it the appearance of a giant swift.

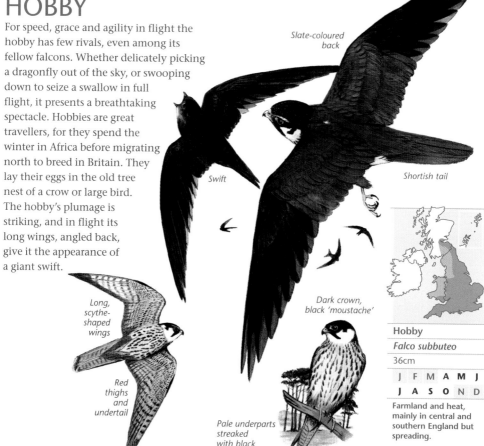

Slate-coloured back

Swift

Shortish tail

Long, scythe-shaped wings

Red thighs and undertail

Dark crown, black 'moustache'

Pale underparts streaked with black

Hobby

Falco subbuteo

36cm

J F **M A M J**
J A S O N D

Farmland and heat, mainly in central and southern England but spreading.

Whitish beneath, barred with black

Dark crown

Juvenile brown above, streaked below

Broad-based pointed wings

Cheek 'moustache'

Grey upper parts

Breeds mainly on high rock ledges

PEREGRINE FALCON

When hunting, the peregrine is a mere speck in the sky as it keeps a lonely, circling watch for prey. When it sights its victim it suddenly snaps back its wings and dives towards it in a rapid 'stoop' estimated as reaching up to 180mph (290km/h). If contact is made the quarry – typically a pigeon or duck – is usually killed instantly as the falcon strikes it with its toes bunched.

Courting male loops the loop after mock dive at female

Peregrine falcon

Falco peregrinus

38-48cm

J F M A M J
J A S O N D

Breeds on cliffs and crags; now also on tall buildings as well.

WATER RAIL

The calls of the water rail from dense waterside vegetation include sounds like a pig squealing with fear. A glimpse, however, is enough to identify the bird, for its long, red bill, black-spotted brown upper parts and black and white striped flank markings on slate-grey underparts are distinctive. The water rail's long legs and toes are adapted for walking on floating vegetation, and its narrow body helps it to slip between close-growing stems.

The rare spotted crake, a summer visitor to a few marshes in Britain, differs in having a much shorter bill, white spots on its upper parts and buff under its tail.

Usual flight weak and fluttering

Brown wings

Dangling legs

Brown back

Striped flanks

Male

Female has duller colouring; chicks black

White spots; buff under-tail

Short bill

Spotted crake
Porzana porzana

On migration, flight is stronger, with legs extended behind tail.

Normally secretive, when migrating or in winter, the birds may be much bolder, coming right out into the open

Red bill

Juvenile colouring is duller, with black barring on breast

Long toes

Water rail

Rallus aquaticus

28cm

J F M A M J
J A S O N D

Reed-beds and marshes in most of Britain and Ireland, except north-west Scotland.

CORNCRAKE

Although fields of corn are sometimes used by the corncrake as breeding grounds, its common name is less appropriate than the alternative, land rail. Formerly the bird nested in large numbers throughout the British Isles, and its double 'crex crex' grating call, like a stick drawn across a notched piece of wood, was a feature of summer days and nights in country areas. Today, due to drainage and agricultural intensification, the corncrake is a rarity, and its numbers are still decreasing.

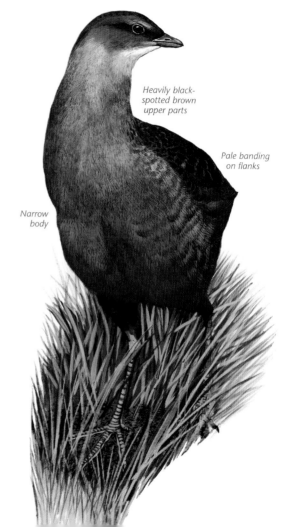

Heavily black-spotted brown upper parts

Pale banding on flanks

Narrow body

The nest is a pad of dead grass built on the ground among long grass or weeds. The female alone incubates the eggs

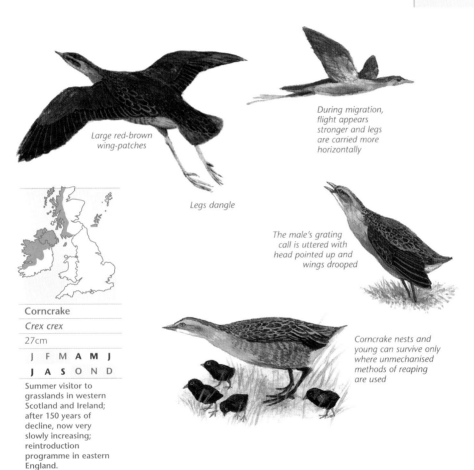

Large red-brown wing-patches

During migration, flight appears stronger and legs are carried more horizontally

Legs dangle

The male's grating call is uttered with head pointed up and wings drooped

Corncrake nests and young can survive only where unmechanised methods of reaping are used

Corncrake

Crex crex

27cm

J F **M A M J**
J A S O N D

Summer visitor to grasslands in western Scotland and Ireland; after 150 years of decline, now very slowly increasing; reintroduction programme in eastern England.

MOORHEN

In spite of its name this is not a moorland species; the name comes from the Anglo-Saxon *more*, meaning mere or bog. It eats water plants, insects, spiders, worms and other invertebrates which it picks from the surface or by up-ending. Like its cousin the coot it is aggressive in defence of its territory, attacking any encroaching neighbour with feet and bill. The feet are exceedingly long, but have no webbing, so its swimming action is jerky and laboured. If alarmed, the bird will dive and stay submerged with only its bill above the water. The nest is usually a woven structure, anchored to aquatic vegetation.

As with coot needs long pattering run to take-off

Dark brown and black plumage

White undertail and flank streak

Bare red forehead shield

Green legs with small red 'garter'

Juvenile has dull brown body and pale throat and belly

Chicks have bare red crown and blue patch above eye

Moorhen

Gallinula chloropus

33cm

| J | F | M | A | M | J |
| J | A | S | O | N | D |

Watersides of all sorts, from ponds and ditches to large lakes and rivers; often feeds in fields.

COOT

In striking contrast to their black plumage, coots of both sexes have an area of bare skin on their forehead that matches their shiny white bill. Males squabble frequently over territory, with the white shield playing an important part in their aggressive displays. It is held forward, low on the water, with wings and body fluffed up behind, presenting a menacing impression. As two birds approach each other they produce an unmusical ringing call – rather like a hammer striking a steel plate. The coot's diet consists mainly of plant material for which it dives to bring to the surface to eat.

Long legs trail in flight

All-black body

White bill and forehead shield

Huge lobed feet

Coot

Fulica atra

38cm

J F M A M J
J A S O N D

Large lakes and reservoirs, slow-moving rivers; feeds in fields; in winter also on estuaries.

Juvenile has pale throat and breast

Chicks have bare red and blue head with ruff of orange down

STONE CURLEW

The plaintive 'cooorr-leee' cry of this odd-looking wader hangs hauntingly over the chalk downs and sandy heaths of south and east England. It is most active between dusk and dawn. Snails, slugs and insects are its main food, although it may also take larger prey such as frogs and field mice. Stone curlews winter in southern Europe and North Africa. After a long major decline, there has recently been a slight recovery, aided by conservation; over 250 pairs now breed.

Courting birds face opposite ways

Large staring yellow eyes

Shortish, heavy black-tipped yellow bill

Striking wing pattern revealed in flight

Two white wing-bars

Long, sturdy yellow legs

Birds leap and wave wings in communal displays in autumn

Stone curlew

Burhinus oedicnemus

40cm

| J | F | M | A | M | J |
| J | A | S | O | N | D |

Downs and heaths in south and east.

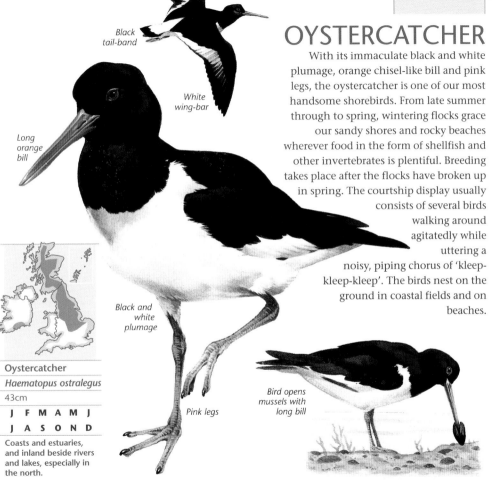

Black tail-band

White wing-bar

Long orange bill

OYSTERCATCHER

With its immaculate black and white plumage, orange chisel-like bill and pink legs, the oystercatcher is one of our most handsome shorebirds. From late summer through to spring, wintering flocks grace our sandy shores and rocky beaches wherever food in the form of shellfish and other invertebrates is plentiful. Breeding takes place after the flocks have broken up in spring. The courtship display usually consists of several birds walking around agitatedly while uttering a noisy, piping chorus of 'kleep-kleep-kleep'. The birds nest on the ground in coastal fields and on beaches.

Black and white plumage

Oystercatcher

Haematopus ostralegus

43cm

**J F M A M J
J A S O N D**

Coasts and estuaries, and inland beside rivers and lakes, especially in the north.

Pink legs

Bird opens mussels with long bill

AVOCET

This striking black and white wader owes its presence in Britain to the Second World War. By the early 1890s it had ceased to breed among the brackish pools and low islets of the east and south-east English coast when the land was reclaimed. During the war, however, access to the coast was restricted and avocets returned. Now strictly protected, they thrive in many colonies in east and south-east England. Avocets feed on tiny invertebrates which they sift from the water by sweeping movements of their distinctly upcurved bills. In a ritual aggressive display, known as 'grouping', pairs of birds join in groups, often in a circle with lowered heads. Fighting sometimes occurs. Avocets are bold defenders of eggs and chicks, chasing off larger birds with noisy calls.

Legs project well behind tail

Black wing and back bars and wing-tips

Black cap

Thin, black, strongly upturned bill

The female shelters the eggs with outstretched wings

Avocet

Recurvirostra avosetta

43cm

J F M A M J
J A S O N D

Breeds mainly on coastal lagoons in east and south-east England; winters also in south-west England.

Mainly white plumage is dazzling in good light

Very long blue-grey legs

Pairs form circle in ritual aggression display

Good swimmers, avocets also up-end to feed like ducks

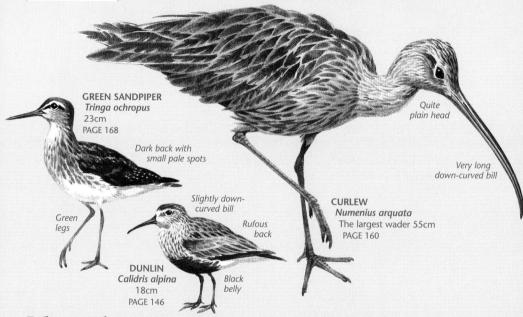

GREEN SANDPIPER
Tringa ochropus
23cm
PAGE 168

Dark back with
small pale spots

*Quite
plain head*

*Very long
down-curved bill*

*Green
legs*

*Slightly down-
curved bill*

*Rufous
back*

CURLEW
Numenius arquata
The largest wader 55cm
PAGE 160

DUNLIN
Calidris alpina
18cm
PAGE 146

*Black
belly*

Identifying waders by size

Wading birds are confusing to the eye because
they are often similar in shape – long-legged,
long-necked and thin-billed. They do, however,
differ in size, habitat and feeding habits. The
waders shown are painted to scale, in their
summer plumage.

Among the larger waders, the biggest of all is
the curlew, about the size of a mallard overall,
but longer and more slender in all parts. Striding
across mud-flats it probes deep with curved bill,
but on upland grasslands it snatches insects
from the surface. The tall black-tailed godwit
may wade up to its belly to probe the
underwater mud of estuary or coast with its
long, straight bill; but it breeds in wet, grassy
meadows. Brackish lagoons are the home of the

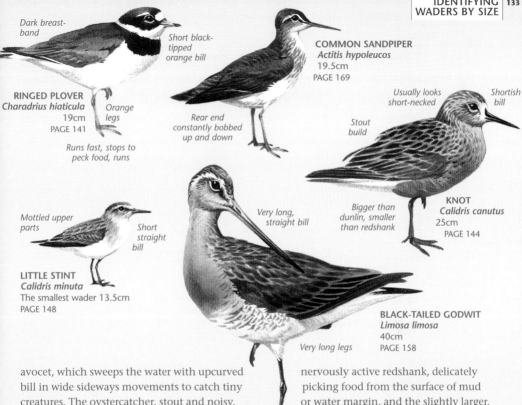

Dark breast-band

Short black-tipped orange bill

COMMON SANDPIPER
Actitis hypoleucos
19.5cm
PAGE 169

Usually looks short-necked

Shortish bill

Stout build

RINGED PLOVER
Charadrius hiaticula
19cm
PAGE 141

Orange legs

Rear end constantly bobbed up and down

Runs fast, stops to peck food, runs

Mottled upper parts

Short straight bill

Very long, straight bill

Bigger than dunlin, smaller than redshank

KNOT
Calidris canutus
25cm
PAGE 144

LITTLE STINT
Calidris minuta
The smallest wader 13.5cm
PAGE 148

BLACK-TAILED GODWIT
Limosa limosa
40cm
PAGE 158

Very long legs

avocet, which sweeps the water with upcurved bill in wide sideways movements to catch tiny creatures. The oystercatcher, stout and noisy, ranges widely from meadows and moors to seacoasts, probing and digging with its strong orange bill.

Among the middle-sized birds, about as big as town pigeons, are the nervously active redshank, delicately picking food from the surface of mud or water margin, and the slightly larger, more elegant greenshank that feeds more vigorously, running through puddles with quick sideways movements of its bill. The knot is nearly as big, but stouter and more compact, and feeds in close-packed flocks

Brown above, strongly streaked below

Medium length orange-red legs

REDSHANK
Tringa totanus
28cm
PAGE 162

Black and white plumage

Long, stout, bright orange bill, flattened from side to side

Sturdy pink legs

OYSTERCATCHER
Haematopus ostralegus
43cm
PAGE 129

Complex mottled and barred plumage pattern

Broad dark bars on nape

Long, tapering bill

WOODCOCK
Scolapax rusticola
34cm
PAGE 157

Short legs

Extremely long, straight bill

Striped head and upperparts

SNIPE
Gallinago gallinago
27cm
PAGE 156

on estuary mud-flats with a steady downward jabbing of bills. Two long-billed waders avoid mud-flats: the woodcock, unlike any other wader, mainly feeds in damp areas of woodland, while its smaller relative, the snipe does so among vegetation in marsh, damp fields and water's edge. Both probe deeply into soil or mud with their long straight bills, which, like those of many other waders, are richly supplied with sensitive nerve-endings at their tips.

HOW SMALLER WADERS FEED AND BEHAVE
Smaller waders include the dunlin, which is about two-thirds the size of the knot, similar in build, and also feeds in flocks on mud. In summer it seeks food on wet upland moors.

Grey upper parts

White below with streaks on head and breast

AVOCET
Recurvirostra avosetta
43cm
PAGE 130

Black cap

Long, slender black up-curved bill

GREENSHANK
Tringa nebularia
30cm
PAGE 168

Long, greenish legs

Long crest

Golden speckles

GOLDEN PLOVER
Pluvialis apricaria
Northern form has more black than southern form 18cm
PAGE 138

Black face, chest and belly in summer breeding plumage

Face markings and breast black

Back and inner wings dark green with blue and purple gloss

LAPWING
Vanellus vanellus
30cm
PAGE 142

There are three more or less dunlin-sized but more slender species: the common and green sandpipers are seen in summer on the edges of inland waters; and the rare grey phalarope is usually found swimming rather than wading.

The plovers are plump birds with a 'run-and-snatch' method of feeding. The dunlin-sized ringed plover lives on bare sand, shingle or gravel by water, while the bigger, pigeon-sized lapwing occupies meadows, fields and marshes; and the golden plover – a bird of similar size – breeds on high moorland and winters on coastal marshes. Smallest of all British waders is the sparrow-sized little stint, which runs about very fast on muddy estuaries and feeds with a very rapid action.

DOTTEREL

Unusually in the bird world, the male dotterel has duller plumage than the female, who takes the lead in courtship displays. This gives him camouflage as he incubates the eggs – for the female, after laying, loses interest in her offspring and leaves all parental duties to the male. She may then go off to mate with another male. In addition to visiting birds, a few dotterels breed on barren mountain tops above about 800m in the north of Britain. They feed on insects, other invertebrates and seeds. The population is small, including about 630 breeding males.

White stripes above eyes meet at back of head

Plain upperwings

Winter plumage much duller

Summer

Male, duller than female, guards and broods young

Male feigns broken wing to distract predators from nest

Adult female has a plump body and a small head. In both sexes, chestnut underparts and white breast-band are distinctive

Grey chest

White breast-band

Chestnut underparts

Female

Juveniles lack the adult's chestnut belly; and have an indistinct breast-band and pale-edged feathers on their upper parts

Dotterel

Charadrius morinellus

22cm

J F **M A M J**

J A S O N D

Scarce breeder on northern mountains, mostly in Scottish Highlands; migrants pause at traditional sites especially in East Anglian fenlands.

GOLDEN PLOVER

The plaintive 'klew-ee' call of the golden plover is a characteristic sound of the high moors where it breeds in summer. During late summer, the adult's black belly moults to white, and some birds migrate south as far as Spain or even into northern Africa to spend winter. More northerly nesting birds, from Iceland and Scandinavia, move south to Britain to winter, and form large flocks that roam about, sometims together with flocks of lapwings, landing in lowland grassland, arable fields or marshland sites, where they feed on grubs and insects. The flocks often roost in ploughed fields.

Gold speckles

Black belly in summer, more extensive in male (and individual variation)

Flocks seen in spring may include birds already in summer plumage.

Grey plover hunched

Golden plover upright

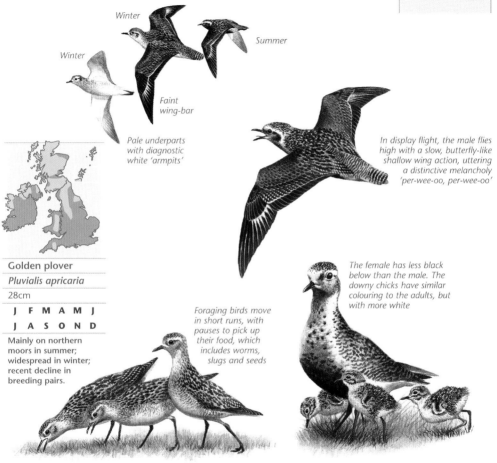

Winter

Winter

Summer

Faint
wing-bar

Pale underparts
with diagnostic
white 'armpits'

In display flight, the male flies
high with a slow, butterfly-like
shallow wing action, uttering
a distinctive melancholy
'per-wee-oo, per-wee-oo'

The female has less black
below than the male. The
downy chicks have similar
colouring to the adults, but
with more white

Golden plover

Pluvialis apricaria

28cm

J F M A M J
J A S O N D

Mainly on northern
moors in summer;
widespread in winter;
recent decline in
breeding pairs.

Foraging birds move
in short runs, with
pauses to pick up
their food, which
includes worms,
slugs and seeds

GREY PLOVER

Most grey plovers are mottled grey
and white when they visit Britain in
autumn and winter from breeding
grounds in the Arctic tundra. Some,
in handsome breeding plumage,
occur in late spring or early autumn.

*Mottled grey and
white, bolder wing-bar
than golden plover*

Summer

Winter

Winter

*Black
under-
parts*

*Diagnostic
black
'armpits'*

*At high tides
plovers at
different
stages of
moult roost
in flocks on
sandbars or a
short distance inland*

*The birds forage
like golden
plovers, but
unlike them they
usually feed on
muddy or sandy
shores. They
eat quite large
crabs as well as
molluscs and
marine worms*

*Striking black,
white and silver
breeding plumage
appears from
late spring*

*The adult in winter is
mottled grey and white.
The bill is heavier than
the golden plover's. Both
sexes look very similar.
The call is different – a
longer, three-syllabled
'hee-oo-wee'*

Grey plover

Pluvialis squatarola

28cm

| J | F | M | A | M | J |
| J | A | S | O | N | D |

Mainly on large muddy
estuaries, also on sandy
shores; rare inland.

Bright yellow eye-ring

All-dark bill

No wing-bar

White wing-bar visible in flight

Little ringed plover
Charadrius dubius

White wing-bar visible in flight

RINGED PLOVER

When feeding, ringed plovers run along the seashore for a few paces, pause, then suddenly tilt forward to seize food from the mud with a swift dip of the beak. The adult is brown and white, distinctly marked about the head and breast with black; the base of the bill and the legs are bright orange. Juveniles have indistinct black markings, incomplete breast-bands and pale legs. The little ringed plover is smaller, with a yellow eye-ring, an unbroken white stripe over the eyes and across the forehead, and dull, pinkish or yellowish legs. It is a scarce summer visitor to inland waters (especially disused gravel pits and industrial sites) in England and South Wales.

Black-tipped orange bill

Black breast-band

Ringed plover
Charadrius hiaticula
19cm

J F M A M J
J A S O N D

Coastal areas all around Britain and Ireland, scarce in south-west England; breeds inland in parts of England and Scotland.

Mottled plumage disguises chicks on sand or shingle

Orange legs

LAPWING

The lapwing is sometimes known as the green plover because of its iridescent back plumage, or the peewit because of its distinctive call. At one time, it was a common sight on farmland, but numbers have fallen dramatically due to modern farming methods. The male's territorial display – involving twisting, rolling dives – is a delight to watch. It is accompanied by a loud song incorporating bubbling, wheezy variations on its call note, as well as a throbbing sound produced by its wing-beats.

Male

Broad, round-ended wings

Long, wispy crest is unique

Black tail-bar

Female

Black breast-band

Metallic-green back

White wing-tips

Male

Orange undertail

Purple gloss on shoulders

White underparts

A male lapwing making a nest-scrape

Lapwings will often join forces to drive off an invading crow from their territory

Lapwings in flight outside the breeding season often travel in large flocks in somewhat ragged formations

Lapwing

Vanellus vanellus

30cm

J F M A M J
J A S O N D

Open country throughout most of Britain and Ireland. Breeds chiefly on farmland, especially among fields with bare soil and short grass; some on wet grassland, marshes and other damp habitats; visits estuaries and shores in winter.

A male lapwing in his 'tumbling' display flight

Female has shorter crest and white mottling on black of forehead

KNOT

The knot standing at the tide's edge has been likened to a tiny King Canute standing on the shore and ordering the tide to retreat. Its common name, however, is probably derived from the bird's call, a low-pitched 'knut'. This medium-sized, stocky, short-necked wader is a winter visitor to coasts, especially big estuaries, where many thousands often gather to probe for food that consists of marine invertebrates. A few late departees in May sport the splendid brick-red breeding plumage, lost in winter; others show traces.

Straight bill

Grey above

Breeding plumage

Brick-red underparts

White below

Winter

Summer

Winter

Pale rump

Narrow white wing-bar

Juvenile has pale-edged feathers on upper parts and a pale apricot tinge below

Knot

Calidris canutus

25cm

J F M A M J
J A S O N D

Coastal mud and sand-flats, especially on estuaries.

SANDERLING

With frenetic bursts of energy, flocks of these little waders scurry along the seashore, their heads down in pursuit of retreating waves. They snatch a few morsels of food, then race back in advance of the next wave to avoid getting washed off their feet. If disturbed they rise with a chorus of liquid 'twick, twick' calls and move along the beach to resume their feeding. In winter, sanderlings can be found on most sandy shores in Britain, but in summer they are birds of the high Arctic where they breed. In spring the plumage changes from almost white to reddish, marked with black on the back, head and breast.

Sanderling

Calidris alba

20cm

J F M A M J
J A S O N D

Especially on sandy coasts and estuaries; small numbers in summer

Winter

White wing-bar

Summer

Pale grey back

Dark shoulder

Short, straight black bill

Winter

White underparts

Black legs

Rusty head and body

Summer

DUNLIN

These little birds blend so well into the background of Pennine and Scottish moorland that they are not easily seen, though they breed there in quite large numbers. The nest is a neat little cup, hidden in a grass tussock. After breeding, our dunlins migrate in autumn to spend winter in southern Europe and northern Africa. They are replaced in Britain and Ireland by more northerly breeders, which come to spend winter here. In their grey and white winter plumage they can be seen in their thousands feeding on coastal mud-flats on molluscs, crustaceans and worms.

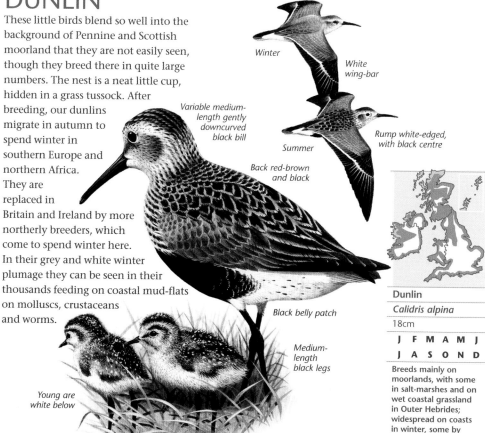

Winter

White wing-bar

Summer

Rump white-edged, with black centre

Variable medium-length gently downcurved black bill

Back red-brown and black

Black belly patch

Medium-length black legs

Young are white below

Dunlin

Calidris alpina

18cm

J	F	M	A	M	J
J	A	S	O	N	D

Breeds mainly on moorlands, with some in salt-marshes and on wet coastal grassland in Outer Hebrides; widespread on coasts in winter, some by inland waters.

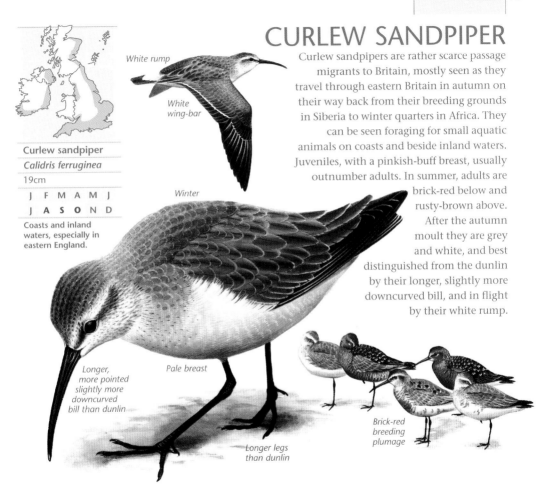

CURLEW SANDPIPER

Curlew sandpipers are rather scarce passage migrants to Britain, mostly seen as they travel through eastern Britain in autumn on their way back from their breeding grounds in Siberia to winter quarters in Africa. They can be seen foraging for small aquatic animals on coasts and beside inland waters. Juveniles, with a pinkish-buff breast, usually outnumber adults. In summer, adults are brick-red below and rusty-brown above. After the autumn moult they are grey and white, and best distinguished from the dunlin by their longer, slightly more downcurved bill, and in flight by their white rump.

Curlew sandpiper
Calidris ferruginea
19cm

J F M A M J
J A S O N D

Coasts and inland waters, especially in eastern England.

White rump

White wing-bar

Winter

Longer, more pointed slightly more downcurved bill than dunlin

Pale breast

Longer legs than dunlin

Brick-red breeding plumage

LITTLE STINT

The smallest wader occurring regularly in Britain, the little stint is a scarce short-stay autumn visitor, passing through on its way from its breeding grounds in northern Russia and Siberia to winter in Africa. Most little stints seen in Britain are juveniles, distinguished by two prominent V-shapes on the back. At this season adults are grey above and white below, with faint streaks on the breast. Temminck's stint, a rare passage visitor to freshwater margins in May, has white outer tail feathers, a finer bill and yellow-green legs.

Winter

Summer

White wing-stripe

Greyish-brown back

White outer tail feathers

Temminck's stint
Calidris temminckii

V-shaped marks on back of juvenile

Mottled russet back

Short straight bill used in pecking very fast at surface of mud as it shuffles jokily along

Grey outer tail feathers

Moves very fast on 'twinkling' black legs

Little stint

Calidris minuta

13.5cm

J F M A **M** J
J **A** **S** O N D

Marshes, freshwater margins and coastal mud-flats, especially on east coast; very few in spring.

PURPLE SANDPIPER

Frequently seen on piers, groynes and slipways at high tide, the plump purple sandpiper is a winter visitor favouring rocky shores and shingle beaches, feeding on insects, molluscs, worms and crustaceans. It is often seen with turnstones. The slate-grey upper parts have a purplish sheen; the short legs are usually dull yellow or orange, and the bill is black with a yellow to orange or reddish base. The contact call is a twittering 'weet-wit' and there is a trilling alarm call. This sandpiper, is a very rare breeder in Britain. Adults have more variegated plumage with rufous on back and 'shoulders' and duller legs in summer.

Narrow wing-bar

Dark above: slate-grey, with purple sheen

Tail projects beyond wing-tips

Slightly curved bill

Yellow-ochre legs, shorter than dunlin's

Short swims are taken

Purple sandpiper

Calidris maritima

21cm

J F M A M J
J A S O N D

Rocky coasts all around Britain and Ireland in winter; a few pairs nest on Scottish mountains.

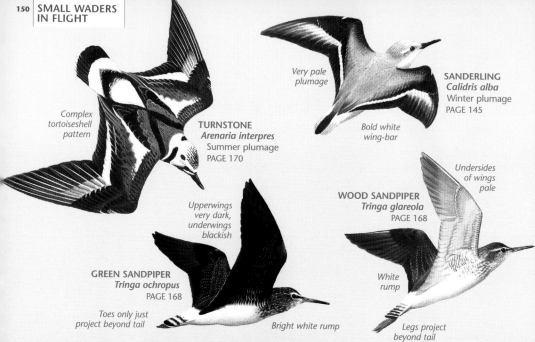

Complex tortoiseshell pattern

TURNSTONE
Arenaria interpres
Summer plumage
PAGE 170

Very pale plumage

SANDERLING
Calidris alba
Winter plumage
PAGE 145

Bold white wing-bar

Undersides of wings pale

WOOD SANDPIPER
Tringa glareola
PAGE 168

Upperwings very dark, underwings blackish

GREEN SANDPIPER
Tringa ochropus
PAGE 168

Toes only just project beyond tail

Bright white rump

White rump

Legs project beyond tail

Small waders in flight

The best way to identify these fast-flying and rather similar birds is by the presence or absence of white patterns and markings on their wings and rumps. Most species also have recognisable, short call-notes, which they constantly utter in flight. Other identification features are the flight patterns and habitats of the different groups. For instance, although most small waders are found on shores and mud-flats, the snipe is a mainly inland bird and is usually seen in marshy areas and on watersides. The common snipe is an extremely long-billed bird that rises steeply in flight; it has some white on its outer tail feathers and its call is a harsh 'scarp'. The smaller jack snipe, which is a much scarcer passage migrant and winter visitor, is a quieter bird that is far more reluctant to fly.

Extremely
long, straight
bill

SNIPE
Gallinago gallinago
PAGE 156

Pair of pale
'tramlines' down
each side of face

**CURLEW
SANDPIPER**
Calidris ferruginea
Winter plumage
PAGE 147

White rump

Narrow
white
wing-bar

DUNLIN
Calidris alpina
Winter plumage
PAGE 146

Narrow white
wing-bar

Grey sides
to tail

Thin,
white
wing-
bar

Dark streak
on rump contrasts
with white sides

Greyish
sides
to tail

Narrow, thin
wing-bar

TEMMINCK'S STINT
Calidris temminckii
Winter plumage
PAGE 148

White sides
to tail

LITTLE STINT
Calidris minuta
PAGE 148

FRESHWATER AND COASTAL BEACHES

Three species of sandpiper are found beside fresh
water, and of these, the common sandpiper
tends to skim just above the surface. It has short,
downward-flipping wing-beats and gives a shrill
call of 'twi-wi-wi-wee'. In contrast to this, the
green and wood sandpipers rise steeply when
disturbed; the green sandpiper has a sharp call of
'kee-weet-tweet', and the wood sandpiper utters
a softer 'whit-whit-whit'. Another freshwater
small wader is the much rarer tiny Temminck's
stint which, when flushed, rises high with a
startled, spluttering call. Plovers are short-billed
birds with black face-patches and breast-bands.
With its loud call of 'pee-oo', the little ringed
plover occurs almost always beside fresh water.

LITTLE RINGED PLOVER
Charadrius dubius
Adult summer plumage
PAGE 141

Black breast-band and head markings

Obvious white wing-bar

Black breast-band and head markings

No wing-bar (or very faint one)

Thin white wing-bar

Pale grey rump

RINGED PLOVER
Charadrius hiaticula
Adult summer plumage
PAGE 141

Very distinctive flight, low over water with bursts of wing-beats and glides on stiffly bowed wings

KNOT
Calidris canutus
Winter plumage
PAGE 144

Tail mainly dark

COMMON SANDPIPER
Actitis hypoleucos
PAGE 169

White wing-bar

Short plump body, long wings

On the other hand, the ringed plover, with its attractive musical 'thlu-i' call, mainly frequents coastal beaches.

Coastal waders tend to move in close, fast-manoeuvring flocks and are recognised by their calls. For example, the dunlin gives out a harsh 'treep'. The call of the longer-billed curlew sandpiper is a distinctive, liquid 'chirrip'; but the

bird is usually first noticed by its white rump. A soft 'wee-whit' is the call of the purple sandpiper, which is usually seen on rocky shores. The turnstone is also found in rocky and pebbly places and its call is a rapid, staccato 'tuk-a-tuk'. But the small, plump sanderling prefers sandy regions and its flight call is a sharp 'twik'. The remaining small waders occur on passage in

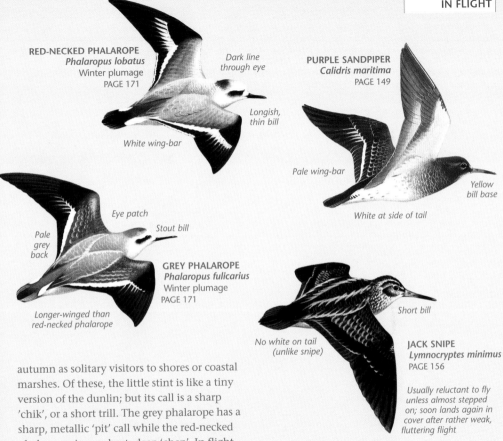

RED-NECKED PHALAROPE
Phalaropus lobatus
Winter plumage
PAGE 171

Dark line through eye

Longish, thin bill

White wing-bar

PURPLE SANDPIPER
Calidris maritima
PAGE 149

Pale wing-bar

Yellow bill base

White at side of tail

Eye patch

Stout bill

Pale grey back

GREY PHALAROPE
Phalaropus fulicarius
Winter plumage
PAGE 171

Longer-winged than red-necked phalarope

No white on tail (unlike snipe)

Short bill

JACK SNIPE
Lymnocryptes minimus
PAGE 156

Usually reluctant to fly unless almost stepped on; soon lands again in cover after rather weak, fluttering flight

autumn as solitary visitors to shores or coastal marshes. Of these, the little stint is like a tiny version of the dunlin; but its call is a sharp 'chik', or a short trill. The grey phalarope has a sharp, metallic 'pit' call while the red-necked phalarope gives a short, deep 'chep'. In flight, the red-necked species is usually faster and more buoyant.

RUFF

Courting male ruffs present an extraordinary sight. They gather together on display grounds called 'leks' in plumage as extravagant as that of an Elizabethan dandy to overawe their rivals and dazzle the females. The neck ruffs and ear-tufts can be black, red-brown, deep purple, white or creamy, or else striped, barred or spotted. Most fly south to Africa in autumn. The petoral sandpiper is a rare wanderer from the Arctic to the British Isles, especially south-west Ireland, Cornwall and East Anglia. Most are juveniles, seen in August or September.

Female

The thickened neck of the male in summer plumage shows in flight. All plumages show a white wing-bar and white rump tail patches

Male in summer

White wing-bar and rump/tail patches

Male in winter

Small head, slightly down-curved bill; short-necked and often looks hunch-backed, but stands very erect when alert

Mottled buff, with white belly and undertail

Resembles a small female ruff, but juvenile has two pale V-shaped lines down back and sharper contrast between neatly streaked breast and white belly

Female

The plumage of the female, or reeve, is a variable brown with dark mottling above and on chest and pale below; the bill is pale, and legs yellowish, greenish or flesh-coloured. Plumage of male in winter is similar although the male is larger

Pectoral sandpiper
Calidris melanotos

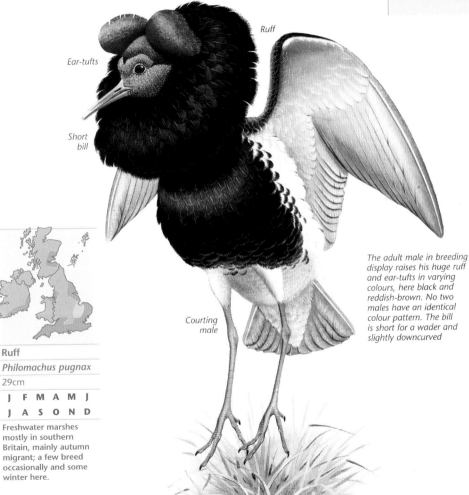

Ear-tufts

Ruff

Short
bill

Courting
male

The adult male in breeding
display raises his huge ruff
and ear-tufts in varying
colours, here black and
reddish-brown. No two
males have an identical
colour pattern. The bill
is short for a wader and
slightly downcurved

Ruff

Philomachus pugnax

29cm

J F M A M J
J A S O N D

Freshwater marshes
mostly in southern
Britain, mainly autumn
migrant; a few breed
occasionally and some
winter here.

SNIPE

Endowed with a bill which is about a quarter of its total length, the snipe is easy to identify. The tip of the bill is flexible and highly sensitive, allowing the bird to detect the worms and invertebrates on which it mainly feeds, and then probe deeply into the mud for them. The snipe has a spectacular courtship display in spring.
The jack snipe is smaller, and is only a scarce passage migrant and winter visitor to Britain.

Shorter bill

Jack snipe
Lymnocryptes minimus

No white on tail

Stiff outer tail feathers produce bleating sound ('drumming')

Courtship display

Buff and dark striped head and back

Extremely long bill

Short reddish-brown tail fringed with white

Nest in tussock of grass; chicks dark

Snipe

Gallinago gallinago

27cm

| J | F | M | A | M | J |
| J | A | S | O | N | D |

Boggy areas with good cover; recent major decline in lowlands but up to a million northern breeders winter here.

WOODCOCK

Eyes set high for wide vision

Russet plumage

Bars on head and breast

Short legs

Long bill

It is difficult to believe that the woodcock is a member of the wader group, so firmly established is it as a bird of damp woodland with plenty of bracken and bramble for cover. Woodcocks need soft ground in woods or nearby pastures or scrubland in which to feed, probing with their bills for worms, insects and their larvae, centipedes spiders and other invertebrates. The male's territorial 'roding' display is very distinctive. He flies over his territory at dusk, on slow-beating wings, uttering a throaty 'og-og-og' followed by a sneezing 'chee-wick'. When disturbed, the woodcock's flight is fast and twisting as it manoeuvres deftly between the trees.

Owl-like appearance in flight except for long bill

Broad wings

Woodcock

Scolopax rusticola

34cm

J F M A M J
J A S O N D

Widespread breeder in damp woodlands, such as young conifer plantations; some nest in bracken-covered moorland; in cold winter weather may feed in streams and other damp places.

BLACK-TAILED GODWIT

Re-established since the 1950s as a breeding bird in Britain, the black-tailed godwit now has a very small population. Males in summer have chestnut, grey and white plumage (females are duller); but in winter, when large flocks can be seen around the coast, the plumage is mainly grey-brown. At all times the prominent black and white tail and broad, white wing-bar distinguish this species in flight from its cousin, the bar-tailed godwit.

Winter

Summer

Black band at end of white tail

White wing-bar

Chestnut head, neck and breast

Very long, almost straight bill

Usually breeds on inland grasslands

Male, summer

Plainer above

Winter

White tail ends in black band; white undertail

Long legs

Grey-brown, darker above, with white belly and undertail

Black-tailed godwit

Limosa limosa

40cm

| J | F | M | A | M | J |
| J | A | S | O | N | D |

In Britain, most breed in seasonally flooded lowland grassland. In winter mainly on muddy estuaries and coastal grassland.

BAR-TAILED GODWIT

Unlike the black-tailed godwit, the bar-tailed godwit does not breed in Britain, but large flocks can be seen in spring on their way to nest in Scandinavia and Russia. Returning here in autumn, many stay for winter, feeding in estuaries or sheltered coasts. The adult male in summer has chestnut head, neck and underparts (the female being duller, pale apricot, down to the breast only), while the winter plumage is mainly a buffy brown, with more streaking than in the black-tailed godwit. The rump is white and the tail barred all year.

Flocks may plunge down in twisting spirals

Barred tail

Plain wings

Winter

White rump

Barred tail

Plumage brownish, with dark-chequered upper parts

Chestnut underparts

Male, summer

Bill probes deeply into sand

Streaked above

Bill slightly upturned

Winter

Legs much shorter than black-tailed godwit

Bar-tailed godwit

Limosa lapponica

38cm

| J | F | M | A | M | J |
| J | A | S | O | N | D |

Estuaries around all coasts and sandy or muddy shores.

CURLEW

Europe's largest wader, the curlew is distinguished by its long, down-curved bill and its loud 'coor-li' call and sad 'whaup' calls. On the marshes, moors and heaths where curlews breed, males establish their territories by flying in wide circles delivering their lovely song, a series of liquid variations on the call notes rising in pitch and intensity to an ecstatic, bubbling crescendo. In winter the birds move to coastal estuaries.

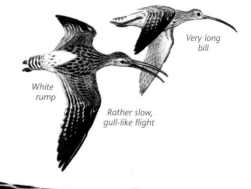

Very long bill

White rump

Rather slow, gull-like flight

Quite uniform head colouring

Very long, quite evenly down-curved bill

The adult bird's very long bill and unstriped head colouring distinguish the curlew from the whimbrel. Small shore crabs are a favourite food

Curlew

Numenius arquata

55cm

| J | F | M | A | M | J |
| J | A | S | O | N | D |

Breeds mainly in uplands of western and northern Britain and Ireland; winters on estuaries and coasts throughout British Isles.

WHIMBREL

The whimbrel is one of Britain's rarest breeding waders, confined to the far north–east mainland of Scotland and the Orkneys and Shetlands. Its shorter bill, distinctive striped crown and whistling 'pee-pee-pee-pee-pee-pee-pee' call distinguish it from the larger curlew. Most birdwatchers see it as a passage migrant in spring and autumn.

Head pattern consists of a dark stripe on either side of the crown with a pale stripe along the top

In flight the whimbrel, like the curlew, shows its long V-shaped white rump, but its shorter bill is distinctive.

Whimbrels, like curlews, often flock in line or V-formations

Bill shorter than curlew's

Striped crown

The whimbrel likes to feed in pasture-land on insects such as grasshoppers

Whimbrel

Numenius phaeopus

40cm

J F M A M J
J A S O N D

Seen mainly migrating along most coasts in spring and autumn; small numbers breed in northern Scotland, almost all in Shetland.

REDSHANK

A volley of harsh, piping notes issues from the so-called 'sentinel of the marsh' as soon as any intruder approaches. This ear-piercing cry contrasts sharply with the redshank's musical, liquid call of 'tew-tew-ew-ew'. The bird is a common breeder in both inland and coastal marshes, where it makes a root-lined nest hidden in a grass tussock. It feeds on all sorts of invertebrates, small fish and frogs, seeds, buds and berries. In winter, redshanks often form large flocks on estuary mud-flats. The spotted redshank is larger, greyer and more elegant with a longer bill, no wing-patch and finely barred and speckled upper parts. It wades in deeper water than the redshank to find food and often swims and upends like a duck. It is mainly an autumn passage migrant.

Long bill, black on upper side and curving down at tip

Grey and white winter plumage

Spotted redshank
Tringa erythropus

Red-based bill

White 'V' on back and rump

Summer

Orange-red legs

Large, white hind wing-patches

Redshank

Tringa totanus

28cm

J F M A M J
J A S O N D

Breeds on coastal salt-marshes and inland on freshwater marshes, wet grassland and moorland; frequents estuaries and coasts in winter.

GREENSHANK

With its long greenish legs and sleek streamlined body, the greenshank is one of Britain's most elegant waders. It is generally to be found on estuaries and pools and lagoons in freshwater marshes. Most north European breeders migrate to Africa in autumn, but some may spend winter in the south and west British Isles. In the breeding season they move to the wild remote bogs of the Scottish Highlands and the Hebrides.

Long, white 'V' on back and rump

Uniform wing colour

Long, slightly upturned bill

Greenish legs

Greenshank

Tringa nebularia

30cm

J F M A M J
J A S O N D

Breeds in Scottish Highlands and Hebrides; winters in Ireland and south and west Britain.

Parent bird fiercely defends young

Winter plumage greyer, with fewer dark centres to feathers above and less streaked below with unstreaked foreneck

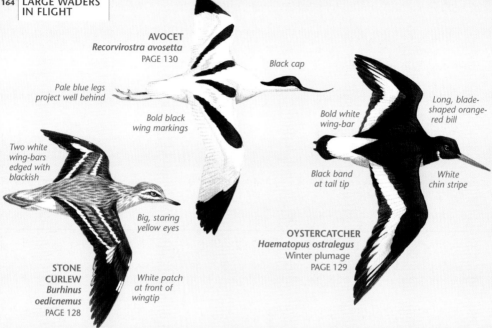

AVOCET
Recorvirostra avosetta
PAGE 130

Black cap

Pale blue legs
project well behind

Bold black
wing markings

Bold white
wing-bar

Long, blade-
shaped orange-
red bill

Two white
wing-bars
edged with
blackish

Big, staring
yellow eyes

Black band
at tail tip

White
chin stripe

**STONE
CURLEW**
*Burhinus
oedicnemus*
PAGE 128

White patch
at front of
wingtip

OYSTERCATCHER
Haematopus ostralegus
Winter plumage
PAGE 129

Large waders in flight

Waders are fast-flying birds and many look rather alike. Usually there is opportunity to notice little more than a bird's general shape, a few conspicuous patches of contrasting colour, and distinctive flight calls and flight patterns. Habitat may help to identify some birds: the stone curlew, for instance, rises suddenly from open, stony areas on long, brown, blackish and white barred wings, and usually drops to run and hide after a short flight. The plump woodcock, with its long bill, short, broad wings and plumage patterned like dead leaves, is most often seen at dusk in spring, as it patrols above the treetops of its breeding wood. Lapwings, with their broad, blunt, slowly flapping wings, appear black-and-white at a distance; just as

White at base of under-wing

RUFF
Philomachus pugnax
Winter plumage
PAGE 154

Golden plover from below

GOLDEN PLOVER
Pluvialis apricaria
Winter plumage
PAGE 138

Grey plover from above

White rump

Mottled gold and black back and rump

Oval white rump-patches

Mottled grey and black above

Indistinct thin, white wing-bar

Indistinct white wing-bar

Broad wings

Very plump body

Black patch at base of under-wing

Long bill, angled downwards

WOODCOCK
Scolopax rusticola
PAGE 157

GREY PLOVER
Pluvialis squatarola
Winter plumage
PAGE 140

easily recognised is the avocet, with its quick flickering flight and a 'klooit' call-note. Other large waders have less obvious differences. The curlew and whimbrel are both large brown birds with white rumps and long, down-curved bills; but while the whimbrel has a pale-striped crown and trills a tittering series of whistling notes, the curlew utters 'cur-lew' and 'whaup' calls. Godwits are a little smaller; they are straighter-billed, and often silent in winter, apart from occasional sharp nasal or whickering calls. The black-tailed godwit shows black and white patterns on wings and tail, and feet that in flight project well beyond the tail; the bar-tailed godwit has shorter legs, a longer white rump and a barred tail. The oystercatcher has a stout

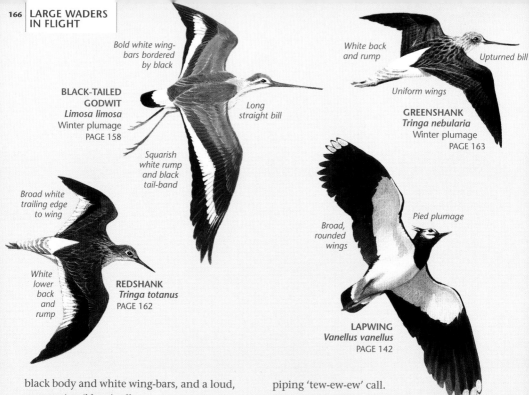

Bold white wing-bars bordered by black

BLACK-TAILED GODWIT
Limosa limosa
Winter plumage
PAGE 158

Long straight bill

Squarish white rump and black tail-band

White back and rump

Upturned bill

Uniform wings

GREENSHANK
Tringa nebularia
Winter plumage
PAGE 163

Broad white trailing edge to wing

White lower back and rump

REDSHANK
Tringa totanus
PAGE 162

Broad, rounded wings

Pied plumage

LAPWING
Vanellus vanellus
PAGE 142

black body and white wing-bars, and a loud, penetrating 'kleep' call.

PLUMAGE AND CALLS AS IDENTIFICATION

Three of the waders shown are smaller than the rest, with long bill and white rump and lower back. Of these, the redshank has prominent white trailing edges to its wings and a plaintive, piping 'tew-ew-ew' call. The greenshank and spotted redshank lack bold white wing marks, but the greenshank has an emphatic 'tew-tew-tew' call, while the spotted redshank gives a loud 'chi-weet', and its long legs project beyond the tail. Ruffs (page 165), except for males in summer plumage, are duller, more

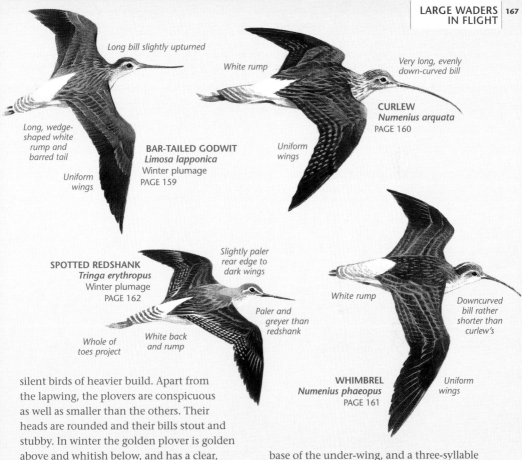

Long bill slightly upturned

White rump

Very long, evenly down-curved bill

CURLEW
Numenius arquata
PAGE 160

Uniform
wings

Long, wedge-shaped white rump and barred tail

Uniform
wings

BAR-TAILED GODWIT
Limosa lapponica
Winter plumage
PAGE 159

Slightly paler
rear edge to
dark wings

SPOTTED REDSHANK
Tringa erythropus
Winter plumage
PAGE 162

Paler and
greyer than
redshank

White rump

Downcurved
bill rather
shorter than
curlew's

Whole of
toes project

White back
and rump

WHIMBREL
Numenius phaeopus
PAGE 161

Uniform
wings

silent birds of heavier build. Apart from the lapwing, the plovers are conspicuous as well as smaller than the others. Their heads are rounded and their bills stout and stubby. In winter the golden plover is golden above and whitish below, and has a clear, whistling 'thlui' call. The grey plover is similar but has a white rump and a black patch at the base of the under-wing, and a three-syllable 'tee-oo-ee' whistle. Both species are black on the belly and face in summer.

GREEN SANDPIPER

Usually seen only when disturbed, as it rises into the air calling 'klee-weet-tweet', the green sandpiper looks black and white at any distance – only its legs are green. It is seen here mainly as a passage migrant in spring and autumn. The nest is unusual for a wader: normally the old nest of a little thrush in a tree. The wood sandpiper is smaller and paler. A few stay for summer in Scotland and one or two pairs breed.

Blackish underside to wings

'Eyebrow' extends clearly behind eye

Paler brown back with large pale spots

Almost vertical rise when flushed

Longer paler yellowish legs

Wood sandpiper
Tringa glareola

Tail bars are narrow

Broad bars on tail

Small white speckles on dark brown back

Greenish legs

White breast speckled brown

Green sandpiper

Tringa ochropus

23cm

| J | F | M | A | M | J |
| J | A | S | O | N | D |

Marshes, ditches and other wetlands, mainly inland; breeds in wet open forests.

Common sandpiper

Actitis hypoleucos

19.5cm

J F **M A M J**
J A S O N D

Breeds by fast streams and rivers and lakes in upland Britain and in Ireland; more widespread migrants and few winter visitors in western Britain and ireland; common migrant elsewhere.

White wing-bar

COMMON SANDPIPER

The restless rear end, bobbing or wagging, is a distinctive feature of the common sandpiper. Its flight is also characteristic: shallow bursts of wing-beats are followed by glides on stiffly down-bowed wings, often accompanied by the loud, musical 'twi-wi-wi-wee' call. The bird feeds on insects and other small creatures. Its upper parts are olive-brown and the underside is white; a dark line runs through the eye.

The nest is a sparsely lined scrape in the ground. A hundred or so birds winter in Britain, but most migrate to Africa.

Straight bill

Bobbing rear

Greenish legs

Distinctive extension of white underparts between brown chest and shoulder

TURNSTONE

As it walks busily across the sands and rocks at low tide in search of food, this colourful plump-bodied little wader quickly reveals the origin of its name. Not only stones, but also seaweed, shells and driftwood are diligently lifted by the bird's probing bill in the hope of finding sandhoppers and other food. Many Scandinavian and Russian birds winter here, and a few first-year birds stay for summer. Young birds resemble winter adults, with dark brown and white plumage. Other adults, breeding in north-east Canada and Greenland, pass through the British Isles in spring and autumn.

Bold piebald pattern in flight

White wing-bar, shoulder stripe and centre to back

Summer

Bright chestnut and black back

Broad black tail-band

Orange legs

White head, flecked black on crown

Winter

Less brightly coloured than summer with dark brown breast and back and less clear-cut pattern of markings

Turnstone

Arenaria interpres

23cm

J F M A M J
J A S O N D

May be seen on almost all shores, especially rocky and pebbly stretches covered with seaweed.

The birds winter at sea, where groups of them sometimes follow in the wake of whales to catch the plankton they disturb or even to land on their backs to catch hard-shelled crustacean parasites

Female, summer

Winter plumage

In flight, the birds show a white wing-bar.

GREY PHALAROPE

The grey phalarope does not breed in the British Isles. Typically, from 200-400 are seen here anually, mostly juvenile and first winter birds blown off course by storms on their journeys between high Arctic breeding grounds in Greenland, Spitzbergen and northern Siberia and the Atlantic Ocean wintering areas. It feeds while swimming on small invertebrates, spinning round to bring its prey to the surface. The normal sexual roles are reversed as the female establishes a territory in the Arctic tundra and courts a male of her choice, who incubates the eggs.

Male, summer

Summer plumage, rarely seen here, is brick-red with a whitish face

Female, summer – brighter

Adult in winter plumage

Grey phalarope

Phalaropus fulicarius

20cm

J F M A M J
J A S O N D

Numbers vary year on year; occasionally strong Atlantic depressions drive relatively large numbers into coastal or even inland waters. Most are seen off Cornwall.

ARCTIC SKUA

Distinctly smaller than a herring
gull, and with less prominent
wing-patches than the great skua,
the Arctic skua is, like the latter
a pirate from which no other
seabird's nest or prey are safe. Eggs
and nestlings are often plundered by a pair
of birds working together, one fighting
off the parents while the other robs the
nest. Passing terns, gulls and auks are also
preyed upon and pursued relentlessly
until a bird disgorges its food. Although
most often seen as a passage migrant, the
Arctic skua breeds on windswept moors
in northern Scotland, especially Shetland.
Smaller and more graceful, the long-
tailed skua is a passage migrant.

Very long, fine flexible
tail streamers

Long-tailed skua
Stercorarius longicaudus

No wing-
flash

White
'flash'
on wing

Arctic skua

***Stercorarius
parasiticus***

45cm

J F M **A M J
J A S O** N D

Passage migrant along
coasts, often closer
to shore than other
skuas; some breed in
far north.

Dark cap

Projecting, pointed
central tail feathers

Pale underparts

Adult

Adult, pale form (all-dark-
brown form also occurs,
plus intermediates)

Immature birds brownish

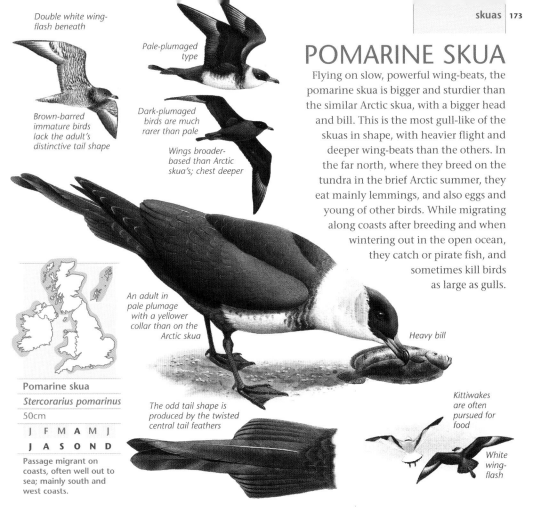

Double white wing-flash beneath

Brown-barred immature birds lack the adult's distinctive tail shape

Pale-plumaged type

Dark-plumaged birds are much rarer than pale

Wings broader-based than Arctic skua's; chest deeper

POMARINE SKUA

Flying on slow, powerful wing-beats, the pomarine skua is bigger and sturdier than the similar Arctic skua, with a bigger head and bill. This is the most gull-like of the skuas in shape, with heavier flight and deeper wing-beats than the others. In the far north, where they breed on the tundra in the brief Arctic summer, they eat mainly lemmings, and also eggs and young of other birds. While migrating along coasts after breeding and when wintering out in the open ocean, they catch or pirate fish, and sometimes kill birds as large as gulls.

An adult in pale plumage with a yellower collar than on the Arctic skua

Heavy bill

Pomarine skua

Stercorarius pomarinus

50cm

J F M A M J
J A S O N D

Passage migrant on coasts, often well out to sea; mainly south and west coasts.

The odd tail shape is produced by the twisted central tail feathers

Kittiwakes are often pursued for food

White wing-flash

GREAT SKUA

The largest of the skuas – the size of a herring gull, it is known as the bonxie in the Shetlands where it nests. A sturdily built and powerful bird, it feeds partly by stealing other seabirds' most recent meals, grasping a wingtip of its victims, including gannets far larger than itself, in its bill and making the bird plunge into the sea where it disgorges its food. As with other skuas, animal and human intruders to the nesting territory are attacked by 'dive bombing'.

Bird swoops on intruders head-on

White wing-patch conspicuous

Flight heavy and purposeful

Thick neck, streaked yellowish

Large, white wing-patch

Stoutest bill of all the skuas

Almost all-brown plumage

Kittiwake chicks are frequent victims

Great skua

Catharacta skua

58cm

| J | F | **M** | **A** | **M** | **J** |
| **J** | **A** | **S** | **O** | **N** | D |

Passage migrant along coasts, often well out to sea; some breed in far north of Scotland.

BLACK-HEADED GULL

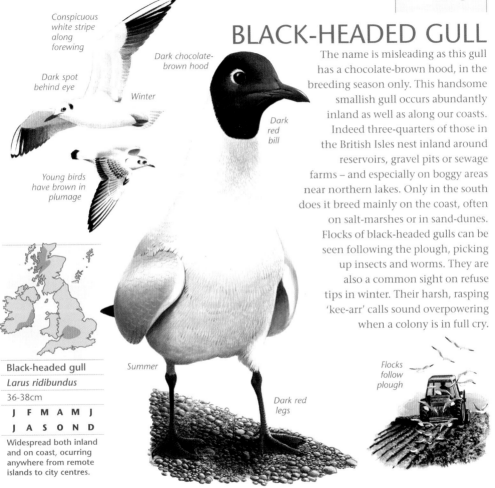

Conspicuous white stripe along forewing

Dark spot behind eye

Winter

Dark chocolate-brown hood

Dark red bill

Young birds have brown in plumage

The name is misleading as this gull has a chocolate-brown hood, in the breeding season only. This handsome smallish gull occurs abundantly inland as well as along our coasts. Indeed three-quarters of those in the British Isles nest inland around reservoirs, gravel pits or sewage farms – and especially on boggy areas near northern lakes. Only in the south does it breed mainly on the coast, often on salt-marshes or in sand-dunes. Flocks of black-headed gulls can be seen following the plough, picking up insects and worms. They are also a common sight on refuse tips in winter. Their harsh, rasping 'kee-arr' calls sound overpowering when a colony is in full cry.

Summer

Dark red legs

Flocks follow plough

Black-headed gull

Larus ridibundus

36-38cm

J F M A M J
J A S O N D

Widespread both inland and on coast, ocurring anywhere from remote islands to city centres.

LITTLE GULL

Unlike its cousin the black-headed gull, this smallest of the world's gulls really does have an entirely black head in adult breeding plumage rather than a brown hood. It has a tern-like, buoyant flight, dipping to the surface to pick up small crustaceans, fish or insects. The pale grey upper parts, black head and the short, spiky red bill and red legs are distinctive in the breeding season; thereafter, the black head colouring is replaced by a dark smudge on the crown and behind the eye. It is mostly seen on passage. The Mediterranean gull, which has whiter wings, now breeds locally in England.

All-white flight feathers and silvery upperparts

All-white under-wing

Summer

Mediterranean gull
Larus melanocephalus

Winter

Jet black head

Small bill

Pale grey upperparts

Winter

Wings all dark below

Young bird

Bright red legs

Little gull

Larus minutus

28cm

J F M A M J
J A S O N D

Fairly widespread on passage; scarcer, mainly coastal, in summer and winter.

KITTIWAKE

The strident calls of 'kitti-wa-a-k' were once supposed to be the ghostly cries of souls lost at sea. These seabirds certainly had a sad time when they were slaughtered for sport, and to supply feathers for Victorian ladies' hats. But under official protection the kittiwake population has spread rapidly. With its combination of short black legs, slightly forked tail and all-black wing-tips, this elegant gull is distinctive. Forming large colonies on the narrowest, most precipitous cliff ledges, kittiwakes build their nests of seaweed and moss, cemented together with their droppings. They feed on small fish, molluscs and shrimps.

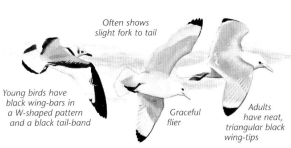

Often shows slight fork to tail

Young birds have black wing-bars in a W-shaped pattern and a black tail-band

Graceful flier

Adults have neat, triangular black wing-tips

Soft grey plumage

Kittiwake

Rissa tridactyla

40cm

J F M A M J
J A S O N D

Breeds around all coasts except for those without cliffs in south-east England; scarcer in Ireland; most winter well out to sea; rare inland.

Yellow-green bill; red mouth

Short black legs

COMMON GULL

The common gull is, in fact, not nearly as common as a breeder as the name suggests, except in Scotland and western Ireland. Few breed in the southern half of Britain and eastern Ireland. However, it is common as a winter visitor. Its varied diet includes insects and worms, water creatures other birds' eggs and young and waste food at refuse tips. Sometimes it chases seabirds to steal food. The adult resembles a small herring gull with its grey back and white head, but the bill and legs are yellow-green; the wing-tips are black, with white spots or 'mirrors' (unlike the otherwise quite similar kittiwake). Its voice is a high-pitched mewing 'keeeyar'. The common gull nests in small colonies on rocks, islets or boggy areas of grass and moorland.

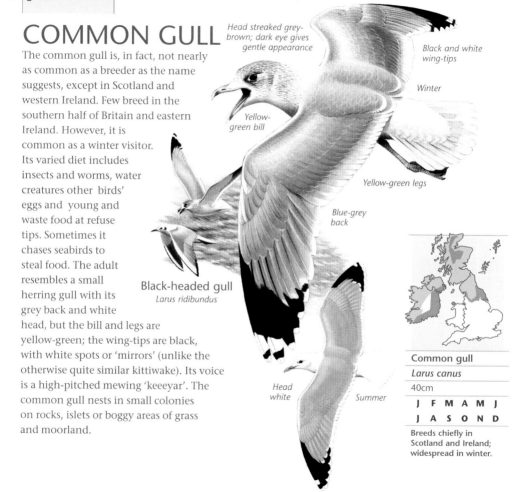

Head streaked grey-brown; dark eye gives gentle appearance

Black and white wing-tips

Winter

Yellow-green bill

Yellow-green legs

Blue-grey back

Black-headed gull
Larus ridibundus

Head white

Summer

Common gull

Larus canus

40cm

| J | F | M | A | M | J |
| J | A | S | O | N | D |

Breeds chiefly in Scotland and Ireland; widespread in winter.

HERRING GULL

The harsh, loud 'kee-owk-kyowk-kyowk-kyowk' call of the commonest of our larger gulls evokes the very spirit of the seashore. It is heard at close quarters in coastal towns where the birds are increasingly breeding on rooftops. Although herrings may form part of its diet, it also eats shellfish, small mammals and birds and, like many other gulls, refuse from rubbish tips. Hard-shelled prey like mussels are dropped from a height to smash them. The yellow-legged gull, with its darker grey upperparts, has become a regular visitor and a few pairs now nest in southern England.

Herring gull

Larus argentatus

55–66cm

J F M A M J
J A S O N D

Coasts all round Britain and Ireland; widespread inland in winter including in towns and cities.

Blackish bill, paler at base

Juvenile mottled grey-brown; tail speckled, with black band

Red spot on bill

Hard-shelled prey is dropped to be smashed on hard ground below

Young take several years to acquire full adult plumage

Pink legs

Grey upperparts long, broad wings and black wing-tips with white spots

LESSER BLACK-BACKED GULL

This handsome bird is about the same length as the herring gull, but with a slimmer build and darker grey back and upperwings. These are slate grey in the race breeding in Britain and Ireland, while in the race breeding in Scandinavia and western Russia – which is a common winter visitor here, they are blackish, though not quite as black as the wingtips. They can be distinguished from the great black-backed gull by their smaller size, smaller head and slimmer bill.

Slender build

Dark grey upper parts

First-year bird is darker than herring gull

Large winter roosts form on inland waters

Varied diet includes crabs

Yellow legs

Lesser black-backed gull

Larus fuscus

53-55cm

| J | F | M | A | M | J |
| J | A | S | O | N | D |

Breeds mainly in north and west. Found both on coast and inland, including urban areas.

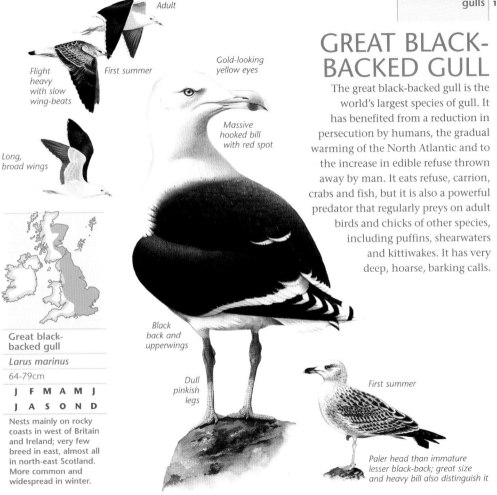

Adult

Flight heavy with slow wing-beats

First summer

Long, broad wings

Gold-looking yellow eyes

Massive hooked bill with red spot

GREAT BLACK-BACKED GULL

The great black-backed gull is the world's largest species of gull. It has benefited from a reduction in persecution by humans, the gradual warming of the North Atlantic and to the increase in edible refuse thrown away by man. It eats refuse, carrion, crabs and fish, but it is also a powerful predator that regularly preys on adult birds and chicks of other species, including puffins, shearwaters and kittiwakes. It has very deep, hoarse, barking calls.

Black back and upperwings

Dull pinkish legs

Great black-backed gull

Larus marinus

64–79cm

J F M A M J
J A S O N D

Nests mainly on rocky coasts in west of Britain and Ireland; very few breed in east, almost all in north-east Scotland. More common and widespread in winter.

First summer

Paler head than immature lesser black-back; great size and heavy bill also distinguish it

GLAUCOUS GULL

This very large gull is an uncommon but regular visitor to Britain; some birds come back to the same spot year after year. Their nearest breeding grounds are Greenland, Iceland, Spitzbergen and Russia, where they nest on cliffs and rocky coasts. Glaucous here means greyish-blue – the colour of the adult's back. The gull is a powerful predator and scavenger and also steals food from other birds. Young birds have pale brownish mottled plumage.

The Iceland gull, like a small glaucous gull, visits Britain in small numbers in winter.

Mottled pale brown plumage in first winter

Paler in second winter

Very heavy bill with red spot

Ponderous wing-beats

Glaucous gull

Larus hyperboreus

68cm

J F M A M J
J A S **O N D**

Mainly on coasts; especial in north (most in Scotland).

Very pale grey wings and back

Rounder crown; smaller bill

Iceland gull
Larus glaucoides

White wing-tips and white edges to flight feathers

No black
at wingtips

Leading
edge
white

BLACK-HEADED GULL
Larus ridibundus
Winter plumage
PAGE 175

Small yellow
bill with
red spot

ICELAND GULL
Larus glaucoides
PAGE 182

Red bill

Distinctive white
wedge-shaped leading
edge to outer
wing

Dark outer
flight feathers

Dark brown
hood, red bill

**BLACK-
HEADED GULL**
Larus ridibundus
Summer plumage
PAGE 175

Dark grey
under-wing

LITTLE GULL
Larus minutus
Winter
plumage
PAGE 176

Black hood, red bill

LITTLE GULL
Larus minutus
Summer
plumage
PAGE 176

Outer
flight feathers
black-tipped

Dark grey under-wing

Gulls in flight

Though all gulls are basically similar in appearance, each species has features which distinguish it when seen in flight. It helps to be close enough to glimpse the bill and feet. These features include differences in size and variations in marking. It is helpful to compare an unidentified bird with a known species. The two most readily seen species, the herring gull

and the black-headed gull, provide standards for comparison. The herring gull is a large species with an ash-grey back and the familiar wailing and laughing 'seagull' calls, whereas the black~headed gull is a smaller, more slender bird with a lighter flight and quicker wing-beat.

A number of large gulls have a stout yellow bill with a red spot near the tip. Among these are

COMMON GULL
Larus canus
PAGE 178

Greenish-yellow bill

Dark eye

Black upper parts

Massive bill; yellow, red spot

Dark grey upper-parts

Yellow bill, red spot

LESSER BLACK-BACKED GULL
Larus fuscus
PAGE 180

GREAT BLACK-BACKED GULL
Larus marinus
PAGE 181

the herring gull, lesser black-backed gull and great black-backed gull. All have black wingtips with white spots at the extreme tips, but they stand out more on the herring gull, which is pale grey on its upper back and upperwings. The lesser black-backed gull has a dark grey or greyish-black mantle, and the much larger great black-backed gull, whose deep-toned barking call is unmistakable, has a sooty-black mantle. Leg colours vary; the British race of herring gull has pinkish legs, as has the greater black-backed gull, but the lesser black-backed gull has yellow or yellowish-grey legs. Glaucous Iceland gulls have yellow, red-spotted bills like other large gulls and pinkish legs like herring gulls but are pale grey on the mantle and wings, and lack black wingtips.

Large yellow
bill with red
spot

No black
at wingtips

GLAUCOUS GULL
Larus hyperboreus
PAGE 182

HERRING GULL
Larus argentatus
PAGE 179

Pale grey
upperparts

Yellow bill,
red spot

MEDITERRANEAN GULL
Larus melanocephalus
Summer plumage. Increasingly
common visitor
PAGE 176

MEDITERRANEAN GULL
Larus melanocephalus
Winter plumage
PAGE 175

White under-
wing

Black hood,
white round eye

Black wingtips
with white
spots

No black
at wingtips

IDENTIFYING THE SMALLER GULLS

The common gull is between the herring and smallest gulls in size, with quicker wing-beats like all smaller birds. Its wing colour is like that of the herring gull, but it has a more slender, greenish-yellow bill and no red spot; its legs are greenish-yellow. Many small gulls have a dark head in summer and a white head with a dark spot behind the eye in winter. Distinguishing features are the bill and under-wing colour. In summer, the black-headed gull, little gull and Mediterranean gull, all have dark heads. Viewed from below, the little gull has dark under-wings, the Mediterranean gull all-white under-wings, and the black-headed gull light under-wings with dark outer flight feathers.

BLACK TERN

Once a regular breeder in south-eastern Britain, the black tern now occurs only as a spring and autumn migrant apart from a few in summer. Its extinction as a breeder is due to drainage of the fens, swamps and marshes it favours, plus egg-collecting and trophy-hunting. A black body, dark grey wings and tail and white undertail make the black tern easily recognisable in summer. In autumn the main distinguishing feature is the black smudge at the side of the breast. Black terns usually swoop and dip over the water, taking insects from the surface.

White forehead

Black smudge at side of breast

Winter

Dark grey wings

Summer

Black body

White undertail

The nest is a floating platform of vegetation

Black tern

Chlidonias niger

24cm

J F M A M J
J A S O N D

Passage migrant mainly to lakes and reservoirs in southern and eastern England. A few recent attempts at breeding.

Summer

Short, forked tail lacks
long thin streamers

*Young
bird*

LITTLE TERN

After wintering in Africa, the
little tern arrives in Britain between
late April and the end of May. The
smallest of Britain's breeding terns,
it breeds on sandy beaches and
shingle banks, though invasions
of holidaymakers have severely
reduced its numbers. Unlike other
British terns, the little tern has a
white forehead in summer as
well as winter. The narrow
wings flicker rapidly in fast
flight as it dives for small
fish, shrimps and marine
worms. It makes distinctive
shrill, rasping 'kree-ik' cries.

Little tern

Sterna albifrons

24cm

J F **M A M J**
J A S O N D

Scattered breeding
colonies around coasts,
especially in east and
south England; rare
inland.

Black
edges to
wings

*Wings held
in 'V' on
courtship
flight*

Summer

Yellow
or orange-
yellow legs

White forehead;
black-tipped yellow bill

Breeding
sites often
disturbed
by humans

*Birds share incubation and
catch fish for each other*

COMMON TERN

Although not Britain's most numerous tern, it is the most widely distributed. It differs from the Arctic tern in having a black tip to its red bill, longer legs and shorter tail streamers; it has a translucent patch in the wing. These features can be seen in a good view, but the two species are very similar, and unidentified birds are often referred to as 'commic terns'. The common tern eats small fish, crustaceans, marine worms and molluscs. Breeding takes place in coastal and inland colonies which sometimes number many hundreds of pairs. The nest is a scrape in the ground. Incubation and care of the young are undertaken mainly by the female.

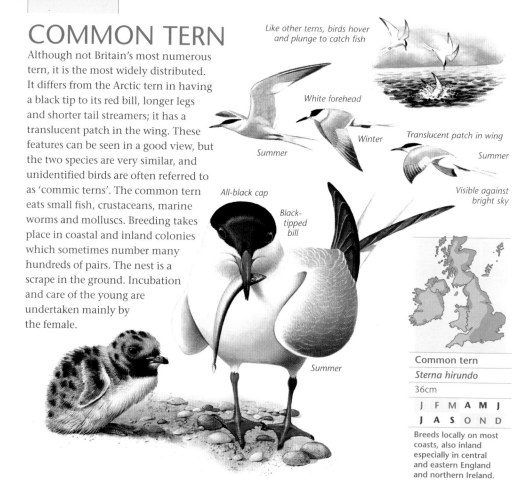

Like other terns, birds hover and plunge to catch fish

White forehead

Winter

Summer

Translucent patch in wing

Summer

Visible against bright sky

All-black cap

Black-tipped bill

Summer

Common tern

Sterna hirundo

36cm

| J | F | M | A | M | J |
| J | A | S | O | N | D |

Breeds locally on most coasts, also inland especially in central and eastern England and northern Ireland.

ARCTIC TERN

The Arctic tern is the most numerous breeding tern in Britain, with 50,000 or so nesting pairs. Like the common tern, this summer visitor may breed in mixed colonies. It is an aggressive bird and will attack any intruders, including humans, by striking with its bill. In flight, the Arctic tern appears darker on the underparts than the common tern, and its underwing is wholly translucent apart from a narrow dark trailing edge around the wingtip. Breeding begins in May, when eggs are laid in a bare scrape and incubated by both parents.

A mixed group of Arctic and common terns are often almost indistinguishable

Arctic tern

Sterna paradisaea

36cm

J F M **A M J**
J A S O N D

Mainly Scottish islands and coast. Some go south to coasts of north Wales and Ireland; some inland.

Summer

Winter

White forehead

Summer

All-black cap

All-red bill

Translucent underwing

Other birds, such as eiders, often nest in Arctic tern colonies, protected by the terns' aggressive reaction to intruders

Short legs

ROSEATE TERN

Rarest of all the terns that breed regularly in the British Isles, the roseate tern gets its name from the soft rosy flush on the breast which appears briefly in the breeding season. In flight the roseate tern shows the longest tail streamers of any tern; it also has a whiter overall appearance, and a longer, blacker bill than the common tern. Like other terns it dives into the water to catch small fish.

Stiffer flight action than common and Arctic terns with shallower wing-beats. Wings appear shorter

Summer

White forehead

Winter

Very long tail streamers

Chicks are vulnerable to cold, wet weather and predation

All-black cap

Dark bill, only red at base

Summer

Rose tint on breast

In courtship display, wings droop and tail and neck point upwards

Roseate tern

Sterna dougallii

38cm

| J | F | M | A | M | J |
| J | A | S | O | N | D |

Rare summer visitor to coasts of Ireland and north-east England; largest numbers in Ireland.

SANDWICH TERN

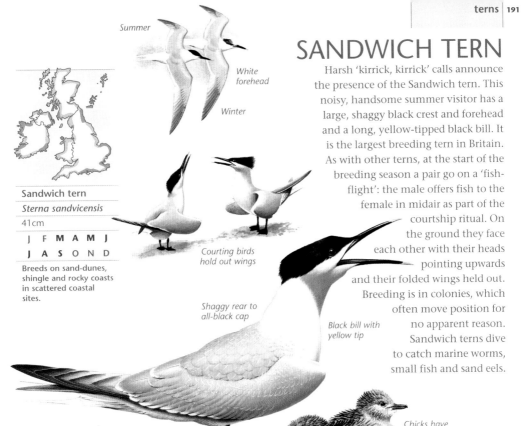

Harsh 'kirrick, kirrick' calls announce the presence of the Sandwich tern. This noisy, handsome summer visitor has a large, shaggy black crest and forehead and a long, yellow-tipped black bill. It is the largest breeding tern in Britain. As with other terns, at the start of the breeding season a pair go on a 'fish-flight': the male offers fish to the female in midair as part of the courtship ritual. On the ground they face each other with their heads pointing upwards and their folded wings held out. Breeding is in colonies, which often move position for no apparent reason. Sandwich terns dive to catch marine worms, small fish and sand eels.

Summer

White forehead

Winter

Courting birds hold out wings

Shaggy rear to all-black cap

Black bill with yellow tip

Chicks have spiky plumage

Summer

Black legs

Sandwich tern

Sterna sandvicensis

41cm

J F **M A M J J A S O** N D

Breeds on sand-dunes, shingle and rocky coasts in scattered coastal sites.

Large dark area at tip of under-wing

Bill short, stout, all-black

Looks very pale

Huge, bright red bill

Almost as large as a herring gull

GULL-BILLED TERN
Gelochelidon nilotica
Winter plumage
Rare visitor, has bred in UK

CASPIAN TERN
Hydroprogne caspia
Winter plumage
Rare visitor

Black behind eye extends onto nape

Bill long, narrow, yellow-tipped

Short, shallow forked tail

SANDWICH TERN
Sterna sandvicensis
Winter plumage
PAGE 191

Terns in flight

There are two distinct types of terns: the grey-and-white sea terns and the black marsh terns of inland waters. The sea terns can be mistaken for small gulls, but fly faster with deeper wing-beats. Another characteristic is their habit of hovering over the water and then plunging in after a fish. Their bodies and bills are generally slender and their tails are forked. Most have little black on their wings, but a neat black cap on their heads, which turns white at the front after the breeding season. In summer they breed along parts of the British coastline. Most of the sea terns are quite small, but the Caspian tern, with its stout, tapering red bill and slow, majestic flight, is the size of a large gull. The next largest is the Sandwich tern, with a long, black, yellow-tipped

LITTLE TERN
Sterna albifrons
Winter plumage
PAGE 187

Tail streamers between those of
common and roseate in length.

Body pale
grey below

Yellow and
black bill

ARCTIC TERN
Sterna paradisaea
Winter plumage
PAGE 189

Wings narrow
with dark fore-
edge to outer wing

All flight feathers
translucent

Translucent
wing-patch

ROSEATE TERN
Sterna dougallii
Winter plumage
PAGE 190

Very long
tail streamers

Very pale
upper parts

Outer flight
feathers dark

COMMON TERN
Sterna hirundo
Winter plumage
PAGE 188

Underwing lacks
dark trailing edge

bill. Almost as big is the heavily built gull-billed tern, whose plumage is whiter than that of the two larger birds.

The smaller grey and white terns can be hard to identify in flight. The Arctic and common terns are very much alike, especially when not breeding. When breeding, the Arctic tern's body is distinctly grey, its bill is red and flight feathers are translucent. The common tern has a white body, a dark scarlet bill with black tip, and a small, translucent wing-patch. In a mixed flock, the roseate tern is told apart by its shorter wings, whiter appearance, pink-tinged breast in spring and very long tail streamers. Smallest of all is the little tern, a miniature species with rapid wing-beats that hovers very frequently.

Forewings white on top

WHITE-WINGED BLACK TERN
Chlidonias leucopterus
Summer plumage

Underwing has black coverts

WHITE-WINGED BLACK TERN
Chlidonias leucopterus
Summer plumage

Grey back and rump

Black head

WHITE-WINGED BLACK TERN
Chlidonias leucopterus
Winter plumage

Streaked crown and dark ear spot

Pale rump

No black breast patch

BLACK TERN
Chlidonias nig...
Summer plumage
PAGE 186

Grey upper parts

BLACK TERN
Chlidonias niger
Winter plumage
PAGE 186

Solid black patch extending to crown

Grey rump

Black patch on breast side

BLACK TERN
Chlidonias niger
Summer plumage
PAGE 186

Black underparts

TERNS THAT FLY INLAND

Marsh terns are mainly found beside lakes, lagoons and marshes, but on spring or autumn migrations may fly along the coast. They usually feed by skimming over the water, swooping to snatch insects from the surface. In summer, the black tern (*Chlidonias niger*), a regular migrant, is sooty-black with white on its under-tail feathers and wings; while the white-winged black tern (*Chlidonias leucopterus*), rare though annual, has white wings with black under-wing feathers, a white rump and tail and red bill. In winter, both birds are much paler: white beneath and mainly dark grey above. The black tern has a dark spot on the sides of its neck, forming a wedge, and the white-winged tern retains its white rump.

PUFFIN

Webbed feet spread as 'brakes' when landing

Rapid whirring wing-beats

White face

Huge, colourful triangular bill

Brown chick fed for about 40 days, then left to find own way to sea where it fends for itself

Unmistakable in summer with its huge red, blue and yellow triangular bill, clown-like face and orange feet, the puffin is one of Britain's best-known birds. The distinctive bill has given rise to such popular names as 'sea parrot' and 'bottlenose'. In winter the face is darker and the bill becomes smaller and less colourful. Totally marine, it catches fish, a breeding adult being capable of carrying many (the record is 62) at a time crossways in its bill. The birds breed in large colonies and lay their single egg in an old rabbit burrow, or a hole excavated from the soft turf on cliff tops.

Puffin

Fratercula arctica

30cm

J F M A M J
J A S O N D

Breeds on cliffs and islands mainly in north and west; seen elsewhere on migation; winters far out to sea.

Bright orange legs

Little auk
Alle alle

Summer

Starling-sized auk; rare winter visitor offshore

GUILLEMOT

When standing upright with its black-brown upper parts and pure white underparts fully visible, the guillemot presents the nearest approximation in Britain to the penguin of Antarctic waters (though penguins are not related to auks). Breeding in dense colonies on precipitous cliff ledges, the guillemots pack themselves together, often with just room to stand. The single egg, laid on the bare ledge, is tapered so that it rolls in a circle without falling off. Both sexes incubate the egg, balancing it on their feet and covering it with their belly plumage.

The black guillemot has black breeding plumage, broken only by a white wing-patch. It is rare except in Ireland, Scotland and the Isle of Man.

Upper parts barred black and white

Winter

Summer

Black body

Black guillemot
Cepphus grylle

Red feet

Large white wing-patch

Winter

White throat and breast, with black line behind eye

Slim pointed bill

Summer

Variably streaked flanks

Dark brown above and white below

Guillemot

Uria aalge

42cm

| J | F | M | A | M | J |
| J | A | S | O | N | D |

Breeds mainly on sea-cliffs in north and west; off all coasts in winter.

RAZORBILL

The stout, much deeper, almost square-ended bill is the razorbill's main distinction from the guillemot, but it also has blacker upper parts and a thicker neck. In winter the black throat changes to white. Razorbills are often seen floating in the sea in great 'rafts', when their dumpy silhouettes and upward-pointing tails are distinctive. They breed in the same areas as guillemots, but mostly in small groups or pairs scattered among guillemots, usually in more protected rock crevices. As in other auks, both parents share the incubation of the eggs.

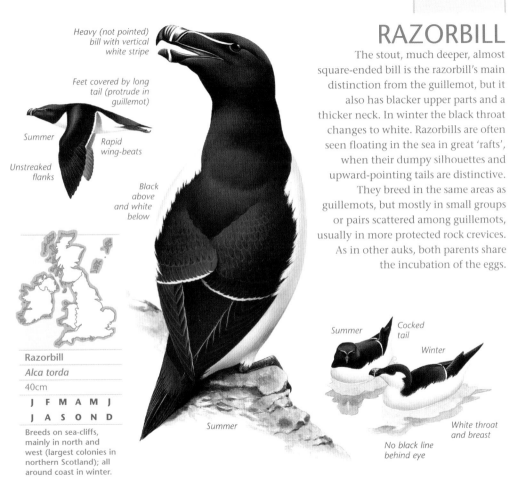

Heavy (not pointed) bill with vertical white stripe

Feet covered by long tail (protrude in guillemot)

Summer

Rapid wing-beats

Unstreaked flanks

Black above and white below

Summer

Cocked tail

Winter

White throat and breast

No black line behind eye

Summer

Razorbill

Alca torda

40cm

J F M A M J
J A S O N D

Breeds on sea-cliffs, mainly in north and west (largest colonies in northern Scotland); all around coast in winter.

WOOD-PIGEON

To many farmers, the largest of Britain's pigeons is 'public enemy number one'. The wood-pigeon does immense damage to crops, particularly in winter when the population is joined by continental immigrants, and huge flocks feed on rape, other brassicas and clover – plentiful alternatives to their traditional foods of ivy berries, acorns and weed seeds. At other times of the year they feed on cereals, potatoes, beans, peas and greens. The wood-pigeon is distinguished from other pigeons by its white neck-patch and wing-patches, the latter conspicuous in flight. The lovely song is a soft, husky cooing, 'coo-coo, coo, coo . . . cuk'. In display flight the bird climbs steeply, noisily claps its wings together and then glides down.

White neck-patch

Pinkish breast

White wing-patches

Broad black band at end of tail

Wood-pigeon
Columba palumbus
40cm

| J | F | M | A | M | J |
| J | A | S | O | N | D |

Most on arable farm-land near woods, but breeds everywhere except on high ground; residents joined by immigrants in winter.

STOCK DOVE

This plump dove is basically all grey with two black bars on the wing, and a greenish neck-patch. It nests in holes in trees and rock faces and old buildings and, very occasionally, in disused rabbit burrows. A similar species breeding in remote coastal areas of Ireland and northern Scotland is called the rock dove. This is most readily distinguished from the farmland-dwelling stock dove by its white rump. Most pigeons found in urban areas are descended from a domesticated form of the rock dove, even though few resemble the wild bird in plumage. They roost on buildings instead of cliffs, and are often known as feral, town or London pigeons.

Short black wing-bars

Grey rump

Stock dove

Columba oenas

33cm

J F M A M J
J A S O N D

Breeds widely in woods and cliffs; often feeds on arable farmland.

No white on neck or wings

Longer wing-bars

White under-wing

White rump

Rock dove
Columba livia

COLLARED DOVE

Before the 1930s the range of the collared dove in Europe was largely restricted to parts of the Balkans. Since then, in an amazing population explosion, it has colonised much of Europe as far north as Iceland. By 1955 it was nesting in Britain, and it has now colonised almost the entire British Isles.

Favourite habitats are in the vicinity of farms, chicken runs, corn mills and docks, where grain and other animal feed is often spilled, and in gardens where birds are fed. The birds nest mainly in conifers, and can produce five broods – each of one or two young – between March and November. The song is a loud, monotonously repeated 'coo-coo-cuk'.

Flocks gather around grain stores

Black half-collar on nape of neck

Buffish-grey body

Frail nest of twigs often built low among brambles

Dark wingtips

Broad white tail-band

Buffish-grey above

Collared dove

Streptopelia decaocto

32cm

| J | F | M | A | M | J |
| J | A | S | O | N | D |

Widespread, except for uplands and city centres.

TURTLE DOVE

The throbbing, purring coo of the turtle dove is a bird call of high summer that mingles well with the sound of cricket on the village green. This dove visits Britain in summer from its winter quarters in sub-Saharan Africa. Adults sport a heavily chequered black and chestnut back and a black and white half-collar, while the underparts have a pinkish tinge. In flight the undertail shows a rounded white tip. Juveniles are duller. Sadly this lovely bird has suffered massive declines over the past 30 years.

Rounded white tip to tail

Male bows in courtship ritual

Turtle dove

Streptopelia turtur

28cm

J F M A M J
J A S O N D

Open woodlands and tall, dense hedges, mainly in southern and eastern England.

Black and white neck-patch

Pink breast

Chestnut and black above

BARN OWL

A white shape silently leaving a barn or quartering a field is all an observer often sees of the barn owl. A closer view reveals golden-buff upperparts lightly mottled with grey, a white heart-shaped face with dark eyes, white underparts and long white-feathered legs. The barn owl feeds mostly on rats, mice and voles, which it catches mainly at night. It breeds in barns, ruins and church towers, and also in natural sites such as cliff holes and hollow trees. This very beautiful bird has suffered a huge decline, due to intensification of agriculture, poisoning by rodenticides and lack of natural nest sites as old trees are felled and traditional barns converted to housing.

White face

Golden-buff upper parts

White under- parts

Long legs

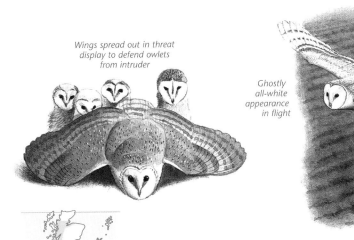

Wings spread out in threat display to defend owlets from intruder

Ghostly all-white appearance in flight

Barn owl
Tyto alba
34cm

**J F M A M J
J A S O N D**

Widespread but local in agricultural country, but scarce in north-east England, upland Scotland and north-west Ireland.

Hollow elm trees are a favourite nest site but they are fast disappearing from the countryside

LITTLE OWL

The smallest of our breeding owls was introduced to this country from the Continent in the late 19th century. Although mainly nocturnal, it can be seen in daylight, especially on warm summer evenings. The birds breed in holes and crevices, and frequent agricultural land, parks, orchards, quarries and sea-cliffs. Insects, small birds and mammals form the main part of the little owl's diet. Its main calls are a plaintive 'kiew', and a yelping 'werrrow'.

Flight low, swift and undulating

Like adults, fledglings bob heads when anxious

Plumage grey-brown and white

Yellow eyes

'Frowning' expression due to white eyebrows

Fence post used as day-time perch

Little owl
Athene noctua
22cm

J F M A M J
J A S O N D

Most numerous in southern and central Scotland; scarce in the south-west.

Big rounded face

Fledglings have barred downy underparts

TAWNY OWL

The male's long, quavering, 'hoo-hoo-hoo-hoo-hooooo', often described as 'to-whit-to-wooo' incorporating the 'ke-wick' call of a responding female, is one of the best known of British bird calls. During the day, the tawny owl's presence is often given away by the alarm calls of small birds mobbing an adult dozing on the branch of a tree. Its wholly dark eyes distinguish the tawny owl (sometimes called the brown owl) from other owls. As with other owls, soft plumage and specially adapted wing feathers make it silent in flight.

Brown body with dark streaks below

Dark eyes

Owl watches for prey from tree perch, then pounces without warning

Tawny owl

Strix aluco

38cm

J F M A M J
J A S O N D

Woodlands throughout Britain; absent from Ireland; occurs in farmland with trees, large gardens and city parks as well as large woods.

LONG-EARED OWL

The apparent 'ears' are in fact no more than tufts of feathers – the actual ears are under the feathers on the sides of the head. The prominent, bright orange eyes in the facial disc, combined with the 'ear' tufts, distinguish this species from our other owls. Strictly nocturnal, roosting in dense tree cover or scrub during the day, the long-eared owl is the only owl, apart from the barn owl, to live in Ireland. Communal roosts often form in winter. The owls usually breed in the old nest of another bird, or in a squirrel's drey. The call is a low, drawn out 'ooo-ooo-ooo-ooo', and the young make a noise like a creaking gate.

Long 'ear' tufts

Orange eyes

Uniformly streaked underparts

Slender posture adopted when alarmed

Finer, fainter bars on tail; and four to five dark bars on wing-tips

Dark 'wrist' patches

Long-eared owl

Asio otus

34cm

| J | F | M | A | M | J |
| J | A | S | O | N | D |

Widespread but uncommon, breeding in woodland and tall hedges near open country for hunting; continental visitors in winter.

SHORT-EARED OWL

Of all the owls, the short-eared owl is the one most often seen hunting in daylight. It looks like a huge moth as it hunts low over moorland, estuaries and marshes. In display the bird makes a loud clapping noise as the wingtips meet below the body. The short ear-like tufts are often difficult to see, but the bright yellow eyes stare from the round face. It preys mainly on voles.

Blacker 'wrist' patches

Two to three dark bars on wing-tips, endmost one larger

Streaks clustered on chest producing dark front and paler rear

Bold tail-bars

Yellow eyes

Short 'ear' tufts

Rounded wings show white trailing edge

Nest is on ground

Short-eared owl

Asio flammeus

38cm

J F M A M J
J A S O N D

Open country, breeding mainly in northern England and Scotland; more widespread in winter.

CUCKOO

The familiar 'cuc-coo, cuc-coo' call of the male bird in April is a sure sign that summer is on its way. The female has a very different loud bubbling call. Cuckoos are notorious for their parasitic breeding habits. The female finds a suitable nest, built by a much smaller bird, in which to lay her eggs. One egg is deposited in each nest, after the cuckoo has carefully removed one of the host's eggs. The nests of meadow pipits, dunnocks and reed warblers are mostly used. Individual cuckoos parasitise particular species. When hatched the young cuckoo ejects the remaining eggs or nestlings of the host.

Reed warbler feeds hungry young cuckoo

Newly hatched cuckoo ejects host bird's eggs

Reed warbler drives off cuckoo

White spot on nape

Some juveniles have red-brown plumage

Female cuckoo removes egg from host nest

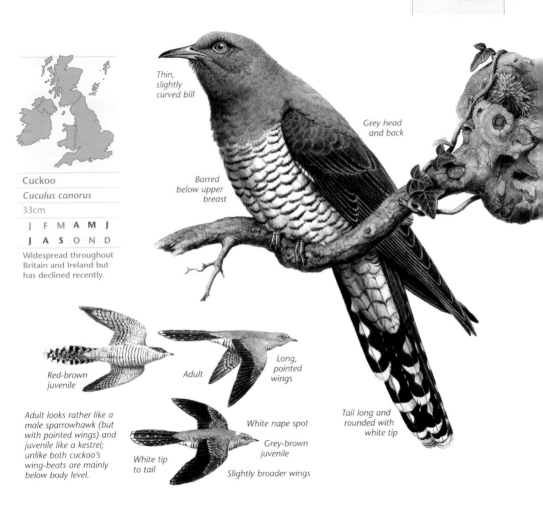

Thin, slightly curved bill

Grey head and back

Barred below upper breast

Cuckoo

Cuculus canorus

33cm

J F **M A M J**
J A S O N D

Widespread throughout Britain and Ireland but has declined recently.

Red-brown juvenile

Adult

Long, pointed wings

Adult looks rather like a male sparrowhawk (but with pointed wings) and juvenile like a kestrel; unlike both cuckoo's wing-beats are mainly below body level.

White nape spot

Grey-brown juvenile

White tip to tail

Slightly broader wings

Tail long and rounded with white tip

NIGHTJAR

The nightjar's churring, long drawn-out song, uttered at night, rises and falls in pitch. It is most often seen at dusk when it hawks for flying insects such as large moths, which it catches in a huge open gape. The bird is also known as the 'goatsucker' from the old (but erroneous) belief that it milks goats with its large mouth. Nightjars are localised summer visitors, that have suffered major declines in the past 70 years.

Intricately patterned grey-brown plumage

Tiny bill but wide hair-fringed gape

Male

During display flight male claps his wings together audibly over his back

Bright white tail-spots and wing-spots

Birds may be seen feeding or displaying at dusk. Wings and tail look very long and flight is light and agile, with sudden long glides, twists and turns and brief hovering

Bird perches along branch, not across it

Nest is a scrape in the ground, with parent, eggs and young camouflaged among sticks and dead leaves

Female

No white spots on tail or wings

Nightjar

Caprimulgus europaeus

27cm

J F M A **M J**
J A S O N D

Heaths, moors and open woodland, mainly in southern England and East Anglia.

KINGFISHER

A flash of iridescent blue speeding along the river bank is the most that many people see of the stunningly coloured kingfisher. A closer view shows blue-green upper parts, orange cheeks and orange underparts. The bird has a white throat and neck patch, tiny red feet and a long, dark, dagger-like bill. It perches on a branch, watching for small fish. When a suitable prey is spotted, the bird dives into the water and catches its victim in its bill. The kingfisher returns to its perch, beats the fish against the branch to kill it, then swallows it head first. Both adults dig a long tunnel in the river bank to make their nest.

Iridescent blue-green above

Dagger-like bill

Orange-chestnut below

Red feet

Vivid blue back

Short wings and tail

Afer making a capture, the
kingfisher beats the fish
against the branch

Adult feeds
young bird

Nest is in tunnel dug in river bank

Kingfisher

Alcedo atthis

16.5cm

**J F M A M J
J A S O N D**

Along slow-moving
rivers; scarce in
Scotland.

White tip to beak of young

Juveniles duller, with a
white bill tip and duller legs

HOOPOE

When erected, the long, black-edged crest of the hoopoe is unmistakable. This is a bird that spends winter in Africa and migrates to southern and central Europe in summer. Some birds extend their journey northwards to southern England, and a few may stay to breed. Surprisingly for such a boldly marked bird it can be difficult to see when perched or when feeding on the ground. In flight, which is undulating with lazy flaps on broad, rounded wings, the striking appearance is unmistakable. The song is a low 'poo-poo-poo', often repeated and far-carrying.

Barred wings and tail

Crest flattened into hammer shape

Bee-eater
Merops apiaster

Another rare wanderer to Britain from the south, this equally unmistakable bird has bred here a very few times

Black-edged crest raised in alarm or when alighting

Long down-curved bill; feeds on insects and grubs

Pink-brown body

Hoopoe

Upupa epops

28cm

| J | F | **M** | **A** | **M** | **J** |
| **J** | **A** | **S** | O | N | D |

Rare. Woodland edges, orchards and other open woodland; feeds on bare soil or short grass (including lawns).

WRYNECK

Its habit of twisting and turning its neck when startled is responsible for this bird's name. Camouflaged with mottled grey and brown plumage, this unusual member of the woodpecker family spends much of its time on the ground, feeding on ants. Holes in trees are usual nesting places. Once common in England as a breeding bird, the species had virtually vanished by 1965. Although a few pairs, apparently from Scandinavia, have bred in the Scottish Highlands since 1969, these too may disappear. Up to 300 passage migrants are seen annually in spring and, especially, autumn.

Flight slow and hesitant

Barred underparts and tail

Plumage has intricate camouflage pattern

Wryneck

Jynx torquilla

16.5cm

| J | F | M | A | M | J |
| J | A | S | O | N | D |

Rare migrant, particularly on Shetland and east and south coasts of England.

GREEN WOODPECKER

The loud, ringing 'kew-kew-kew' call of this largest of British woodpeckers sounds like laughter and gives this bird the local country name of 'yaffle'. It is brightly and distinctively coloured. Both sexes have the black face-patch; the female has a black 'moustache', which on the male is red and black-edged. The green woodpecker seldom 'drums' like its two spotted relatives. And unlike them, it feeds mainly on the ground, using its dagger-like bill to hack into short grass to extract ants and their eggs, larvae and pupae from their nests.

Red crown

Longish, powerful tapering bill

Red 'moustache' edged in black

Green back

Male

Vivid greenish-yellow rump, conspicuous in flight

Ring-necked parakeet
Psittaccula krameri

Since about 1970, this long-tailed small green parrot has been breeding in gardens and parks, and orchards in south-east England; almost 7,000 birds were counted at one Surrey roost site

The adult female has a black 'moustache'. Juveniles have pale-spotted upperparts and dark spotted and barred underparts.

Green woodpecker

Picus viridis

32cm

J F M A M J J A S O N D

Widespread in woods in England and Wales, spreading in Scotland; not in Ireland.

GREAT SPOTTED WOODPECKER

Rapid blows with its bill on a dead branch produce the characteristic drumming sound of a great spotted woodpecker establishing territory. It is also known as the pied woodpecker because of its mainly black and white plumage. The large white shoulder patches are easily recognised. Both sexes have bright red under-tail patches, but only the male has a red patch on the nape. Young birds have a red cap.

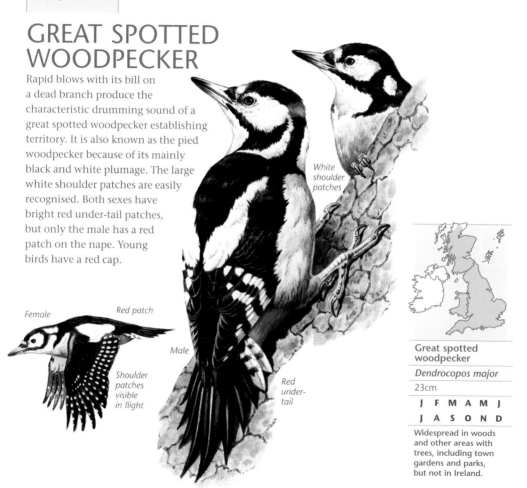

White shoulder patches

Female

Red patch

Male

Shoulder patches visible in flight

Red under-tail

Great spotted woodpecker

Dendrocopos major

23cm

J F M A M J
J A S O N D

Widespread in woods and other areas with trees, including town gardens and parks, but not in Ireland.

LESSER SPOTTED WOODPECKER

Only the size of a house sparrow, the lesser spotted woodpecker can be elusive among the top branches of trees where it likes to live. Its other name, the barred woodpecker, better describes its plumage; the black upper parts are barred with white. The male's cap or crown is red, the female's buff. The bird drums in spring; each burst is longer, softer, yet more rattling than that of the great spotted woodpecker.

Female has buff cap

Black and white pattern noticeable in flight

Young bird brownish on head

Red cap

White bars on black back

Male

Lesser spotted woodpecker

Dendrocopos minor

14.5cm

J F M A M J
J A S O N D

Woods and hedgerows in England and Wales; not in Scotland or Ireland.

The lesser spotted woodpecker often nests in orchards and rural parkland

SWIFT

Few birds spend more of their lives in the air than the swift. They collect all their food and nesting material in flight, and drink and bathe without alighting. Swifts even mate on the wing, and at dusk parties of them can be seen circling higher and higher into the sky to spend the night 'cat-napping' while airborne. Insects are funnelled into the large gape with the help of stiff bristles around the mouth. Food for the young is stored in a throat pouch which can often be seen bulging with gorged insects. Alighting only to nest and feed the young, the swift breeds in holes and crevices in cliffs and buildings.

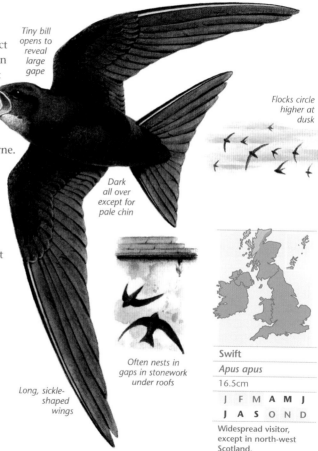

Tiny bill opens to reveal large gape

Flocks circle higher at dusk

Dark all over except for pale chin

Often nests in gaps in stonework under roofs

Long, sickle-shaped wings

Screaming mobs dash around rooftops

Swift

Apus apus

16.5cm

| J | F | M | A | M | J |
| J | A | S | O | N | D |

Widespread visitor, except in north-west Scotland.

WOODLARK

The woodlark's generic name *Lullula* is derived from its highly distinctive song, a rich medley of various phrases often repeated and interspersed with an occasional 'loo-loo-loo'. The song is delivered in a circular song flight, or from a tree or bush. Similar in appearance to the skylark, the woodlark has a shorter tail, buffish eye-stripes meeting across the nape, a white-black-white patch on the edge of the wing and a much smaller crest.

Woodlarks once bred in nearly every county in England and Wales, but were hit hard by cold winters in the 1960s. Mild winters and helpful woodland and heathland management have brought about a resurgence.

Seeds supplement insect diet in autumn

Long pale stripe over eye extends to nape

Small crest

No white trailing edge to wing

Buff nape band

Black-and-white patch near bend of wing

Very short tail with white tips

Woodlark

Lullula arborea

15cm

J F M A M , J A S O N D

Wooded areas and heaths with trees and scrub, mainly in south-west England and East Anglia.

SKYLARK

As it flies above the open fields and downs, giving voice loudly, the skylark is a difficult bird to ignore. It breeds more widely in Britain than any other bird, occurring on all types of open habitats including farmland, grassland, meadows, commons and sand-dunes. It is larger than the woodlark and has a plainer face and a bigger crest. Rising almost vertically in a hovering flight, often to several hundred feet, the skylark sustains its clear warbling song for several minutes, before sinking gradually to the ground, still singing. Sadly, this much loved bird has suffered major declines over the past 25 years, due to agricultural intensification.

The shore lark, a scarce winter visitor, mainly to the east coast of Britain, is distinguished by its boldly patterned head.

Crest may be lowered or raised

Dark-streaked brown upper-parts and breast and off-white below

Longish tail with white outer feathers

Long hind claws typical of larks

Yellow and black head with tiny black 'horns' in adult male in late winter

Male

Shore lark
Eremophila alpestris

Song sustained while in flight, often when hovering

Tail longer than woodlark's

Skylark

Alauda arvensis

18cm

J F M A M J
J A S O N D

Widespread; joined by migrants from northern and eastern Europe in winter.

Migrant skylarks on open sand-dunes

SWALLOW

Although swallows are regarded as harbingers of summer, the first birds often arrive from their African wintering grounds as early as March. Swallows rarely land on the ground except to gather nest material. They hunt and drink on the wing, skimming over the water. Their pleasant, twittering song is often heard as they perch on telephone wires. The swallow's russet throat and the long tail streamers of the adults (longest in males) are unmistakable. Swallows usually nest in barns, stables and other buildings, frequently return to the same locality, even the exact site, to breed. The nest is a cup of mud and straw, typically on a ledge or rafter.

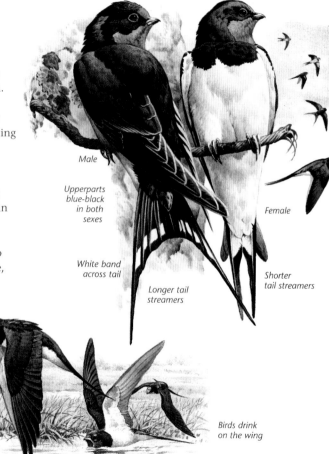

Male

Upperparts blue-black in both sexes

Female

White band across tail

Longer tail streamers

Shorter tail streamers

Russet throat and forehead in both sexes

Birds drink on the wing

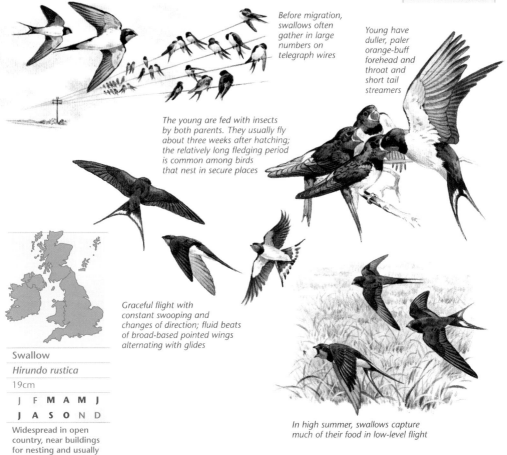

Before migration, swallows often gather in large numbers on telegraph wires

Young have duller, paler orange-buff forehead and throat and short tail streamers

The young are fed with insects by both parents. They usually fly about three weeks after hatching; the relatively long fledging period is common among birds that nest in secure places

Graceful flight with constant swooping and changes of direction; fluid beats of broad-based pointed wings alternating with glides

Swallow

Hirundo rustica

19cm

J F **M A M J**
J A S O N D

Widespread in open country, near buildings for nesting and usually water.

In high summer, swallows capture much of their food in low-level flight

HOUSE MARTIN

A short tail and a white rump distinguish the house martin from the swallow. Traditionally it is a cliff-nesting species, but it has adapted to nesting under house eaves. Its nest of mud and plant fibres is cup-shaped, with only a small entrance at the top. Arriving from Africa in April or May, house martins start breeding almost immediately and raise two or even three broods each year. The birds swoop and wheel to catch flying insects for food. Nests built by house martins that arrive early are often re-used by later migrants.

White underparts and bold white rump

Insects are caught in flight

Tail less forked than swallow's

Nests in small colonies

A thousand or more little pellets of mud are gathered to make the cup-shaped nest

Blue-black upper parts

House martin

Delichon urbica

12.5cm

J F M **A M J**
J A S O N D

Widespread in and around villages and towns, and farmland; scarce in north and west Scotland and western Ireland.

SAND MARTIN

The sand martin population is prone to fluctuations caused by the weather in its African winter quarters. Periodic droughts drastically reduce the numbers of aerial insects on which the birds feed. Slightly smaller than the house martin, the sand martin takes its name from its nesting habits: it digs out a 35-120cm long tunnel in a sand-bank, leading to a nesting chamber lined with plant material and feathers. In good weather years, sand martins may raise two broods.

Birds roost in reed-beds

Sand martin

Riparia riparia

12cm

J F **M A M J**
J A S O N D

Widespread where there are sandy banks for nesting, usually by rivers or in sand or gravel pits.

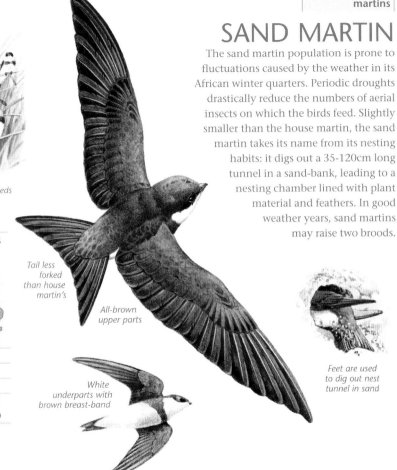

Tail less forked than house martin's

All-brown upper parts

White underparts with brown breast-band

Feet are used to dig out nest tunnel in sand

TREE PIPIT

From mid April onwards the tree pipit arrives in Britain to breed, after a winter spent in Africa. Fluttering up steeply from its perch high in a tree, the bird delivers a loud, far-carrying trill ending in 'zeea-zeea-zeea'. The bird continues to sing as it floats down, wings and tail held out like a parachute. The tree pipit is slightly more elongated than the meadow pipit, and has a slightly stouter bill, shorter hind claws and pinker legs. Its call is different – a strong, sharp 'teeaze'. It breeds in heathland, open woodland and young conifer plantations, the nest being well hidden in vegetation on the ground.

Male 'parachutes' down in song flight from tree

Flanks have only a few fine streaks

Bill slightly shorter than the meadow pipit, pinkish at base

Tree pipit

Anthus trivialis

15cm

| J | F | M | **A** | **M** | **J** |
| **J** | **A** | **S** | O | N | D |

Widespread in mainland Britain in open woodland; needs mix of open areas for feeding and trees or shrubs for song-posts.

Birds feed mainly on ground insects, also some seeds and berries

Pink legs; short hind claws visible at close range

Long tail, white-edged

'Parachuting' song flight starts and ends from ground

Fine bill

Slightly smaller, less elegant than tree pipit with plumper belly

Flanks more streaked than tree pipit

Long hind claws

Brownish legs

MEADOW PIPIT

Present all year, although many migrate south to France or Spain for winter, the meadow pipit is a bird of open country and one of Britain's commonest song-birds. Its long hind claws and more densely streaked breast, and its thinner 'eest' or 'tissip' call, distinguish this bird from the tree pipit. The conspicuous song flight by the male starts as the bird flies up to 30m from the ground, uttering an accelerating series of 'pheet' notes. These reach a climax and are replaced by slower and more liquid notes as the bird 'parachutes' down.

Meadow pipit

Anthus pratensis

14.5cm

J F M A M J
J A S O N D

Widespread, especially on heaths and moor-land; also on downs, rough grassland and salt-marshes.

ROCK PIPIT

Longer and darker-billed and darker-legged than other breeding pipits, the rock pipit inhabits rocky shores and cliffs. Other distinctive features are its heavily streaked breast and olive-brown upperparts, and grey outer tail feathers. Its alarm call, an explosive 'phist', is also distinctive. The nest of grass, moss and fine seaweed, built by the female, is usually concealed in a hole among rocks or in a cliff. The water pipit, a continental species, is a very scarce visitor to Britain in winter, often to marshes and watercress beds. It is identified by its white outer tail feathers, more prominent stripe over the eye and less streaked, whiter breast.

Relatively long, dark bill

Dark greyish-olive above, strongly streaked below

Grey outer tail feathers

Dark brownish legs

Whitish eye-stripe

Bold, pale stripe above eye

Whiter under-parts and fewer streaks than rock pipit

Water pipit
Anthus spinoletta

Bird feeds on seaweed insects

Rock pipit

Anthus petrosus

16.5cm

| J | F | M | A | M | J |
| J | A | S | O | N | D |

Breeds widely on rocky coasts; in winter also on other coasts and saltmarshes.

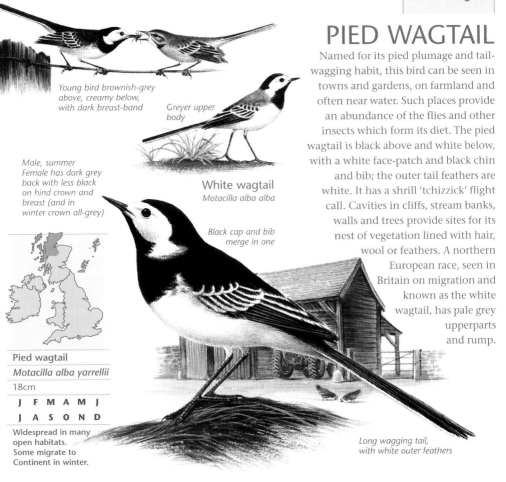

Young bird brownish-grey above, creamy below, with dark breast-band

Greyer upper body

Male, summer
Female has dark grey back with less black on hind crown and breast (and in winter crown all-grey)

White wagtail
Motacilla alba alba

Black cap and bib merge in one

Pied wagtail
Motacilla alba yarrellii

18cm

J F M A M J
J A S O N D

Widespread in many open habitats. Some migrate to Continent in winter.

Long wagging tail, with white outer feathers

PIED WAGTAIL

Named for its pied plumage and tail-wagging habit, this bird can be seen in towns and gardens, on farmland and often near water. Such places provide an abundance of the flies and other insects which form its diet. The pied wagtail is black above and white below, with a white face-patch and black chin and bib; the outer tail feathers are white. It has a shrill 'tchizzick' flight call. Cavities in cliffs, stream banks, walls and trees provide sites for its nest of vegetation lined with hair, wool or feathers. A northern European race, seen in Britain on migration and known as the white wagtail, has pale grey upperparts and rump.

YELLOW WAGTAIL

The slender yellow wagtail, a summer visitor, can often be seen sitting on a fence or tall plant calling with a loud, 'tsweep' or 'tsee-eep'. It lives in flooded areas: arable fields, water-meadows and marshes. It feeds on insects, and is frequently found near fly-bothered cattle and dung-heaps. The male bird is bright greenish above and yellow below; the female is duller. Migrant birds from the Continent with varying head colours appear from time to time; the blue-headed wagtail is the most often seen. The yellow wagtail's cup-shaped nest is built in a hollow on the ground.

Adult male, summer

Olive-green upper-parts and bright yellow face and underparts

Flying insects are caught

Blue-grey crown and cheeks; white stripe above eye

White edges to tail which is shorter than the other two wagtails

Young birds buff below, with black 'necklace' on throat

Male, summer

Blue-headed wagtail
Motacilla flava

Yellow wagtail

Motacilla flava

16.5cm

J F M **A M J**
J A S O N D

Marshes and wet meadows and other damp areas in most of England.

Birds roost together in winter

Young bird yellow under tail, unlike young yellow wagtail

Blue-grey above

Tail very long – longest of the wagtails

Female duller

White stripe over eye and between blue-grey cheeks and black throat

Black throat

Yellow below

Male

GREY WAGTAIL

A walk beside one of the rushing, tumbling streams in Britain's hill country may afford a glimpse of this elegant little bird. It spends much of its time walking along the water's edge or perching on a boulder, twitching its long tail as it watches for insects such as flies, midges, dragonflies and water beetles. Its yellow underparts are as bright as those of the yellow wagtail; but unlike the migrant yellow wagtail the grey wagtail is present all year. The nest is always by fast-flowing water and usually in a crevice or hollow. The usual call is a loud, sharp 'tswick', which is shorter than the pied wagtail's.

Grey wagtail

Motacilla cinerea

18cm

| J | F | M | A | M | J |
| J | A | S | O | N | D |

Widespread, but most abundant in northern and western uplands.

DIPPER

Unlike any other British bird, the dipper walks underwater on the bed of fast-flowing streams seeking food – mainly aquatic insects and their larvae. As it walks upstream with its head down, the force of the current against its slanting back holds it on the bottom. It also swims underwater and on the surface, propelling itself with its wings. Looking like an outsized wren with a white throat and breast, it is often seen on a rock, bobbing up and down and flexing its legs before plunging in. Both male and female build a domed nest under a bridge, behind a waterfall or beneath the overhang of a river bank.

Young bird has grey plumage that is darker with a scaly pattern above and with grey crescents below

Fast, whirring flight on short, straight wings

Short tail, often cocked

White throat and breast

Chestnut waistband

Bird walks underwater with back slanted and head down

Dippers often prefer swimming to flying

Dipper

Cinclus cinclus

18cm

| J | F | M | A | M | J |
| J | A | S | O | N | D |

Breeds mainly along fast streams and rivers, with some around lakes, mostly in upland north and west; some along slower lowland rivers in winter.

WREN

Tiny and inconspicuous, the wren can most easily be located by its voice, which is so loud for such a little bird. An explosive 'tit-tit-tit' is the call; the song is a very loud, shrill, rattling warble. The male builds a number of domed nests, one of which the female chooses and lines with feathers. With a diet of small insects and spiders, it is hard hit by severe winters but being a prolific breeder, it can soon make good losses of up to 80 per cent mortality in a particularly hard winter. They may huddle together in communal roosts in cold weather.

Fast, straight, whirring flight on short rounded wings

Bird briefly glimpsed flitting between patches of undergrowth

Tail often cocked

Eats small insects

Reddish-brown with dark barring above; buff below with barred flanks

Call is often made from a rock or wall

Wren

Troglodytes troglodytes

9.5cm

J F M A M J
J A S O N D

In most habitats throughout Britain and Ireland, from city centres to remote islands.

DUNNOCK

The dunnock uses its wings in a curious display. A pair or even a small party of birds will perch in the open and wave their wings at each other in a sort of semaphore – this is an aggressive display during territorial disputes. The dunnock has long been called the hedge sparrow, but it is not a member of the sparrow family. It is identified by its grey head and underparts and thin bill. Its song is a jingling warble, rather like the wren's but less aggressive in tone. It lines its cup-shaped nest with hair and feathers.

Blue-grey head and breast

Rich brown upperparts with dark streaks

Thin bill

Plumage brightest in spring

Streaked flank

Male

Often rears cuckoo from egg laid in nest

Dunnock's song is a short rapid warble quite similar to wren's

Young bird is duller and streaked all over its underparts

Dunnock

Prunella modularis

14.5cm

J F M A M J
J A S O N D

Widespread in gardens, woodland, farmland and other habitats with cover.

ROBIN

The robin's association with Christmas is appropriate, for it is during winter that its colours are most marked, with its breast at its reddest and its back a warm brown, both contrasting with whitish underparts. Young birds have speckled plumage and look like juvenile nightingales, though without the latter's reddish tail. The bird is tame in town and city gardens, and often accompanies gardeners to search for insects and worms as the ground is dug over. Away from habitation, however, it is shy and retiring, inhabiting woodland and hedges. Males are very aggressive and guard their territory possessively. The song is a high, pleasant warble and the loud alarm call a penetrating 'tic-tic'.

Male defends territory aggressively

Nest built in any convenient container such as an old teapot

Whitish belly

Robin

Erithacus rubecula

14cm

J F M A M J
J A S O N D

Widespread throughout Britain and Ireland in woods, hedgerows, gardens, parks and other places with trees, shrubs and undergrowth.

Red breast, with pale blue-grey border separating it from olive-brown upperparts

Song is thinner and more melancholy after moulting in autumn

NIGHTINGALE

The most famous songster of all, the nightingale is a shy bird more often heard than seen. Renowned for singing at night, it can also be heard by day. The rich song has short phrases, single notes and harsh trills. It is far louder, richer and very different from that of the robin, although often confused with it, since that species also often sings by night. Nightingales live in coppiced woodland, thick hedges, bramble thickets and other areas with dense cover.

Chestnut tail and rump, conspicuous in flight

Large dark eye, with pale ring

Buff underparts

Rich, brown back

Longish tail, reddish-brown

Juveniles heavily spotted and mottled; differs from young robin in having longer rufous tail

Nightingale

Luscinia megarhynchos

16.5cm

J F **M A M J**
J A S O N D

In wooded or scrubby habitats in England with dense cover, often near water; mainly in south and east.

REDSTART

A flash of bright, rusty red, low down in a tree or bush, reveals the redstart as it 'shimmers' its tail. This flickering motion plays an important part in courtship. A summer visitor from northern Africa, the male has a blue-grey back, black face and throat, white forehead, reddish belly and rusty rump and tail. The female is brown above and paler below, but has a rusty rump and tail like the male. The call is loud 'hooeeet-tac'; the song is a brief warble ending with a jingling rattle. The nest is in a crevice or hole in a wall or tree.

Scarce spring and autumn migrant, mostly on Shetland and east and south coasts; has bred a few times here; often skulks on ground among vegetation

Bluethroat
Luscinia svecica

Female brown above and paler below

Female in flight

Blue-grey back

Black mask

Reddish belly

Male, summer

Rusty tail

Young is mottled, like young robin, but with a rufous tail

Redstart

Phoenicurus phoenicurus

14cm

J F **M A M J**
J A S O N D

Widespread in British woods and parkland; mainly in northern and western uplands (most numerous in Wales); rare in Ireland.

BLACK REDSTART

The black redstart population in Britain began to grow during the Second World War, when bombed and derelict buildings and old docks made ideal nesting sites. Even today, fewer than 100 pairs breed in Britain, on sites that include factories, power stations and railway yards. Males are sooty black above, females browner. The song is a loud, reedy warble. The birds usually nest on a ledge or crevice.

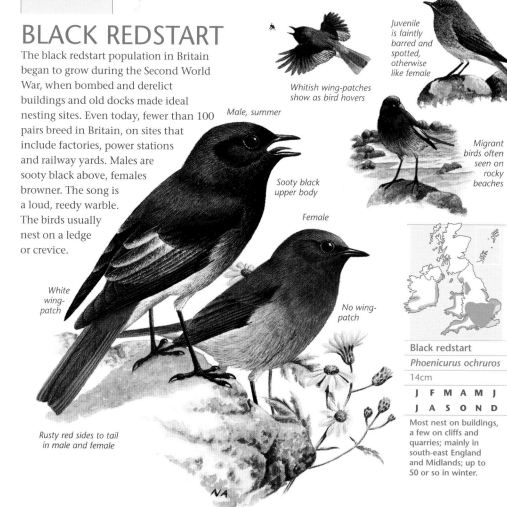

Whitish wing-patches show as bird hovers

Male, summer

Juvenile is faintly barred and spotted, otherwise like female

Migrant birds often seen on rocky beaches

Sooty black upper body

Female

White wing-patch

No wing-patch

Rusty red sides to tail in male and female

Black redstart

Phoenicurus ochruros

14cm

| J | F | M | A | M | J |
| J | A | S | O | N | D |

Most nest on buildings, a few on cliffs and quarries; mainly in south-east England and Midlands; up to 50 or so in winter.

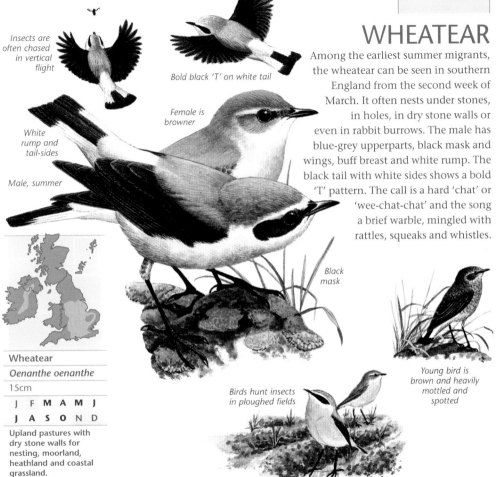

WHEATEAR

Among the earliest summer migrants, the wheatear can be seen in southern England from the second week of March. It often nests under stones, in holes, in dry stone walls or even in rabbit burrows. The male has blue-grey upperparts, black mask and wings, buff breast and white rump. The black tail with white sides shows a bold 'T' pattern. The call is a hard 'chat' or 'wee-chat-chat' and the song a brief warble, mingled with rattles, squeaks and whistles.

Insects are often chased in vertical flight

Bold black 'T' on white tail

Female is browner

White rump and tail-sides

Male, summer

Black mask

Wheatear

Oenanthe oenanthe

15cm

J **F M A M J J A S O** N D

Upland pastures with dry stone walls for nesting, moorland, heathland and coastal grassland.

Birds hunt insects in ploughed fields

Young bird is brown and heavily mottled and spotted

WHINCHAT

The attractive little whinchat, a breeding visitor, has disappeared from many areas in recent years. Heathland with plenty of gorse and bracken is the likeliest place to see breeding birds – 'whin' is another name for gorse. The male is noticeable for the white stripe above each eye and below the cheek and orange-buff breast; the female is less boldly marked. The whinchat builds its nest in thick ground cover. Prominent perches are used for fly-hunting and spotting prey on the ground. The whinchat winters in central and southern Africa.

Dark cheeks isolated by white stripes

One large and one small white patch on each wing

White sides to base of tail

Blackish-streaked brown upperparts

Orange-buff breast

Male, summer

Female less boldly marked

White wing and tail-patches visible in flight

Whinchat

Saxicola rubetra

12.5cm

J	F	M	A	M	J
J	A	S	O	N	D

Mainly on upland moorland, rough grassland and young conifer plantations.

STONECHAT

Small white rump

White wing-patch

No white markings on tail

Female has duller plumage

White half-collar

Black head

Male, summer

Stonechat

Saxicola torquata

12.5cm

J F M A M J
J A S O N D

Widespread on lowland heaths and coastal areas with gorse and young conifer plantations with heather, scarce in eastern England.

Perching on a high vantage point, the little, plump-bodied stonechat scolds intruders with its alarm call, a hard 'wee-tac-tac', like two pebbles being knocked together – hence the bird's name. Unlike the whinchat, it is a resident. It has a similar diet, of insects, worms, spiders and some seeds and blackberries. This enables it to rear up to three, or even four broods a year compared with the whinchat's maximum of two. The male has a black head, white half-collar, white patches on the wings and rump, and an orange-red breast. A nest of moss, grass and hair is well concealed, low in a bush.

SONG THRUSH

Broken snail shells littering the ground around a large stone indicate the presence of the song thrush. Tapping noises coming from cover may be the sound made by the bird as it smashes open the snails on a favourite 'anvil' to get at the contents. Aptly named, the bird is noted for its loud, rich song, which consists of a series of repeated musical phrases together lasting for 5 minutes or more. This impressive aria is usually delivered from a high perch. The bird's call is a thin 'sipp' in flight or a 'tchuck-tchuck' alarm note. It feeds mainly on snails, worms, insects and berries. There has been a 50 per cent decline in numbers between 1970 and 2001, with only a slight recent recovery.

Redwing

Golden-buff under-wing distinguishes song thrush from redwing

Song thrush

Warm brown above

Blackish spots on golden-buff breast and flanks; fewer spots on whitish belly

Song thrush

Turdus philomelos

23cm

J F M A M J
J A S O N D

Widespread in woods, hedgerows, gardens and other areas with trees and shrubs for nesting. Passage migrants and winter visitors from Continent.

White underwing

White tail tips

MISTLE THRUSH

The largest of the British thrushes is also the most boldly marked, with bigger and blacker spots than those of the song thrush. In flight, its white underwing and white tips to the tail help to distinguish it from other thrushes. The call is a harsh, rattling chatter and the song is a prolonged series of short, repeated phrases and fluty notes of considerable carrying power. This is usually sung from the top of high trees, and can be heard throughout winter as well as in spring and summer. Mistle thrushes feed on berries (including mistletoe), slugs, snails, worms and insects. After the breeding season small family groups often feed together.

Grey-brown above

Mistle thrush

Turdus viscivorus

27cm

J F M A M J
J A S O N D

Widespread in open woods and other areas with tall trees for nesting and song-posts and open ground for feeding.

Large, bold spots on whitish underparts

Longer wings and tail than song thrush

Very upright posture

Birds often seen in family groups

RING OUZEL

Similar to the blackbird in appearance, the male ring ouzel is distinguished by the white crescent or gorget across its breast and the pale silvery patches on its wings. Females are brownish-grey, with a less clearly marked crescent. These summer visitors from the Mediterranean are normally shy and nervous, but they can be aggressive at nesting time. The harsh 'chak-chak-chak' alarm call is more metallic than the blackbird's. The song differs too, its simple phrases of a few loud, fluty notes separated by pauses.

Slimmer and longer-winged than blackbird

Departing migrants feed in groups

Male

Female

Crescent is less marked

Pale edges to flight feathers show as silvery patches in flight

Clear white crescent

Ring ouzel

Turdus torquatus

24cm

| J | F | **M** | **A** | **M** | **J** |
| **J** | **A** | **S** | **O** | N | D |

Mountains and moors, mainly in west and north Britain.

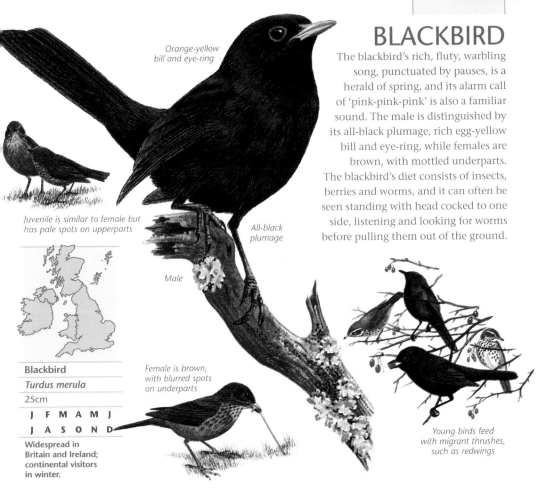

BLACKBIRD

The blackbird's rich, fluty, warbling song, punctuated by pauses, is a herald of spring, and its alarm call of 'pink-pink-pink' is also a familiar sound. The male is distinguished by its all-black plumage, rich egg-yellow bill and eye-ring, while females are brown, with mottled underparts. The blackbird's diet consists of insects, berries and worms, and it can often be seen standing with head cocked to one side, listening and looking for worms before pulling them out of the ground.

Orange-yellow bill and eye-ring

Juvenile is similar to female but has pale spots on upperparts

All-black plumage

Male

Blackbird

Turdus merula

25cm

J F M A M J
J A S O N D

Widespread in Britain and Ireland; continental visitors in winter.

Female is brown, with blurred spots on underparts

Young birds feed with migrant thrushes, such as redwings

FIELDFARE

Autumn and winter see large flocks of these colourful thrushes arriving in the British Isles from Scandinavia and Finland. The birds' 'chack-chack' chattering calls can be heard as they fly onto fields to feed on worms and insects. Noisy scuffles are common among flocks of fieldfares as they feed, and berry-bearing bushes are defended against all-comers. Later in winter, when the berry stocks have been eaten by thrushes and other birds, fieldfares, along with their relatives, visit gardens to gorge on windfall apples.

Grey rump

Chestnut back

Grey head and nape

Noisy scuffles common as birds feed

*Black tail and
flight feathers*

*Bold white
underwing*

*Orange-buff breast
heavily speckled*

Fieldfare

Turdus pilaris

25cm

J F M A M J
J A S O N D

Feeds in fields with
short grass, arable
crops or soil, also in
hedgerows, gardens
and orchards; very few
breed in Scotland and
northern England, but
many visit the British
Isles in winter.

*Black tail contrasts with
grey rump in flight*

REDWING

Leaving its northern European breeding grounds in autumn, the redwing is a passage migrant and winter visitor to the British Isles, although a very few pairs breed in Scotland. In September and October flocks can be heard flying over, uttering their thin 'seeip' contact call. The adults are smaller and darker than the song thrush, brown above, with a pale streak above the eye. Below they are whitish, with a yellowish-buff tinge to the breast, marked with dark spots and streaks, and have reddish flanks and under-wing patches. Their favoured food is hawthorn, holly and other berries. Worms, snails and insects are also eaten.

Rusty-red under-wing patches

Redwings often feed with other thrushes

Eye-stripe

Rust-red flanks

Dark brown upperparts

Redwing

Turdus iliacus

21cm

J F M A M J
J A S O N D

Feeds on fields with short grass or crops, or soil and in hedgerows, gardens and orchards.

Cetti's warbler
Cettia cetti

Dark, reddish-brown upper parts

Narrow pale stripe over eye

Pale underparts

GRASSHOPPER WARBLER

The distinctive trilling song or 'reel', like the sound of a cricket or a fishing reel being wound, is usually the only clue to this secretive warbler's presence. When disturbed, the bird usually creeps away mouselike through the dense vegetation which it favours, and only rarely is it seen flitting between bushes or tussocks. Cetti's warbler, a scarce recent addition to Britain's birdlife, is a secretive bird, resembling a small nightingale but usually located only by its loud, repetitive song. From its first breeding in Kent in 1972, the species has spread to various scattered sites in dense scrub near water, in southern England, East Anglia and south Wales. Unlike most other British warblers, it is a year-round resident.

Heavily streaked brown upper parts

Buff underparts plain or only lightly streaked on upper breast but with large dark streaks under the tail

Long, rounded tail

Grasshopper warbler
Locustella naevia

12.5cm

J F M A M J
J A S O N D

Widespread in wet and dry lowland habitats, from dense scrub and marshes to heaths, farmland and young conifer plantations, except far north.

SEDGE WARBLER

A summer visitor from Africa, the sedge warbler favours dense vegetation in damp areas such as reed and osier beds, and ditches and bushes near water. But it will also breed in standing crops and young forestry plantations. The song, a continuous and hurried mixture of harsh, chattering phrases, sweeter notes and mimicry of other birds, is delivered from the top of a reed or bush or as the male flies vertically upwards, singing, then descends on spread wings and tail.

Flights between patches of cover are low and direct.

Smudgy streaks on back; bright tawny-buff rump

The head pattern, streaked back and more compact shape distinguish the sedge warbler from the reed warbler

Creamy stripe above eye

Sides of breast and flanks have warm buff tinge

Sedge warbler

Acrocephalus schoenobaenus

12.5cm

| J | F | **M** | **A** | **M** | **J** |
| **J** | **A** | **S** | O | N | D |

Among thick vegetation, mainly by water; some breed in drier places, such as bramble thickets, young forestry plantations and fields of crops.

REED WARBLER

A common host of the cuckoo, this summer visitor from Africa breeds mainly in reed-beds, in the parts growing in the water. The harsh repetitive song, 'jag-jag-jag . . . chirruc-chirruc-chirruc', is similar to that of the sedge warbler, but harsher, slower, lower-pitched and more even. Breeding only in a few areas of south-east England, the very similar-looking marsh warbler's most distinctive feature is its song which is much sweeter and richer. A supreme mimic, it has been known to imitate as many as 70 other bird species.

Head looks peaked when singing, otherwise quite flat

Warm brown upperparts

Dark greyish legs

Reed warbler

Acrocephalus scirpaceus

12.5cm

J F M A M J
J A S O N D

Reed-beds in England and Wales.

Rounder head than reed warbler

Colder brown upperparts

Paler brownish or pinkish legs

Marsh warbler
Acrocephalus palustris

BLACKCAP

In recent years some blackcaps have started braving the English winter, visiting bird-tables and gardens for food, but they are normally summer visitors from the Mediterranean, with smaller numbers wintering in Africa. They have a rich, warbling song, shorter and more variable than that of the garden warbler. The male's black cap distinguishes it from all other British warblers. Insects are its main food.

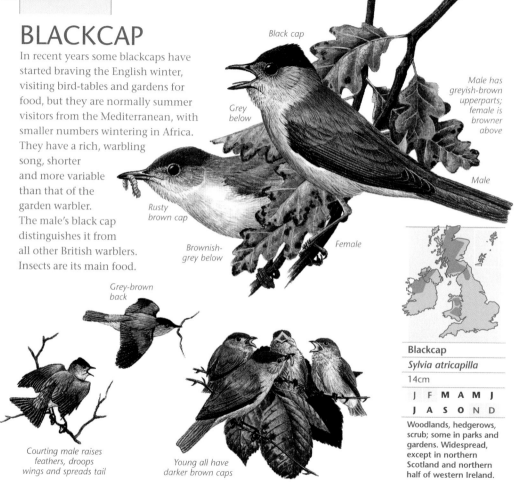

Black cap

Grey below

Male has greyish-brown upperparts; female is browner above

Male

Rusty brown cap

Brownish-grey below

Female

Grey-brown back

Courting male raises feathers, droops wings and spreads tail

Young all have darker brown caps

Blackcap

Sylvia atricapilla

14cm

J F M A M J
J A S O N D

Woodlands, hedgerows, scrub; some in parks and gardens. Widespread, except in northern Scotland and northern half of western Ireland.

GARDEN WARBLER

Despite its name, the garden warbler is found only in large, mature gardens with trees and shrubs. It is more a bird of open woodland and copses, where it announces its presence by its melodic song or harsh 'tacc-tacc' and grating 'churr' calls. In appearance it is a rather heavy-looking, short-billed bird, with no distinctive features. Before migrating back to Africa in winter it fattens up on berries.

Olive-grey-brown upper parts

Short bill

Pale buff underparts

Plain face

Tail spread and wings fluttered in courtship display

Nest built low, often in brambles

Garden warbler

Sylvia borin

14cm

J F M A M J
J A S O N D

Woods and bushy areas, especially in coppice and thickets. Not in much of northern Scotland and Ireland.

WHITETHROAT

Once the commonest warbler to be found in Britain, the whitethroat suffered a severe fall in numbers between the autumn of 1968 and the spring of 1969, because of a severe drought south of the Sahara, where the birds winter. Since then the breeding population has fluctuated at around a million pairs. The whitethroat's song, a short, scratchy warble, is often uttered by the male in a brief dancing display flight.

The barred warbler is a very scarce autumn passage migrant. Almost all records are of first-winter birds along the east coast of Britain.

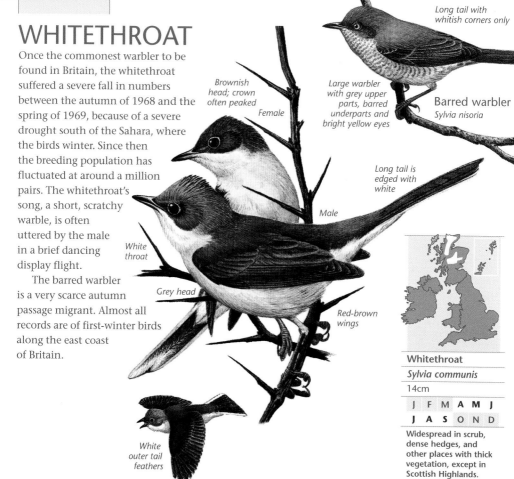

Long tail with whitish corners only

Brownish head; crown often peaked

Female

Large warbler with grey upper parts, barred underparts and bright yellow eyes

Barred warbler
Sylvia nisoria

Long tail is edged with white

Male

White throat

Grey head

Red-brown wings

White outer tail feathers

Whitethroat

Sylvia communis

14cm

| J | F | M | A | M | J |
| J | A | S | O | N | D |

Widespread in scrub, dense hedges, and other places with thick vegetation, except in Scottish Highlands.

Greyish upper parts

Dark cheeks

White throat

Dark cheek (variable) and dull brown wings

Underparts pale buff or have pinkish tinge

Tail rather shorter than whitethroat's, with white outer feathers

Shyer than whitethroat, usually concealed among cover

LESSER WHITETHROAT

Only marginally smaller than the whitethroat, the lesser whitethroat prefers areas with taller trees and shrubs and dense cover, especially bramble, blackthorn or hawthorn hedges or thickets. It is distinguished by its more uniform brown wings, which lack the contrasting reddish tinge of the whitethroat's wings. The bird's song often starts with a low warble, then continues with a rattling note repeated five or six times, audible at some distance.

The song is often delivered from the shelter of a bush or thicket.

Lesser whitethroat

Sylvia curruca

13.5cm

J F **M A M J**
J A S O N D

Rarely breeds in most of Scotland or Ireland; may be declining.

DARTFORD WARBLER

A secretive bird, the diminutive Dartford warbler is usually seen only when flitting between cover, or in spring, on warm, non-windy days when males may sing from the tops of gorse bushes. It is unusual among British warblers in that it does not migrate for winter. In periods of severe frost its numbers may decline substantially, as it cannot find the insects which form its diet. Despite the loss of most of its favoured heathland habitat, a succession of mild winters has enabled it to increase and spread.

Bushy grey head

Long, narrow tail is held cocked

Brown-grey back

Tiny body; head looks big and round

Male; female is less colourful

Tiny white spots on throat

Dark pinkish-brown below

Birds flit furtively between bushes

Dartford warbler

Sylvia undata

12.5cm

J	F	M	A	M	J
J	A	S	O	N	D

Dry, lowland heaths and commons with gorse and heather in southern England. The British breeding population is Europe's most northerly.

WOOD WARBLER

This handsome bird is named after its favoured habitat of oak or beech woods. Foraging for insects high in the tree canopy, the bird can be elusive and would be easily overlooked were it not for its distinctive voice. It has two different songs: one is a series of 'stip' notes accelerating into a very fast trilling 'sirrrr', which is repeated now and then, interspersed with the second song, a series of 5-20 plaintive 'pew' notes. Larger, more brightly coloured than the willow warbler and chiffchaff, it is greener above, clear lemon-yellow on the breast and above the eyes, with a pure white belly.

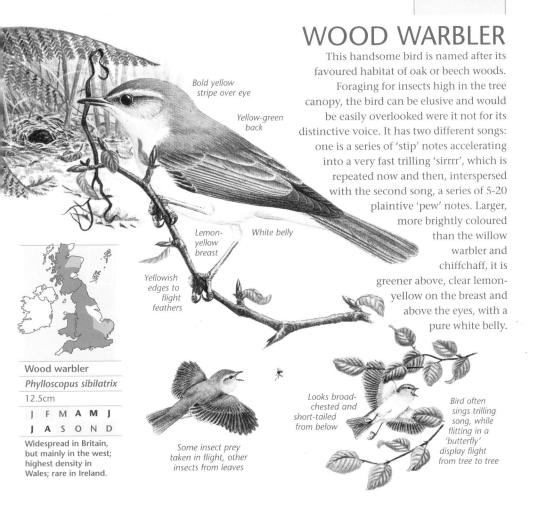

Bold yellow stripe over eye

Yellow-green back

Lemon-yellow breast

White belly

Yellowish edges to flight feathers

Looks broad-chested and short-tailed from below

Bird often sings trilling song, while flitting in a 'butterfly' display flight from tree to tree

Some insect prey taken in flight, other insects from leaves

Wood warbler

Phylloscopus sibilatrix

12.5cm

J F M A M J
J A S O N D

Widespread in Britain, but mainly in the west; highest density in Wales; rare in Ireland.

WILLOW WARBLER

By far the commonest of all warblers in the British Isles, the willow warbler is a summer visitor from Africa. Some 3 million pairs inhabit open woodland and bushy places – for the bird is in no way confined to willows. Its song, a wistful cadence of soft, liquid notes that descend in a pitch and end in a flourish, can be heard all summer as the bird darts restlessly among the foliage, feeding on its insect prey. Unusually, the willow warbler moults completely, replacing all its plumage twice a year.

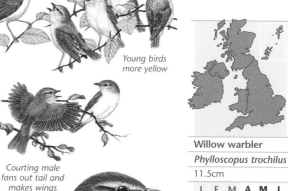

Young birds more yellow

Courting male fans out tail and makes wings quiver

Willow warbler

Phylloscopus trochilus

11.5cm

| J | F | **M** | **A** | **M** | **J** |
| **J** | **A** | **S** | O | **N** | D |

Widespread in woods and scrub.

Flight fast and agile

Greenish or olive above

Larger, more noticeable pale streak above eye

Yellowish below

Legs usually pale

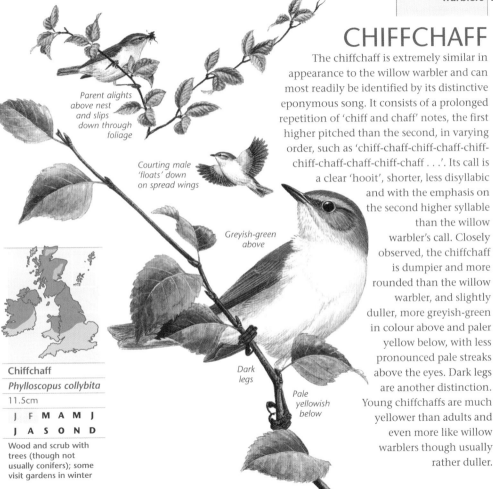

CHIFFCHAFF

The chiffchaff is extremely similar in appearance to the willow warbler and can most readily be identified by its distinctive eponymous song. It consists of a prolonged repetition of 'chiff and chaff' notes, the first higher pitched than the second, in varying order, such as 'chiff-chaff-chiff-chaff-chiff-chiff-chaff-chaff-chiff-chaff . . .'. Its call is a clear 'hooit', shorter, less disyllabic and with the emphasis on the second higher syllable than the willow warbler's call. Closely observed, the chiffchaff is dumpier and more rounded than the willow warbler, and slightly duller, more greyish-green in colour above and paler yellow below, with less pronounced pale streaks above the eyes. Dark legs are another distinction. Young chiffchaffs are much yellower than adults and even more like willow warblers though usually rather duller.

Parent alights above nest and slips down through foliage

Courting male 'floats' down on spread wings

Greyish-green above

Dark legs

Pale yellowish below

Chiffchaff

Phylloscopus collybita

11.5cm

J F **M A M J**
J A S O N D

Wood and scrub with trees (though not usually conifers); some visit gardens in winter

GOLDCREST

This is the smallest bird in Europe. Although often allowing close approach, it spends most of its time flitting from branch to branch in the top of coniferous trees, seeking the spiders, insects and larvae which form its diet. The bright orange centre to the crown of the male is visible only at close range; the female lacks the orange feathers to her all-yellow crest. A thin, blackish 'moustache' at the sides of the bill tends to give the goldcrest a mournful appearance. Juveniles lack the coloured crest, being dull greenish above and pale below.

Yellow crest

Female

Goldcrest

Regulus regulus

9cm

J F M A M J
J A S O N D

Most are in coniferous woodland, but also breeds in churchyard yews, parks and large gardens.

Dull green upper parts

Pale buff underparts

Short tail

Double wing-bars

Male

Crest has much orange mixed with yellow

Nest usually built in conifer

FIRECREST

Similar in appearance to the goldcrest – and only fractionally larger – the firecrest is much less commonly seen, being mainly a passage migrant in autumn and spring. It can be distinguished from the goldcrest by the black and white eye-stripes in both adults and juveniles and, in the adult male, far more orange in the more sharply black-bordered crest. Some females also have a little orange in the crown. Adult firecrests are a brighter green on the back and whiter below than goldcrests, and have bronze-coloured patches on the shoulders, especially in the male.

Firecrest

Regulus ignicapillus

9cm

J F M A M J
J A S O N D

Very scarce breeder in woods and regular passage migrant in southern Britain; some winter in scrub in south-west England.

Black and white eye-stripe

Courting male raises crest

Juvenile lacks crest

Mainly fiery orange crest

Green upper parts

Male

Bronze shoulder-patches

Whitish underparts have shining 'silky' appearance

Scarce autumn migrant seen mainly along east and south coasts of Britain and south-west Ireland

Pallas's warbler
Phylloscopus proregulus

Very scarce autumn migrant mainly along east and south coasts of Britain

Yellow-browed warbler
Phylloscopus inornatus

SPOTTED FLYCATCHER

Sitting on a low branch or other perch, the spotted flycatcher watches for its flying insect prey. Periodically it darts out and catches flies with an audible snap of its broad-based bill and quickly returns to its perch. The bird's plumage is mainly grey-brown above, pale below. Arriving from Africa in May, the birds seek out woodland edges and glades, gardens, parks and heathland. Both birds build a cup-shaped nest of dried grass and lichen among creepers such as ivy on walls or fences, in old nests of other birds or in an open-fronted nest-box. Calls are a squeaky 'tzee' and a sharp 'tzee-chick' of alarm, its simple song a series of quiet squeaky and scratch warbling notes, well spaced out.

Broad-based flat bill makes audible snap when bird flies out to catch insects

Soft, blurred streaks on breast and head

Grey-brown upper parts, silvery-whitish-buff below with pale edges to wing feathers

Juveniles prominently spotted and scaly

Spotted flycatcher

Muscicapa striata

14cm

| J | F | M | A | M | J |
| J | A | S | O | N | D |

Widespread, open wooded areas, large mature gardens, parks; numbers decreasing.

PIED FLYCATCHER

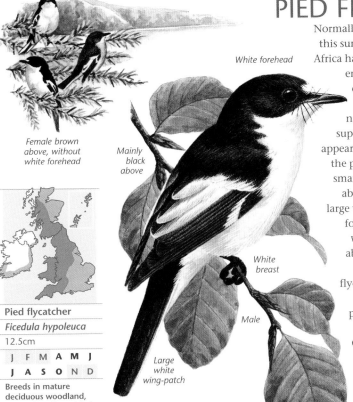

Female brown above, without white forehead

White forehead

Mainly black above

White breast

Male

Large white wing-patch

Pied flycatcher

Ficedula hypoleuca

12.5cm

J F M A M J
J A S O N D

Breeds in mature deciduous woodland, especially oak, mainly in western Britain; most abundant in Wales; elsewhere a regular passage migrant.

Normally breeding in holes in trees, this summer-visiting migrant from Africa has spread in Britain with the encouragement of nest-boxes deliberately placed for them in woodland in areas where natural tree holes are in short supply. Despite this, the species appears to have declined here over the past century. The male in his smart breeding plumage is black above and white below, with a large white wing-patch and white forehead; the female lacks the white forehead and is brown above. The birds catch insects in flight but unlike spotted flycatchers, rarely return to the same perch and also snatch prey such as caterpillars from leaves or even the ground. Calls are a sharp 'whit' and a 'tic' and the song a simple sweet warbling with marked changes of pitch.

LONG-TAILED TIT

The tail of this tiny bird is more than half the bird's total length and very conspicuous, especially in flight. The birds are almost always on the move in woods, commons, wasteland and hedges, feeding on small insects and spiders, as well as some seeds. Severe winters take their toll, and in some years reduce the bird's population by 80 per cent. The deep, purse-shaped nest is a masterpiece in moss, bound together with cobwebs and hair and camouflaged on the outside with lichen and lined with many hundreds of feathers.

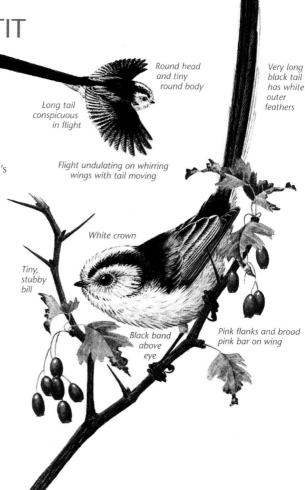

Round head and tiny round body

Long tail conspicuous in flight

Very long black tail has white outer feathers

Flight undulating on whirring wings with tail moving

White crown

Tiny, stubby bill

Black band above eye

Pink flanks and broad pink bar on wing

Head mainly blackish

Juvenile duller, with shorter tail

Birds roam about in small groups

Roosting birds huddle in tightly packed clumps for warmth

Parents feeding a nest of young are often aided by one or more unpaired adults

Long-tailed tit

Aegithalos caudatus

14cm

J F M A M J
J A S O N D

Widespread, but more abundant in the south.

BLUE TIT

For many people the blue tit is the star performer in the garden bird show, combining the talents of acrobat, conjurer and songster. It is small and highly adaptable: it was the blue tit that first cracked the problem of how to pierce milk-bottle tops to reach the layer of cream at the top – a practice that has almost vanished due to the popularity of semi-skimmed milk and decline in doorstep deliveries. Blue tits cannot digest lactose in milk, but cream presents no such problems. Originally a woodland bird, the blue tit will nest wherever there is a suitable small hole in a tree or a nesting-box. It has a large vocabulary of calls and a song comprising two or three thin, high notes followed by a rapid trill.

Birds readily use nest-boxes with small entrance hole c.0.29mm across

Blue cap

Green back

White face with black eye-stripe

Bluish wings and tail with white wing-bar

Yellow underparts

Young birds are duller with greenish caps and yellow faces

Blue tit

Parus caeruleus

11.5cm

J F M A M J
J A S O N D

Woods (largest populations in deciduous woods, especially oak), parks and gardens in all areas, including cities.

GREAT TIT

The great tit is the biggest, brightest and noisiest member of the tit family in the British Isles. Experts have identified over 50 distinct calls and songs, including the scolding 'cha-cha-cha', the chaffinch-like 'chink' calls and the often-heard, loud 'teacher, teacher, teacher' song and its variants. It is also extremely adept at finding ways to reach tempting morsels of food, such as a nut at the end of a piece of string. Its nest is usually in a hole in a tree or a wall, or in a nest-box, but occasional sites include, letter-boxes and drainpipes.

Single, white wing-bar

Bluish-grey and green upper parts

Black and white head

Great tit

Parus major

14cm

J F M A M J
J A S O N D

Woods and gardens in all areas; has gradually expanded its range northwards over the past 100 years, but does not occur in Orkney or Shetland.

Yellow belly, black stripe down body; wider and glossier in males

White outer tail feathers

Young are duller than adults, with yellow cheeks

CRESTED TIT

A common bird on the Continent of Europe, from the Mediterranean northwards to Scandinavia, the crested tit in Britain is found only in a relatively small area in Scotland. It is an extremely sedentary species and thus has not colonised the other large areas of planted pine forests which are its favoured habitat. The bird is easy to identify by its pointed black and white crest, unique among small British birds. Like the coal tit and treecreeper, it moves along the tree-trunks picking insects and their larvae from the bark, as well as eating pine seeds and berries.

Bird picks insects from bark of trees

Pointed black and white crest

Pine forests are a favourite habitat

Crested tit

Parus cristatus

11.5cm

J F M A M J
J A S O N D

Ancient native Scots pine forest and some native Scots pine plantations, between the Spey Valley and Moray Firth.

COAL TIT

The smallest British tit, the coal tit's favourite habitat is coniferous woodland, where its high-pitched 'tsee' call and sweet piping 'wee-choo, wee-choo' song (with the accent on the first syllable) can be heard. It often visits bird-tables, especially for nuts, meat and suet scraps and tends to fly off with them to hide and eat later. It survives prolonged periods of snow by feeding on insects beneath the bark of trees.

Black cap

Olive-grey upperparts

White cheek and nape-patch

Buff underparts

Two white wing-bars

Young have yellow cheeks and nape-patches

Coal tit

Parus ater

11.5cm

J F M A M J
J A S O N D

Widespread in woods, especially conifers but also in mixed and deciduous woods, also in gardens.

Birds eat insects under tree bark

MARSH TIT

In spite of its name, the marsh tit is rarely found in marshland but favours woods, heaths and hedges. It is almost indistinguishable from the willow tit at a distance except by its call and song. Its calls include a distinctive, loud, explosive 'pitchew' or a scolding 'chickabee-bee-bee-bee'. The song is a single, repeated ringing liquid 'chip, chip, chip'. Closely observed, its black crown is glossy and it lacks the pale wing-patch of the willow tit.

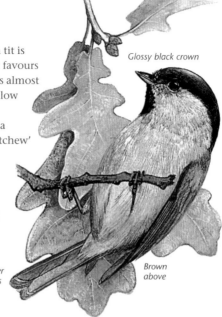

Glossy black crown

Brown above

Juvenile bird has a duller crown and is thus usually impossible to distinguish from willow tit

Plumage usually looks neater and sleeker than willow tit's

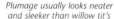

Birds feed mainly on lower vegetation; quite often with other tit species in mixed roving flocks in winter

No pale wing-patch

Marsh tit

Parus palustris

11.5cm

J F M A M J
J A S O N D

Deciduous woods in England and Wales, visits gardens, especially in winter; rare in Scotland and absent from Ireland.

WILLOW TIT

For years the willow tit was mistaken for the marsh tit, and it was not recognised as a separate species until 1897. Gradually it was realised that the willow tit is almost as common as the marsh tit. For unknown reasons, both species have declined in recent years. It is distinguished from the marsh tit by its matt black crown, less extensive white on cheeks, more diffuse black bib and pale panel on the wing. It can also be identified by its voice. The call is a loud, harsh 'tchay' (like a similar call of the marsh tit's) and a diagnostic, quiet buzzing 'zee-zee-zee'; the song is a short, rich, melodious warbling, unusual among tits.

Unlike marsh tit, but like great-crested tit, bird excavates nest-hole in soft tree-trunk

Willow tit

Parus montanus

11.5cm

J F M A M J
J A S O N D

Damp woods, often near rivers, streams or flooded gravel pits and reservoirs; less likely to visit gardens than marsh tit. Found in England, Wales and southern Scotland; absent in Ireland.

Matt black crown

Pale wing-patch

Like marsh tit, has brown upperparts and buff underparts with white on cheeks

BEARDED REEDLING

A twanging 'ping-ping' call-note announces a flock of tit-like bearded reedlings flying low over their territory. These birds inhabit dense beds of reeds. They are also known as bearded tits, but despite their tit-like appearance, they belong to a different family. They are called 'bearded' because of the black face markings on the male bird; these are lacking on the female. Bearded reedlings live mainly on the seeds of the *Phragmites* reeds they inhabit. The nest, built by both adults, is a deep cup of dead reeds and sedges, placed low down among the reed stems and lined with the feathery flower-heads of reeds. Two broods are often raised in a year.

Black 'moustache'

Tawny back

Male

Long tail

Larger than long-tailed tit

Black under-tail

Brown, no 'moustache'

Female

Birds fly low over reeds, tails fanning

Courting male displays 'moustache' and tail

Bearded reedling

Panurus biarmicus

16.5cm

J F M A M J
J A S O N D

Most in reed-beds in East Anglia and parts of southern England, with outlying colonies in northern England.

NUTHATCH

The nuthatch is unique in its ability to move down a tree-trunk as easily as up it. It picks up insects from the bark, and also feeds on hazel and beech-nuts, acorns and seeds. The nuts are placed into a crack in the bark, and the bird hammers them open to reach the kernel. The nuthatch's call is a loud repeated 'chwit' or a rapid, trilling 'chiririri'. Nuthatches breed in tree-holes or nest-boxes, making the entrance smaller by plastering round it with mud, which hardens in the sun.

Female uses mud to reduce size of nesting hole to prevent larger birds from taking it over

Nuthatch

Sitta europaea

14cm

| J | F | M | A | M | J |
| J | A | S | O | N | D |

Deciduous woods and mature gardens with trees in England and Wales; has recently started breeding in southern Scotland.

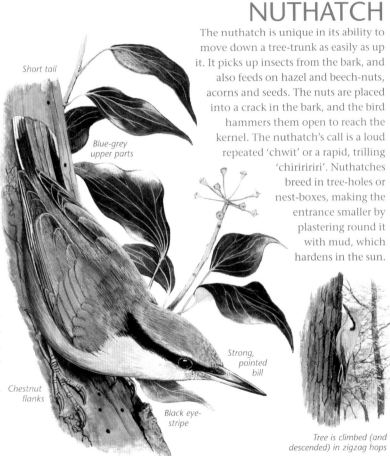

Short tail

Blue-grey upper parts

Chestnut flanks

Strong, pointed bill

Black eye-stripe

Tree is climbed (and descended) in zigzag hops

TREECREEPER

Thanks to its large, sharp claws and stiff, fairly long, frayed-looking tail, the little treecreeper can progress jerkily up tree-trunks in its search for bark-dwelling insects. It climbs spirally up one tree and then – because it cannot hop down like the nuthatch – flies down to the base of another and starts its upward journey again. The treecreeper's song a trill followed by a warble, is thin and very high-pitched, its call a shrill 'tseee'. In winter, treecreepers and nuthatches associate with flocks of tits as they search for insects. The nest is usually behind loose bark or ivy on an old tree. The young climb well, but are poor fliers at first.

Mottled brown and cream above

Pale stripe above eye

Long, down-curved bill

Silvery-white below

Large claws for climbing

Treecreeper

Certhia familiaris

12.5cm

J F M A M J
J A S O N D

Woodlands in most parts of Britain and Ireland; also visits large gardens and hedgerows, especially in winter.

Shuffles mouse-like with fast, jerky movements up tree-trunk

Longish, stiff tail

Pointed tips to tail

JAY

The most colourful member of the crow family in the British Isles, the jay is heavily dependent on trees – especially oaks – and is more often heard than seen. It scolds woodland intruders with a loud, harsh 'skraaark'. When seen, the pinkish-buff plumage, streaked crown, white rump and blue wing-patch are distinctive. A major food is acorns, which are often collected and buried among fallen leaves and twigs to be eaten in the winter. Beech-nuts, peas, fruit and berries are similarly stored. Jays also eat small mammals, insects and worms, and will sometimes raid the nests of other birds for eggs or young.

Streaked crest can be raised in display when alarmed

Prominent white rump and wing-patches

Pinkish-brown back

Blue wing-patch

Jay

Garrulus glandarius

34cm

J F M A M J
J A S O N D

Woodlands in most of the British Isles, but not in northern Scotland and part of western Ireland.

Jay buries acorns and other food

MAGPIE

Once heavily persecuted and considered a pest, the magpie is now increasing in numbers, especially in suburban areas where it was once unknown. Its black and white plumage and long wedge-shaped black tail, with multicoloured iridescence in sunlight, make it one of the easiest of all birds to identify. During the nesting season magpies often stay hidden in overgrown hedgerows and thickets, their presence only revealed by their call, a hoarse, laughing chatter 'chacha-chacha-chak'. The birds build a large, domed nest of sticks. Young birds, which have shorter tails, leave the nest after three to four weeks. Though often accused of wiping out songbirds, detailed research shows that its habit of eating eggs and young has a negligible effect on their overall populations – indeed where magpies thrive, so do songbirds – and it has a wide diet, including berries, seeds and other plant material in winter, and carrion and insects, including many harmful to farming and gardening.

Black head and chest; rest of underparts white

Wedge-shaped tail, spread as rudder

Large, white shoulder patches; outer wing feathers mainly white

Large white patches on shoulders

Flanks and belly white

Pied plumage – on black areas, gloss is bluish-purple on head, breast and back, bluish-green on wings

Tail tinged with purple, reddish, blue and green

Long tail

Juveniles are duller, with far less gloss, and short tails

Magpie

Pica pica

45cm

J F M A M J
J A S O N D

Widespread in many habitats, from farmland, moorland and other open areas to city centres, as long as there are trees for roosting. Absent in northern Scotland.

Magpies steal eggs and sometimes nestlings of other birds, but only as part of a very wide-ranging diet

CHOUGH

Master of the air, performing breathtaking aerobatics as it glides, dives, rolls and soars above rocks or sea, the chough is a bird of mountain crag and sea-cliff. It has purple and blue-glossed black plumage, and unique long red curved bill and red legs. Once fairly widespread, the population has declined due to habitat and food loss and depredation, bad weather, predation and human persecution. In particular, modern agriculture has reduced the areas of low-intensity grazing that create the short open cliff-top or grassland. Choughs feed on worms, caterpillars and other insects, and also eat small shellfish. They are often seen in small flocks, and their wild, excited 'keeaar' call is distinctive. The name 'chough', now pronounced 'chuff' was once spoken as 'chow', being an imitation of its call. The nest is built on a ledge or crevice in a cave, or on a cliff.

Wing-ends upturned in soaring flight with primary flight feathers separated like fingers

Curved red bill, adapted for probing into short turf, soil and cowpats for insects

Acrobatic displays common

Red legs

Glossy purple-black plumage

Chough

Pyrrhocorax pyrrhocorax

39cm

| J | F | M | A | M | J |
| J | A | S | O | N | D |

Coasts of Wales, Isle of Man, Islay, Colonsay and Jura in the Inner Hebrides, and Ireland; a few have just returned to breed in Cornwall.

JACKDAW

Easily identified by its grey nape, which contrasts with its darker grey and black plumage, jackdaws are very sociable and usually found in pairs or flocks. They often feed and roost with rooks. The bird's diet includes cereals, potatoes, fruit and berries as well as insects, mice and worms. Jackdaws often store and hide food and sometimes steal the eggs and nestlings of other birds. They nest in tree holes, old nests of other birds, rabbit burrows or chimney pots. The main call is a loud, explosive 'tchack' , a long 'kyaaar' and a shrill 'keeya'.

Jackdaw

Corvus monedula

33cm

J F M A M J
J A S O N D

Breed on cliffs, quarries, ruins, chimneypots and old woodlands throughout Britain and Ireland.

Short bill

Faster wing-beats than rooks or crows

Whitish-grey eyes

Grey nape

Black back

Dark grey underparts

Relatively short legs

Birds flock together on derelict buildings such as castles

ROOK

As many as 6000 rooks have been counted in one raucous rookery, their nests at the tops of tall trees standing out in springtime against a network of bare branches. They feed in flocks on roadside verges, rubbish tips and fields, especially on permanent pasture on farmland, where the soil contains many of the bird's favourite insect foods – leatherjackets and wireworms. A bare, white face-patch, elongated thigh feathers and highly glossy purplish-black plumage distinguish the adult rook from the similar but more solitary carrion crow. Juveniles lack the pale face-patch but have the adults' distinctive, slim, pointed bill shape.

Crown often looks peaked

Black plumage with strong purple gloss

Bare white face-patch – quite slender pointed bill with un-feathered nostrils

Long thigh feathers

Throat pouch distended when carrying food

Wedge-shaped tail

Rook

Corvus frugilegus

45cm

| J | F | M | A | M | J |
| J | A | S | O | N | D |

Widespread, especially in lowland farmland with tall trees for nesting. Absent only from treeless uplands and large towns.

CARRION CROW

Smaller than the raven but far more common, the carrion crow has few friends. Its scavenging habits and harsh croaking call have not endeared it to man, and it has been persecuted because of its liking for grain and root crops and thieving of the eggs and chicks of game birds. Birds south and east of north-west Scotland are usually all black carrion crows, while a more northerly very close relative (formerly regarded as a subspecies of the carrion crow) have grey bodies and are known as hooded crows. In between, the two species often interbreed, producing hybrids that have black plumage with some grey markings.

Heavier, blunter bill than rook with feathered nostrils

Square-ended tail

Birds often feed on carrion

All-black plumage is only slightly glossy

Carrion crow

Corvus corone

47cm

J F M A M J
J A S O N D

Widespread. Hooded crow in north-west Scotland and Ireland; carrion crow elsewhere; hybrids along zone of overlap.

Square-ended tail

Grey body; black wings

Hooded crow
Corvus cornix

RAVEN

In the past the raven, the world's largest member of the crow family, was regarded as a bird of ill-omen and harbinger of death. It probably acquired its reputation because of its black plumage and its habit of feeding on corpses hanging on the gibbet or slain in battle. Once common throughout the British Isles, it has been forced by man to withdraw to remote sea-cliffs, mountains, quarries, moors and windswept hills. Like most crows, the raven's main method of acquiring food is by scavenging. But it will also kill birds or small mammals, and forage for eggs, reptiles, insects and seeds. Its very large stick nest is usually placed on a rock ledge or in a tree. Calls are distinctive and include a far-carrying deep, resonant, 'prruk prruk' or an echoing, higher-pitched 'tok tok tok', often given in flight.

Stout, heavy bill

Shaggy throat feathers

All-black plumage

When the raven croaks, the feathers on its crown and shaggy throat are raised

Long, finger-like spread wing-tip feathers

The raven will occasionally feed on dead sheep and lambs. The major part of its diet comes from small mammal carrion

Diamond-shaped tail visible in flight

Ravens often perform dramatic aerobatic displays over their territory, soaring, diving, tumbling and characteristically, making a half roll (or occasionally a complete one) in flight

Raven

Corvus corax

64cm

J F M A M J
J A S O N D

Lives mainly in uplands and coasts in north and west British Isles.

GOLDEN ORIOLE

Despite the brilliant golden-yellow and black plumage of the male golden oriole he is seldom visible in its favoured woodland habitat. Usually the only clue to its presence is a fluty, melodious whistle 'weela-wheco'. Like the hoopoe this is a rare summer visitor, with a few pairs staying to breed. Female and juveniles are yellow-green, streaked on the breast, and can be confused with the green woodpecker. Some old adult females can resemble adult males. The female builds the nest, a suspended cup, in the fork of a branch. The eggs are incubated by both parents.

Male

Black tail with yellow corners

Black wings with small yellow patches

Narrow black mask

Male

Bill pinkish-red

Yellow body

Female

Yellow-green plumage

Underparts pale, sreaked

Yellow undertail and rump (not as bright as male's)

Golden oriole

Oriolus oriolus

24cm

J	F	M	**A**	**M**	J
J	**A**	**S**	O	N	D

A few pairs breed in poplar woods in East Anglia; elsewhere, rare spring migrant.

RED-BACKED SHRIKE

The red-backed shrike population has decreased drastically in Europe and it is virtually extinct as a breeder in Britain where it is at the edge of its range. Owing to colder, wetter summers and the effects of insecticides and consequent food scarcity, and to the destruction of the birds' habitat, today none now breed in England or Wales and only a handful of pairs in Scotland. Shrikes like to perch on a bush, fence or telegraph wire, watching for prey. Like its great grey relative, the smaller red-backed shrike often stores its victims by impaling them on thorns.

Hooked bill

Black band through eye

Black, grey and white plumage

The larger great grey shrike is a very scarce migrant and winter visitor to open habitats

Grey cap; black face-stripe

White edge to tail

Male

Great grey shrike
Lanius excubitor

Red-backed shrike
Lanius collurio

17cm

J F M A M J
J A S O N D

Scarce migrant on east and south coasts; a few pairs nest in Scotland.

Female is dull brown above and buff below

Grey rump and white sides to tail

Male

Slightly smaller than a starling

Red back

Juveniles resemble females but usually have dark, fine crescent markings above

WAXWING

Winter visitors to the British Isles, waxwings do not breed here; mostly only 100 or so are seen, but during 'interruption' years when their breeding populations in northern Scandinavia and Russia outstrip the food supplies, several thousands arrive here searching for berries – the rowan, hawthorn and whitebeam are favourites, though they also eat rose, cotoneaster, and many other berries and some seeds. Adults are pinkish-brown, darker on the back, with a unique long, pointed crest, a black mask and throat, grey rump and yellow-tipped black tail. Black, yellow and white appear in the wings with the red waxy-looking blobs that give the bird its name. The call is a shrill, trilling, bell-like 'sirrr'.

Crest

Black on throat and around eyes

Dumpy body

Multi-coloured wings; dull rufous undertail

Yellow tip to tail

Birds fly swiftly and directly in flocks

Flight silhouette and alternate flapping and closed wing flight action resembles starlings, but waxwings have longer, plumper bodies and less dart-like flight

Birds gather in groups to eat berries from trees and shrubs

Waxy red tips on wing feathers visible at close range

Waxwing

Bombycilla garrulus

18cm

J **F** **M** **A** M **J**
J **A** **S** **O** **N** **D**

Shrubs and trees, mainly in east; numerous only in occasional years.

Ponds and puddles are drinking places

STARLING

This assertive and noisy bird is as familiar in towns as it is in the country. Starlings' droppings foul buildings and pavements, and their voracious appetite can strip fields of corn. On the other hand, they eat leatherjackets, wireworms and other garden and farm pests. An expert mimic, the starling imitates other bird-calls and songs, incorporating them into its own song, largely a jumble of squeaks and whistles. Hundreds of thousands of starlings are present in Britain all year, and in winter their numbers are swollen by millions more that arrive from the Continent to take advantage of our milder winter climate. Nevertheless, starlings have declined dramatically in Britain – by almost 70 per cent in the past 35 years.

Starlings often hawk for flying insects in midair

Glossy, iridescent blackish plumage

Sharply pointed yellow bill, with bluish base to lower mandible in breeding season

Female has all-yellow bill. In both sexes, bill is dark grey in winter

Adult male in breeding season, with relatively few buff spots or none

Legs and feet are pinkish in spring, brown in winter

After breeding, starlings often gather in huge flocks, performing amazingly co-ordinated aerobatic manouevres and calling noisily before settling to roost

Starlings often make nests in old woodpecker holes but any hole in a tree or cliff – or in homes and other buildings, including in cities, will do. Males begin making a nest before pairing.

Juveniles mouse-brown, gradually becoming blackish with white spots, giving patchy appearance

Starling

Sturnus vulgaris

22cm

J F M A M J
J A S O N D

Found throughout Britain and Ireland apart from high mountains in many open habitats. Feeds mainly on grassland, from farm fields and parks to garden lawns, also on shores, rubbish dumps, town centres.

Adult in winter plumage heavily speckled with white

Feeds by inserting bill and opening it below ground while looking down and spotting insect larvae food

HOUSE SPARROW

Among the most familiar of British birds, the house sparrow is, surprisingly, less numerous than the chaffinch, blackbird or wren. It is largely dependent on humans for its food and nesting places, but it is also likely to be due to humans that it has suffered the recent much publicised decline – likely factors include agricultural intensification and air pollution in urban areas caused by cars. A persistent 'chee-ip' is the commonest call, and the simple song a series of chirping notes. The sparrow's nest is a rather untidy affair in a hole or under the eaves of a building. Where there are no suitable man-made structures it will build a domed nest in a hedge, bush or tree.

Grey crown and chestnut-brown area on rear of head

Large, untidy black bib

Male, breeding plumage

Dark-streaked chestnut-brown back

Pale grey cheeks and underparts

Sparrows often dust-bathe in suitable spots on open ground in high summer, making small hollows in the dry earth in the process

Female   *Male*

Female's plumage is far duller, without the grey crown or black bib

Young birds beg for food from their parents by holding their bodies low and quivering their wings

Nests are often domed structures of straw and feathers when built in hedges; but in cities and towns an untidily lined hole in a building or tree will suffice

House sparrow

Passer domesticus

14.5cm

J F M A M J
J A S O N D

Towns, villages and farmland throughout Britain and Ireland, but recently in much reduced numbers.

House sparrows mingle with finches in winter to feed on seeds

TREE SPARROW

This slightly smaller and neater country cousin of the house sparrow is distinguished by a chestnut crown, white half-collar, neater bib and black cheek spot. Adults, both males and females, and young are all similarly marked. Populations fluctuate, and distribution is to some extent dependent on the availability of suitable nesting sites. In the 1970s and 1980s there was a massive decline of more than 80 per cent due to agricultural intensification. Breeding is in colonies; both sexes build the domed nest in a suitable hole or cavity in a tree, wall or cliff face or in a nest-box, using dried grass or straw. In flight, tree sparrows give a high, distinctive 'teck-teck' call.

Courting birds bow and run at each other

Neat black bib

All-chestnut crown

Partial white collar

Black patch on cheek

Tree sparrow

Passer montanus

14cm

J F M A M J
J A S O N D

Far scarcer than house sparrow and less linked to humans. Lives mainly in open woodland, farmland with trees, orchards and quarries.

GOLDFINCH

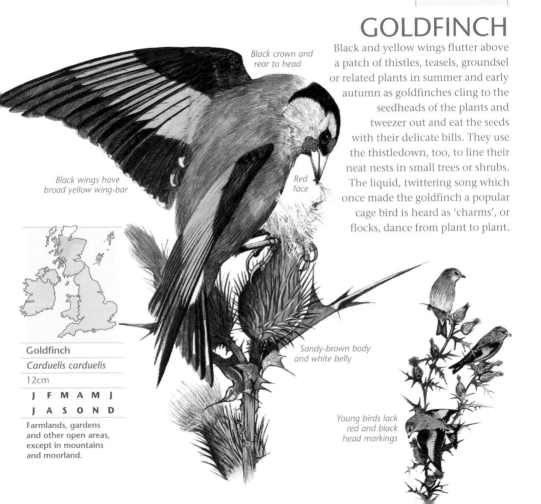

Black and yellow wings flutter above a patch of thistles, teasels, groundsel or related plants in summer and early autumn as goldfinches cling to the seedheads of the plants and tweezer out and eat the seeds with their delicate bills. They use the thistledown, too, to line their neat nests in small trees or shrubs. The liquid, twittering song which once made the goldfinch a popular cage bird is heard as 'charms', or flocks, dance from plant to plant.

Black crown and rear to head

Black wings have broad yellow wing-bar

Red face

Sandy-brown body and white belly

Young birds lack red and black head markings

Goldfinch

Carduelis carduelis

12cm

J F M A M J
J A S O N D

Farmlands, gardens and other open areas, except in mountains and moorland.

CHAFFINCH

One of the British Isles' commonest birds – there are about 6 million pairs in Britain and over a million in Ireland – the chaffinch nests in hedges and trees. It feeds itself and its young on insects, but in winter roams widely in large flocks by day seeking seeds in fields and other open places. There is no mistaking the colouring of the male chaffinch when at rest, while in flight it shows its white shoulder patches and wing-bar. The nest is a cup of grass, moss and lichens, lined with hair. The loud cheerful, sweet rattling song starts slowly, accelerates down the scale and ends with an exuberant flourish; it is repeated up to five or ten times a minute. The alarm call is a loud 'pink, pink, pink'.

White wing-bar and shoulder patch

Chestnut back

Slate-blue crown and neck

Females less colourful but have same wing pattern

Wing pattern visible when perched

Pink-brown below

Male

Chaffinch

Fringilla coelebs

15cm

| J | F | M | A | M | J |
| J | A | S | O | N | D |

Widespread, nesting in woods, scrub, hedges, parks and large gardens.

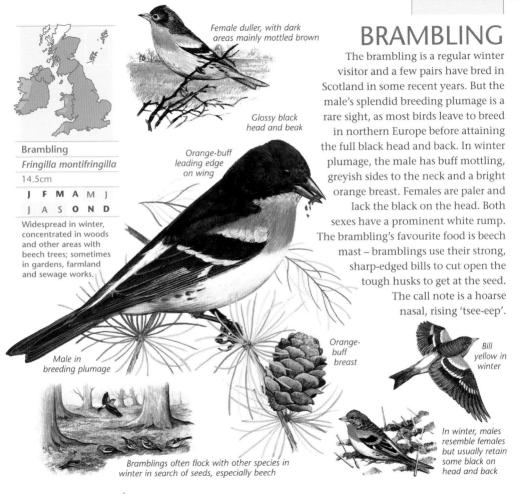

BRAMBLING

The brambling is a regular winter visitor and a few pairs have bred in Scotland in some recent years. But the male's splendid breeding plumage is a rare sight, as most birds leave to breed in northern Europe before attaining the full black head and back. In winter plumage, the male has buff mottling, greyish sides to the neck and a bright orange breast. Females are paler and lack the black on the head. Both sexes have a prominent white rump. The brambling's favourite food is beech mast – bramblings use their strong, sharp-edged bills to cut open the tough husks to get at the seed. The call note is a hoarse nasal, rising 'tsee-eep'.

Brambling

Fringilla montifringilla

14.5cm

J **F M A** M J
J A **S O N D**

Widespread in winter, concentrated in woods and other areas with beech trees; sometimes in gardens, farmland and sewage works.

Female duller, with dark areas mainly mottled brown

Glossy black head and beak

Orange-buff leading edge on wing

Male in breeding plumage

Orange-buff breast

Bill yellow in winter

Bramblings often flock with other species in winter in search of seeds, especially beech

In winter, males resemble females but usually retain some black on head and back

GREENFINCH

Bright yellow wing and tail flashes help to identify the greenfinch against a background of woodland and bushes. It is a frequent visitor to town gardens, especially when there is water for bathing or peanuts on the bird-table. Greenfinches build their bulky cup nests in bushes, using twigs, moss or roots. The flight calls are a fast twittering and hard 'jup jup jup', and they have two different songs: one a loud trill, often followed by a long, wheezy 'djeeeee', the other a jumble of trills, whistles and twitters rather like that of a canary. In song flight the male often flits and weaves erratically with extra-slow wing-beats.

Yellow wing and tail flashes are distinctive in flight

Pink bill

Female duller, with slightly streaked underparts

Brighter green than female

Dark area around eye

Yellow on wing and tail

Male

Greenfinch

Carduelis chloris

14.5cm

J F M A M J
J A S O N D

Widespread in lowlands, in woods, farmland with hedges, gardens and other areas with trees and bushes; in winter also on salt-marshes and other open habitats.

SISKIN

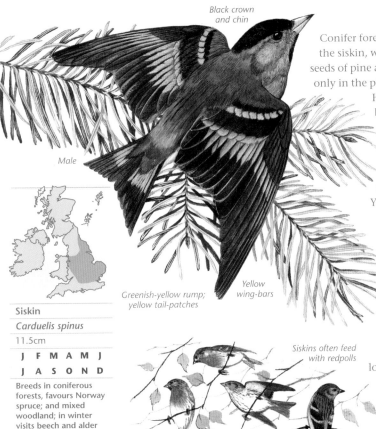

Conifer forests are the main home of the siskin, which feeds largely on the seeds of pine and spruce. It used to live only in the pine forests of the Scottish Highlands; though it now breeds more widely, most birds seen in southern Britain are winter visitors. Siskins like to flock together, often in alder trees during winter. Yellow-green in colouring, like the greenfinch, it is a distinctly smaller bird and the male has a black crown and chin. Siskins build their small, neat, cup-shaped nests high in conifer trees, and towards the tips of branches. The call is a loud, sharp 'tsing' or 'tsuu' and the song a mixture of twittering notes and long wheezy sounds.

Black crown and chin

Male

Greenish-yellow rump; yellow tail-patches

Yellow wing-bars

Siskins often feed with redpolls

Female less yellow, more streaked

Male

Siskin

Carduelis spinus

11.5cm

J F M A M J
J A S O N D

Breeds in coniferous forests, favours Norway spruce; and mixed woodland; in winter visits beech and alder trees, usually near water, and gardens for peanuts.

LINNET

In Victorian and Edwardian times linnets were often kept in cages for their musical song, a varied twittering heard between late March and late July. Now a protected bird, this small, slim finch now faces a new enemy in the increased use of weedkillers, which are depleting the seeds of wild flowers such as chickweeds, fat-hen and dandelions which make up its diet. Linnets build their nests a few feet off the ground, often in gorse or bramble. The call is a dry twittering.

Crimson forehead

Grey head

Chestnut back

Male

Female duller, more streaked

Crimson patches on either side of breast

Tail is quite long and forked

White edges to wing and tail feathers seen in flight

Linnet

Acanthis cannabina

13.5cm

J F M A M J
J A S O N D

Breeds mainly in open country with gorse and other dense bushes, farmland with thick hedges, young conifer plantations and large gardens.

TWITE

Although it breeds in moorland and upland areas, the twite extends its range in winter to salt-marshes, stubble fields and coastal areas, where the birds can be seen in small flocks, often feeding with other finches. It is easily confused with female and young linnets, but has a yellow bill in winter, and the male has a pink (not brownish) rump in spring and summer. It also has a buff throat and a longer, more forked tail. The female has a greyish rump and is drabber. Food is mainly seeds, but insects are also eaten. The call sounds like 'twa-it' and is longer and more nasal or bleating than the linnet's. The nest, a cup on the ground, is built by the female.

Bill brownish-grey in summer, yellow in winter

Streaky brown plumage

Male

Notched tail

Pink rump

Long, deeply forked tail

Twite

Acanthis flavirostris

13.5cm

J F M A M J
J A S O N D

Breeds in uplands of northern England, north Wales, Scotland and western Ireland; winters locally on coasts.

Twites mix with other finches in winter

LESSER REDPOLL

Streaked brown with red and pink patches, like the linnet, the lesser redpoll's main distinguishing mark is its black chin. It nests in a variety of sites, from low gorse bushes and alder thickets to the high branches of silver birches and conifers. The nest is a cup of twigs, grass and plant stems. The redpoll's flight call is a rattling metallic trill. Flocks of redpolls often rise from the treetops and wheel in the air a few times before settling again.

Neat black chin and black around base of bill

Red forehead (dull red to yellowish on females)

Small yellowish bill

Birds feed on tree and wild flower seeds

Red and pink breast and rump – rarely seen on female

Buff wing-bars

In winter, birds feed in flocks on alder and birch seeds, often mixing with siskins

Male

Lesser redpoll

Larger, paler common redpolls such as the bird on the right from northern Europe and Greenland may visit in winter

Common redpoll

Forked tail

Lesser redpoll

Acanthis cabaret

11.5–15cm

J F M A M J
J A S O N D

Widespread in woods, thickets, tall hedges and heaths with trees but has suffered an 80 per cent decline in the past 30 years.

CROSSBILL

Feeding mainly on pine seeds, this bird and related species have developed a peculiar bill, one mandible of which crosses over the other. This enables it to prise open the cones to extract the seeds. Although conifers are greatly preferred, the crossbill at times also eats the seeds of rowan, ivy, hawthorn and thistles; some insects and other invertebrates are taken too. The male has brick-red or orange-red plumage, while the female is yellowish-green. Young birds are greenish-grey with dark streaks. Breeding is usually from February to July but has been recorded for every month of the year; the nest of twigs and grass is built high in a conifer.

Female
Green plumage

Forked tail

Dark wings

Male

Crossed bill

Brick-red head and body

Young have uncrossed bill

Crossbill

Loxia curvirostra

16.5cm

| J | F | M | A | M | J |
| J | A | S | O | N | D |

Widespread though sporadic and shifting breeder in coniferous woodlands; scarcer in Ireland.

BULLFINCH

Despite its beautiful distinctive colouring, the bullfinch is not often seen; it is a secretive bird, generally keeping to cover in hedgerows and bushes. Often the only clue to its presence is the soft piping 'dew' of its call note. The male has bright, pinkish-red underparts, black cap, grey upperparts and a striking white rump. The female has a similar pattern, except for a duller, browner-grey back and dull salmon-pink underparts. Bullfinches often raid orchards to strip fruit trees of their young buds, the stubby bill being specially adapted for this diet. The birds breed mainly in woodlands with dense undergrowth but also in parks, thick hedges and scrubby areas, and large mature gardens. The nest of twigs, moss and lichens varies from a shallow platform to a bulky cup.

Black cap; stubby bill

Male

PInkish-red underparts

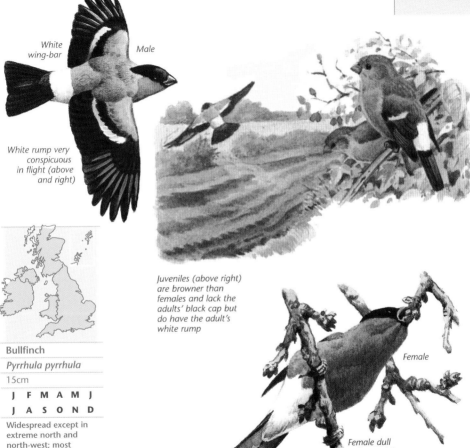

White wing-bar

Male

White rump very conspicuous in flight (above and right)

Juveniles (above right) are browner than females and lack the adults' black cap but do have the adult's white rump

Bullfinch

Pyrrhula pyrrhula

15cm

J F M A M J
J A S O N D

Widespread except in extreme north and north-west; most numerous in southern England and southern Ireland.

Female

Female dull salmon-pink below

HAWFINCH

The largest of Britain's finches also has the most powerful bill. It uses this to crack open the stones of fruit such as cherries and sloes to get at the edible kernels which form much of its diet. It also feeds on beech and hornbeam seeds, tree buds and insects. Hawfinches are very elusive birds, keeping mainly high up in the tree canopy in mature woodlands. An abrupt 'tik' occasionally indicates the bird's presence overhead. The nest, often built in an oak or fruit tree, is bulky, constructed of twigs and moss, and lined with roots and grass.

Female

Female

Female plumage duller than male's with pale grey panel on wing

Large head

Pale grey nape

Massive, strong bill, blue-grey in breeding season, pale buff in winter

Male

Chestnut body and head

Hawfinch

Coccothraustes coccothraustes

18cm

| J | F | M | A | M | J |
| J | A | S | O | N | D |

Mature deciduous and mixed woods, especially with hornbeam. Scattered distribution; most common in south-east England. Rare in Scotland and Wales; absent from Ireland.

Big head, tipped short tail, broad white band on inner wing and white 'flash' on outer wing

Most visible in autumn and winter when they feed more on the ground

Young bird lacks black bib and has dark bars on its belly

Largely white wings

White head

Male, summer

Black back

Female, like male in winter, is brown and white

Snow bunting

Plectrophenax nivalis

16.5cm

J F M A M J
J A S O N D

Up to 100 pairs breed in Scottish Highlands; most winter visitors are seen on or near coasts elsewhere though in north Britain, some winter on moorland and mountains.

SNOW BUNTING

Although snow buntings breed mainly in the Arctic, on rocky coasts, high mountains and tundra, a small population nests on high mountain-tops in the Scottish Highlands and occasional pairs elsewhere on high mountains. As winter visitors they are more common, occuring in small flocks on the shoreline especially in eastern Britain. Possibly more than 10,000 birds winter in Britain and Ireland but it is thought that numbers are declining. In summer, the male is mainly white with black on the wings, back and tail. The female is brown and white, as is the male in winter. The song is a brief fluting 'turee-turee-turee-turiwee'. The nest is usually in a cranny between rocks and is made of moss and grasses, lined with wool or feathers.

REED BUNTING

Once confined to reed-beds, marshes, fens and riversides, the reed bunting has spread to other, drier habitats. In summer the male's black head and throat are distinctive, and both sexes have a white moustache-like streak. Reed buntings often mingle with yellowhammers, house sparrows and finches in winter when they search for food. The song is a very simple, repetitive 'cheep-cheep-cheep-chizzup'. The nest, a cup of grass and moss lined with hair, is built on or close to the ground.

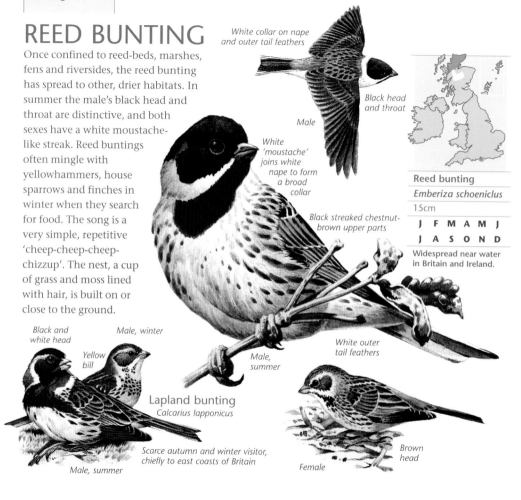

White collar on nape and outer tail feathers

Male

Black head and throat

White 'moustache' joins white nape to form a broad collar

Black streaked chestnut-brown upper parts

Reed bunting

Emberiza schoeniclus

15cm

J F M A M J
J A S O N D

Widespread near water in Britain and Ireland.

Black and white head

Yellow bill

Male, winter

Male, summer

Lapland bunting
Calcarius lapponicus

Scarce autumn and winter visitor, chiefly to east coasts of Britain

White outer tail feathers

Male, summer

Brown head

Female

CORN BUNTING

The largest of the British buntings inhabits cornfields and other lowland arable areas, as well as heaths and downlands. Adult birds of both sexes have streaked brown plumage and a heavy head with a yellowish, stubby bill. The song – usually delivered from the top of a bush, fence post or telegraph wire – consists of a rapidly repeated note speeding up into a flourish. It sounds like a bunch of jangling keys. The fluttering flight is sparrow-like, and the male often leaves his legs dangling during a display flight. A loose cup of grasses and plant stems, lined with hair, forms the nest, which is built on the ground or in a bush or hedge.

Male dangles legs in display flight

Heavy head with stubby bill

Corn bunting
Emberiza calandra
18cm

J F M A M J
J A S O N D

Arable farmland; rare in west; seriously declining everywhere.

Streaked brown plumage

Corn buntings mingle with sparrows to feed in winter

YELLOWHAMMER

'A little bit of bread and no cheese' is a popular human interpretation of the yellowhammer's song – a repeated series of notes ending in 'zeee' or 'chwee' – with some variations. The bird inhabits hedged fields, scrubby heathland and commons, feeding on seeds, berries, grain and insects. The male has a bright yellow head and breast, and a chestnut back streaked with black; its plain chestnut rump distinguishes it from the cirl bunting. Females are duller and more streaked. The nest is a neat cup of grasses. The ortolan bunting is a rare spring and autumn migrant, mainly to Orkney, Shetland and the Isles of Scilly.

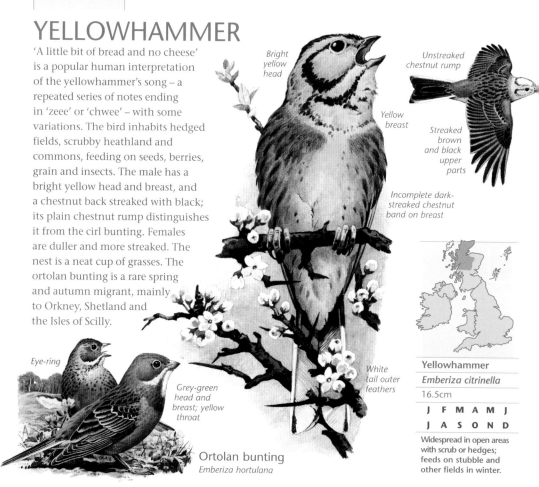

Bright yellow head

Yellow breast

Incomplete dark-streaked chestnut band on breast

Unstreaked chestnut rump

Streaked brown and black upper parts

White tail outer feathers

Eye-ring

Grey-green head and breast; yellow throat

Ortolan bunting
Emberiza hortulana

Yellowhammer

Emberiza citrinella

16.5cm

J F M A M J
J A S O N D

Widespread in open areas with scrub or hedges; feeds on stubble and other fields in winter.

Male

Streaked olive-grey rump

Striped black and yellow head

CIRL BUNTING

Once spread across southern England, cirl buntings have declined greatly in numbers over the past 70 years and are now very localised. The male's black and yellow head, black chin, grey-green breast-band and streaked olive-grey rump distinguish it from the male yellowhammer. Females lack the head pattern and breast markings and are buffish. The song is a rattling, repeated single note. The cirl bunting feeds on seeds, berries and some insects. The nest is made of grass, moss and rootlets.

Male

Greenish breast-band

Birds join yellowhammers to feed in winter

Cirl bunting

Emberiza cirlus

16.5cm

J F M A M J J A S O N D

Arable farms with many hedges and trees; now breed only in South Devon, but a reintroduction scheme is underway in Cornwall.

GREENFINCH
Carduelis chloris
MALE
PAGE 298

Yellow tail flashes

Yellow wing flashes

Yellow rump; much bright yellow on head

Yellow wing-bars

SERIN
Serinus serinus
MALE

Rare spring visitor, mainly to southern England and East Anglia, has bred a few times

SISKIN
Carduelis spinus
MALE
PAGE 299

Green rump

Yellow tail flashes

Yellow wing-bars

White rump

GOLDFINCH
Carduelis carduelis
MALE
PAGE 295

Scarlet face, black and white head

Broad yellow wing-bar

Finches and buntings in flight

Plumage, flight pattern and habitat all help to distinguish these birds, shown here in breeding plumage. Wing, rump and tail patterns usually identify the finches; buntings differ only slightly in wing and outer tail feathers. The flight of most finches is strongly undulating; in smaller species it is especially jerky and dancing. Linnets, twites and goldfinches frequent open, weedy places, while redpolls, siskins and serins flit between trees, bullfinches skulk in woodland and scrub; hawfinches, when disturbed, take refuge high in trees. Crossbills are birds of conifer woods; snow and Lapland buntings keep mainly to mountains and coasts. Reed buntings breed in marshes or other damp spots. The corn bunting has an abrupt 'quit' call-note.

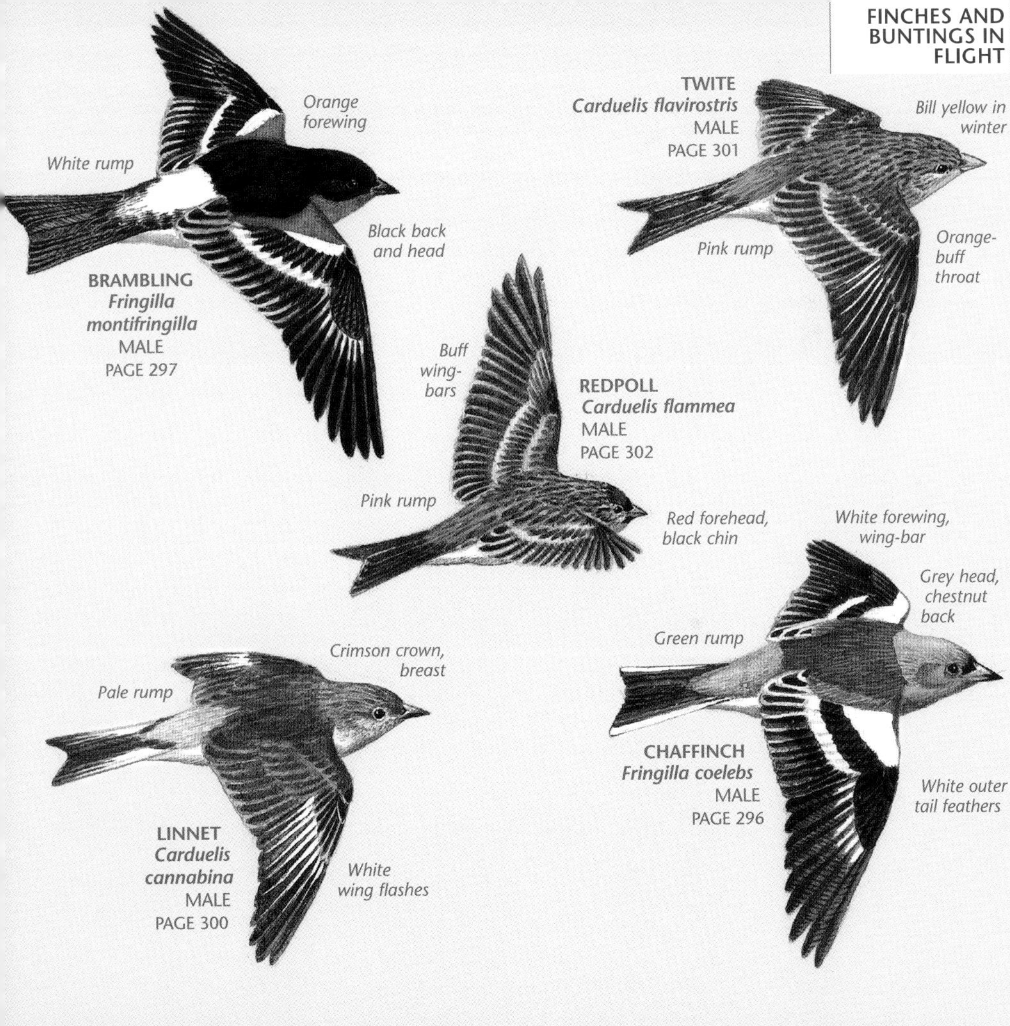

White rump

Orange forewing

BRAMBLING
Fringilla montifringilla
MALE
PAGE 297

Black back and head

TWITE
Carduelis flavirostris
MALE
PAGE 301

Bill yellow in winter

Pink rump

Orange-buff throat

Buff wing-bars

REDPOLL
Carduelis flammea
MALE
PAGE 302

Pink rump

Red forehead, black chin

White forewing, wing-bar

Grey head, chestnut back

Green rump

CHAFFINCH
Fringilla coelebs
MALE
PAGE 296

White outer tail feathers

Pale rump

Crimson crown, breast

LINNET
Carduelis cannabina
MALE
PAGE 300

White wing flashes

BULLFINCH
Pyrrhula pyrrhula
MALE
PAGE 304

Blue-grey back

Bright white rump

Black cap

White wing-bar

Pinkish-red underparts

White wing-bar and shoulder patch

Broad white tip to tail

HAWFINCH
Coccothraustes coccothraustes
MALE
PAGE 306

Heavy head, massive pale bill

Black and yellow face

Dark-streaked olive-brown rump

Black throat

CIRL BUNTING
Emberiza cirlus
MALE
PAGE 311

Bright yellow head and underparts

Unstreaked red-brown rump

YELLOWHAMMER
Emberiza citrinella
MALE
PAGE 310

ORTOLAN BUNTING
Emberiza hortulana
MALE
PAGE 310

Greenish-grey head

Pink bill

Brown rump

REED BUNTING
Emberiza schoeniclus
MALE
PAGE 308

White outer
tail feathers

Black head

White nape,
moustache

Mainly brick-
red body

Greyish-green
streaked head
and body

Red
rump

Crossed
bill

Large white
wing-patches

Large white
tail-patches

CROSSBILL
Loxia curvirostra
PAGE 303

Female

SNOW BUNTING
Plectrophenax nivalis
MALE
PAGE 307

Male

All-brown
wings

Stubby bill

All-brown tail

Rusty
nape
patch

Yellow bill

Dull,
generally
featureless

CORN BUNTING
Emberiza calandra
MALE
PAGE 309

LAPLAND BUNTING
Calcarius lapponicus
MALE
PAGE 308

Bird
Behaviour

SONG THRUSH *A variety of short phrases are repeated in a loud, clear voice, such as 'Did he do it?' 'Did he do it?' 'Philip, Philip, Philip' and 'quick, quick, quick'.*

ROBIN *The passionate cascade of liquid warbling notes mixed with shriller notes and abrupt changes in pitch and tempo come from the robin. It is exceptional as it sings all year round, with both sexes using their voices. It also sings at night, especially when stimulated by a street light, floodlight, or full moon, and may then be thought to be a nightingale.*

MISTLE THRUSH *A bird in full song during rain is likely to be the mistle thrush, also known as the storm cock. His low song is wilder than a blackbird's with broken phrases consisting of three to six short notes followed by a pause.*

DUNNOCK *A cheerful, high-pitched hurried-sounding series of broken warbling phrases comes from the dunnock. He likes to sing from the protection of a hedge or shrub.*

The dawn chorus

As winter retreats, the melodious chorus of early morning birdsong can begin at 4am in the south. Although the pavements may still be wet, and the parks and gardens bare and muddy, just before dawn first one male bird and then another sings at the top of his voice to attract a female to join him and to warn off rivals. The chorus starts at dawn for practical reasons.

One is that the light is not yet strong enough to allow predators to pinpoint the whereabouts of the singer. And an early start also means that the chorus does not cut into valuable feeding time. Most songbirds are primarily insect eaters – at least in the breeding season – and they find it hard to detect their prey when the light is poor. Another reason is that the air is usually calmer at

HOUSE SPARROW *The call of the house sparrow is a rather persistent, rattling 'chissup' or 'chee-ip'. Not known for the quality of their song, sparrows make up for it in enthusiasm and volume.*

GREAT TIT *This vociferous bird's commonest forms of song are a shrill, see-sawing 'tea-cher tea-cher', and a repeated cry of 'pee-too, pee-too'.*

WREN *The wren utters 'tic tic' alarm calls and a remarkably loud, explosive song of clear, high-pitched warbling notes mixed with (and usually ending on) intense, rattling trills.*

LATE CALL *The spring migrants rise later than the permanent residents, and the first to join in is often the chiffchaff, soon followed by a wistful, rippling cascade of sound from the willow warbler (below).*

STARLING *If you think you heard a lapwing, curlew or golden oriole in the city, you've probably just been duped by a starling. These common town birds are excellent mimics.*

dawn and sound transmission is at its best. No two dawn choruses are ever the same: which birds take part and the order in which they begin to sing will vary, but the blackbird is usually one of the first voices to be heard. Its rich melodious song has a flute-like quality. Various phrases are performed, but without the repetition that typifies the song thrush, another one of the first singers, that likes to sing perched high up in the trees or on a TV aerial. Other very early performers include the robin and the surprisingly loud warble of little wrens. Over time, the chorus intensifies, perhaps later incorporating such songs as the thin trill of a bluetit in flight and the cheerful song of a chaffinch.

SHOWING ANOTHER SIDE
The jay turns sideways to meet an enemy, ruffling and spreading its feathers to make itself look bigger.

MARKINGS THAT WARN
When threatening, a male ringed plover bends his legs, raises the featheres on his back and spreads his tail, to make him look bigger and more threatening and faces his rival to display his dramatic black and white markings.

THREAT IN A COLOUR
The male yellow wagtail frightens rivals by stretching himself and showing off the brilliant yellow plumage of his underparts.

Fighting – resolving disputes

Competition between birds for territory, nest sites, food and mates produces hostility, although instead of fighting, most birds use a system of bluff, from frightening calls to physical displays. Rivalry is at its most intense during the breeding season. If song and flying displays fail to do the trick, birds have a repertoire of other menaces. At close quarters they make themselves look as big and fearsome as possible – puffing out their feathers, stiffening crests or crown feathers and executing a series of menacing movements. Real battles do break out, particularly when one bird threatens another's nest during the breeding season. Normally, the males engage in a brief and relatively bloodless contest: perching birds flutter breast to breast,

ADMITTING DEFEAT *Some of the most spectacular battles in the bird world occasionally take place between male mute swans. When the fight is over, the losing bird submits by stretching its neck forward along the water or ground and keeping still, so the winner soon stops pecking.*

SKIRMISH ON A LEDGE *Two gannets, with their dagger-like bills interlocked, battle to topple one another over the edge of a cliff.*

BATTLE IN THE WATER *Long, sharp claws are used by these fighting coots to give vicious effect to each blow of their feet.*

grappling with their bills; pigeons beat each other with their wings. Contests usually end when one bird concedes defeat, often by flying away. But when a bird is cornered, it will employ a set of submissive postures. It stays motionless, head withdrawn, feathers fluffed up, and does its best to hide the markings which, at other times, would be used to frighten enemies.

Birds may attack any animal, or even human, that comes too near the nest. Seabirds can be particularly ferocious: a breeding fulmar will shoot an invader with an oily, evil-smelling liquid from its stomach via its bill; skuas may dive straight at an intruder's head, striking out viciously with their clawed feet. They have even been known to draw blood from a man's head.

MATING COLOURS *A puffin in the mating season (left), and the same bird at other times; the bright new colours help it to attract a mate. A male house sparrow in the breeding season (left) also shows bolder distinctive markings.*

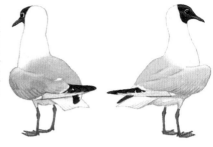

HEAD FLAGGING *Both male and female black-headed gulls take part in courtship displays: here they start threatening one another, then suddenly turn their heads away.*

TRIUMPH CEREMONY *A spectacular display of the breeding season is provided by Canada geese as they race together with necks outstretched, calling loudly.*

Courtship rituals

The 'language' of bird courtship involves song, plumage and display. A bird uses these to spell out a number of messages – where it has established a territory; when it wishes to pair up; its sex and species; where it has found a possible nest site; and when it is ready to mate.

Most courtship begins in spring, before nesting gets under way, the male usually taking the initiative. Many birds have special plumages and ornaments – crests, plumes and wattles – to enhance their displays. The robin has its red breast, herons have plumes, and grebes and ruffs use a variety of head ornaments. The plumage of many male ducks is an almost permanent multicoloured display. In species where male and female plumages are alike, birds are often

MUTUAL PREENING
Two jackdaws strengthen the link between them by preening feathers on each other's heads.

Ghostly penguin display

Cat display

DISCOVERY CEREMONY *Part of the great crested grebes' elaborate dance is known as the discovery ceremony. One bird approaches the other in a shallow underwater 'ripple dive', then rises up beyond it in the 'ghostly penguin display'. The second bird faces it in the 'cat display', and then the first rotates to face it. After this, they shake their heads at one another.*

RITUAL OF THE CARESS
Mutual fear and aggression are reduced between these wood-pigeons by caressing one another.

aggressive towards one another in the early stages of courtship. This enables the male to discover the sex of the bird to which he is displaying: an aggressive response means that the other bird is a male, too. Courtship displays are often mutual between birds of similar plumage – male and female play identical roles simultaneously, as in the 'greeting' ceremonies of herons. The great crested grebe has an intricate courtship dance in which both sexes take part. Not all birds with similar plumages display together, however; in starlings, wrens and various pigeons, display is left to the male.

Courtship displays help to establish a bond by breaking down the aggressiveness and fear birds feel, even towards the opposite sex.

COURTSHIP FEEDING *Like a parent with a nestling, a male robin brings food in his bill and passes it on to the female, so helping to strengthen the bond between them.*

THE FEEDING RITUAL *Courtship feeding between hawfinches is at times totally ritualised, so that although their bills meet, no food passes between them.*

PRESENTING A FISH *A gift of food precedes copulation in kingfishers; the male presents a fish head-first to the female, so that she can swallow it without choking on the fins and scales.*

SHOWING A NEST SITE *The male lapwing flies over his territory (top) to attract a female, and attempts to mate. Then he starts scraping out a hollow in the earth, as if showing the mate where they might build their nest.*

Once birds have become paired, the bond between them is strengthened by mutual preening, courtship feeding and showing a nest-site. It can be further strengthened by the joint defence of territory against rival birds.

Courtship feeding is more widespread than mutual preening. It is found chiefly in species in which the female carries out the duties of incubation alone. The form of the ritual varies, but generally the female behaves like a begging chick and the male feeds her as a parent would.

The courtship feeding of finches is usually extremely stylised in the early stages, with male and female merely touching or 'scissoring' bills in a kind of kiss. As the breeding cycle progresses, the feeding tends to become more

NEST QUIVERING *In the early stages of pair formation, male and female shags often perform 'nest-quivering', both holding an item of nest material and quivering it, first with necks stretched up and then with heads lowered to the level of the nest.*

CHASE AND DISPLAY
A series of vigorous chases (above) starts when a female wren entices a male. Later, the male attracts the female to one of his nests by singing loudly, his tail and wings quivering.

complete. In the bullfinch, for example, the male has often reached the stage of regurgitating food into his mate's bill by the time of nest-building, and this continues during incubation.

Displays designed to show the mate likely nest-sites are especially well developed in birds which nest on the ground or in holes in trees. Little ringed plovers have a scrape ceremony in which the male 'flags' his clearly patterned tail while turning in the hollow. The male great tit displays his black and white head pattern and the black and yellow of its breast conspicuously against the dark entrance of its nest cavity.

Many species have special displays which indicate their willingness to copulate and which stimulate the partner to respond. Mating

COURTING A MATE
The male redstart begins his courtship by chasing the intended mate through the tree-tops.

He shows off his red breast and black and white forehead, or, more usually, turns round and fans out his chestnut tail at the nest-hole.

He then crouches hissing before the female when ready for copulation.

NECK BITING
When a female gannet comes close to a nest site, the male responds by 'neck biting', seizing her neck in his bill. A female that is interested does not retreat but submits.

HERON GREETING
Once the female heron is accepted at the nest site, the male starts flying out and returning with twigs. This leads to mutual 'greeting displays' each time he alights.

displays are not always by male birds only: there are often soliciting displays by females. The female blackbird points her bill and tail up almost vertically, sleeking her feathers and running a little in front of the male, giving a soft, high-pitched call. A female shag sits in the nest with her tail cocked while bending down and moving nest material. The female gannet meekly submits to being bitten firmly on the back of the neck. Among herons, mating often follows the presentation of a stick by the male.

Most birds have no external reproductive organs, though in a few groups, such as ducks, the male has a penis. In the majority, ducts leading from the testes of the male and the ovaries of the female end in their respective

THREAT DISPLAY *In his advertising display, the male black grouse inflates his neck and chest, erects the red bare skin on his head, droops his partly open wings and fans his tail over his back, strutting about and fluttering up in the air, all the while uttering harsh calls and a strange, rhythmic bubbling song. There are occasional fights between males.*

COLOURFUL RUFFS *In the breeding season the male ruff develops a huge mane-like ruff round his head and neck, two long 'ear-tufts' and bare wattles on his face. No two males are identical, so individual recognition is easy. As the breeding season begins, a male's wattle and bill skin colours get brighter and bigger.*

cloaca openings. In copulation, the male stands on the female's back, the cloacae are brought together, and sperm passes from male to female. Mating often occurs several times a day over a period lasting from just before egg laying begins until the last egg is laid. Most bird species form monogamous pairs, at least for part of the breeding season, but in a few species, such as black grouse and ruff, males take no part in nesting, and meet females only at a communal display ground, called the lek, for mating. In most of these promiscuous species, there is intense competition between males for females. Males are usually larger and brighter and have evolved elaborate plumage characteristics matching their highly ritualised displays.

BLACKBIRD'S CUP NEST *After establishing a foundation by lodging material in a bush, hedge or tree, the female blackbird builds a strong, secure nest of grass, roots, moss and twigs plastered on the inside with mud and lined with fine grass. Blackbirds often use the same nest two or three times in a season, relining it each time.*

GOLDCREST'S HANGING NEST *Male and female goldcrests weave an intricate deep, cup-shaped nest of moss and spiders' webs, suspends it from a conifer branch and lines it with feathers. The pair may construct a second nest in which the female lays her eggs before the first brood have left their nest; in this case the male feeds the first family.*

SWALLOW'S BRACKET NEST *A nail on a barn wall can provide all the support a swallow needs for its snug cup nest. Both sexes share the building, catching small straws and grass stems in the air and picking up mud with which to work them into pellets. The nest takes shape as pellets, placed on top of one another, harden.*

Nests and their builders

A nest is a shelter in the battle for survival – a cradle in which eggs and helpless nestlings can be relatively safe from their enemies. The nest-building instinct is not found in all birds – cuckoos, for example, manage well enough without it. There are two main types of nest – simple nests made by birds whose chicks are able to quit the nest and run on the day of

hatching; and intricate nests of birds whose nestlings are born naked and helpless – and there are various stages in between. The simplest nest is, in fact, not a nest at all – the stone curlew, for instance, lays in a depression in the ground; the guillemot deposits its egg on a ledge. To protect their helpless young, hoopoes, woodpeckers, kingfishers and tits nest in holes.

NIGHTJAR'S NEST *Ground-nesting birds build simple nests, relying on camouflage for safety. The nightjar's nest is so simple, in fact, that it is a mere scrape in the ground.*

LAPWING'S NEST *The lapwing's nest is only one stage more complicated than the nightjar's – a rough lining of grass placed in a muddy hollow.*

GREAT CRESTED GREBE'S NEST
Birds which nest on water may need substantial nests, but the nest construction is still basically simple – as with the great crested grebe's floating platform of water-weeds, reeds and rushes, anchored to the adjacent vegetation. When a grebe leaves the nest, it usually covers its eggs with weed as a defence against predators, though there is not always time.

There is often rivalry for sites among hole-nesters, and the same cavity may be used in successive years or even in the same season by different species. Some birds such as the hobby use disused nests that others have built. Song thrushes build cosy cup nests. Magpies protect their cup with a canopy of twigs. Wrens, willow warblers, wood warblers and chiffchaffs build more intricate domes, but none can vie with the long-tailed tit's beautifully made 'bottle' of lichen-covered moss, with the entrance hole placed near the top. House sparrows, starlings and jackdaws often nest on man-made sites; many birds will use nest-boxes, and robins, among other species, may even rear their broods in abandoned motor vehicles.

THE FEET OF LAND BIRDS

WALKING *The ground-dwelling meadow pipit's hind claw is elongated to give the bird greater stability when walking.*

RUNNING *Partridges, which often run, have a shortened hind toe, reducing the area of foot touching the ground.*

PERCHING *The greenfinch's backward-pointing hind toe curls round beneath its perch to meet the other toes, holding the bird firmly in place.*

CLIMBING *Strong claws and two backward-facing toes enable the great spotted woodpecker to climb by gripping bark.*

CLINGING *The swift uses the claws on the four forward-facing toes of its tiny feet as hooks and can cling to almost vertical surfaces.*

HUNTING *The powerful talons of an eagle are used both for perching and for seizing and killing its prey.*

Feet – special adaptations

A bird walks on its toes, not on the entire area of its foot – what looks like a knee joint is in fact the bird's 'heel'. Most birds have four toes; three point forwards and one, the hallux, points back. But there are many variations; the feet of birds suit the kind of life they lead – where they live and even sometimes what they eat. Apart from walking, running, hopping and perching, birds'

feet have many other uses. The toes of the pheasant, for example, have strong claws for scratching to get at roots and worms; the male's feet are also equipped with 'spurs' for fighting. Bitterns and nightjars have a 'pectinated claw' – a notched third toe, acts as a preening comb.

The conditions underfoot beside water are varied, and the adaptations of waterside birds'

THE FEET OF WATERSIDE AND SWIMMING BIRDS

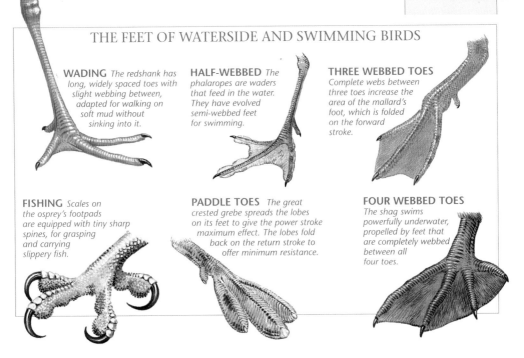

WADING *The redshank has long, widely spaced toes with slight webbing between, adapted for walking on soft mud without sinking into it.*

HALF-WEBBED *The phalaropes are waders that feed in the water. They have evolved semi-webbed feet for swimming.*

THREE WEBBED TOES *Complete webs between three toes increase the area of the mallard's foot, which is folded on the forward stroke.*

FISHING *Scales on the osprey's footpads are equipped with tiny sharp spines, for grasping and carrying slippery fish.*

PADDLE TOES *The great crested grebe spreads the lobes on its feet to give the power stroke maximum effect. The lobes fold back on the return stroke to offer minimum resistance.*

FOUR WEBBED TOES *The shag swims powerfully underwater, propelled by feet that are completely webbed between all four toes.*

feet reflect this. In one area the shore may be firm and dry, and in another soft and marshy. The feeding habits of waterside birds vary considerably, too. Redshanks wade into the shallows, looking for small water creatures; ospreys circle over the water, waiting to dive for fish; and gulls scavenge along the tide-line. Birds that swim have either webbed feet or paddle-shaped toes to move them through the water. To work efficiently, both types of feet must move as much water as possible on the power stroke, and as little as possible on the recovery stroke. The amount of water that can be pushed back by the spread foot on the power stroke is a rough indication of how important swimming is in the life of the species.

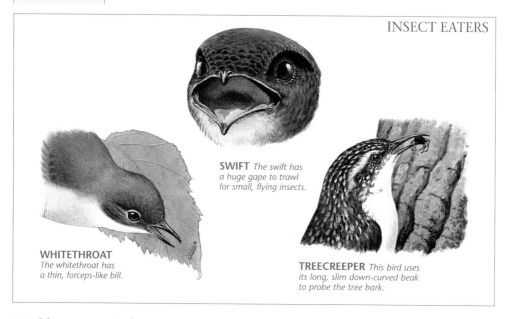

INSECT EATERS

SWIFT *The swift has a huge gape to trawl for small, flying insects.*

WHITETHROAT *The whitethroat has a thin, forceps-like bill.*

TREECREEPER *This bird uses its long, slim down-curved beak to probe the tree bark.*

Bills and feeding techniques

Though birds' bills vary greatly with feeding habits, even an unspecialised bill – like that of the song thrush – can be used to pick a minute gall-wasp from a leaf; to dig a 5cm hole to reach a beetle pupa; to tug an earthworm from the ground; to swing a snail shell against a stone; or to gulp down a ripe cherry. Gulls and crows, nature's scavengers, take a relatively wide range of both animal and vegetable foods with their all-purpose bills. Other birds are specialised feeders and depend on a fairly narrow selection of foods. This helps them to avoid competition within their preferred habitat. The kingfisher and the heron, for example, feed by seizing or spearing fish, and both have evolved dagger-shaped bills. Grey herons stalk through the

PRISING *An oystercatcher strikes into the shell of prey and levers it open with its powerful chisel bill.*

SWEEPING *The avocet feeds on insects caught as it sweeps its slim upturned bill from side to side in water or liquid mud.*

GRASPING *A red-breasted merganser grips slippery fish in its strong, serrated, hook-tipped bill.*

SEIZING AND SPEARING *The grey heron's long, dagger-like bill is well suited to grabbing or stabbing fish.*

SIFTING *Spoonbills sift insects from the shallows with their spatulate bills.*

shadows, seeking prey which they seize or stab with their long bills. Kingfishers catch their prey with a shallow dive from a perch, then batter the heads of the fish they catch on the perch – killing the fish and making it easier to swallow.

Ospreys and gannets hurtle down from the sky. Grebes and divers propel themselves underwater with their feet searching for food;

and auks (razorbills, guillemots and puffins) 'fly' underwater using their wings for propulsion. Owls and falcons use sheer speed to fly their prey down, delivering the killing blow with a bite at the base of the prey's skull.

Nuthatches and great spotted woodpeckers wedge nuts in cracks of trees before splitting open the shells. Herring gulls get at the

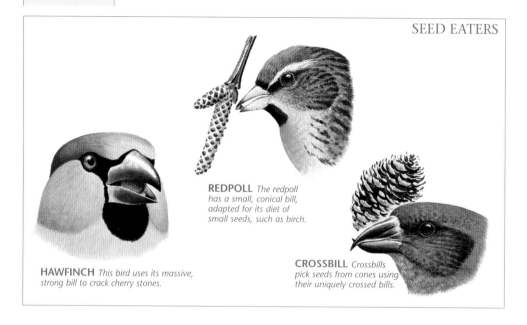

SEED EATERS

REDPOLL *The redpoll has a small, conical bill, adapted for its diet of small seeds, such as birch.*

HAWFINCH *This bird uses its massive, strong bill to crack cherry stones.*

CROSSBILL *Crossbills pick seeds from cones using their uniquely crossed bills.*

succulent flesh of mussels by dropping them from the air to shatter on the rocks below.

The rook, which eats many soil-dwelling insect larvae and earthworms, has a longer bill than that of its nearest relative, the carrion crow, which takes such food less often. Other soft-ground feeders – the snipe, woodcock, curlew, black-tailed godwit, dunlin and other waders which probe for food in soft mud, have long bills; and each species avoids competition with the others by probing at a different depth.

All the finches have the strong conical bills typical of seed eaters; but the bill of each species is slightly different from the rest. The most powerful, that of a hawfinch, can crack a cherry stone. At the other extreme, the far thinner

SHEARING *The wigeon uses its short, wide bill to crop grass and other plants like a goose.*

TEARING *A golden eagle's strong, deeply hooked bill is designed to tear flesh apart.*

PROBING *Woodcocks use their long, thin bills, which have very sensitive tips, to probe for worms in soft earth.*

HAMMERING *A green woodpecker chisels into bark for hidden insects with its powerful bill.*

billed goldfinch tweezers the seeds from teasels by probing for them.

Most birds drink when they have the opportunity, though some species survive on 'metabolic' water – water released in the digestion of food. Seabirds can, and do, drink sea water and get rid of the superfluous salt by the secretion of highly concentrated brine from

glands situated at the base of the beak. Crows bring water to their young by transporting it in the throat. All birds conserve water by producing a very highly concentrated urine – which is almost a paste of uric acid crystals. In very dry weather they reduce the time and effort spent singing and, with it, evaporation of moisture from the lungs.

PREENING *A male blackbird 'zips up' his wing feather barbs; his mate nibbles her undertail feathers.* Preening removes feather parasites – a vital operation; birds that are ill or have malformed or damaged bills, preventing adequate preening, often have an abnormally large number of parasites which eat away the feathers and affect general health.

DIRECT SCRATCHING *With wings closed, a lesser black-backed gull reaches a leg forward to scratch its head feathers.*

INDIRECT SCRATCHING *A chaffinch scratches its head by drooping a wing, then bringing its foot up over its shoulder. The majority of British songbirds and birds of some other groups, such as swifts, nightjars and kingfishers (but not woodpeckers) scratch indirectly.*

Plumage – keeping feathers clean

Feathers are not indestructible and their careful maintenance is vital to a bird's well-being.

PREENING This habit, shared by all birds, is the treatment of feathers by the bill. With body feathers fluffed up, a bird 'nibbles' individual feathers between the tips of its bill, working from the base of the quill outwards, with a series of precise pecking movements. The bird also draws feathers – particularly those of wings and tail – one at a time through its bill, with a single, quick pull of the head. This cleans the plumage, works in oil from the preen gland just above the tail, puts feathers back in place and repairs vanes and webs by 'zipping up' the tiny barbs.

SCRATCHING A bird cannot preen its own head so, it scratches with one foot while balancing on

BATHING *Fluffing up its body feathers, a song thrush hops into the water and first dips forward with head, breast and wing-joints in the water, at the same time shaking its bill violently from side to side and flicking its wings forward. Then it squats back, with tail and belly in the water, and flicks its wings upwards to send the water splashing and showering.*

OILING *A great crested grebe rubs its head on its preen gland (the 'parson's nose'), at the base of its tail, stimulating the gland to produce oil. Many long-necked water birds use their heads as an oily 'mop', spreading oil over the rest of the plumage, rubbing the head on the preen gland and then over the flanks and back.*

the other. A few, such as gannets and herons, have a pectinated claw – a special 'comb' on the inside edge of the third toe – used to scratch the head and neck. Some mated birds, including crows, bearded tits, martins and pigeons, preen one another's heads as part of courtship.

BATHING Apart from cleansing, the main object of bathing for many birds is to dampen the plumage so that preen oil may be spread over it more effectively. Land birds bathe in shallow water where they can stand safely – puddles, the edges of streams or ponds and birdbaths. Water birds spend more time over bathing because they are usually safe on open water. After bathing, birds shake their feathers and flap their wings to dry themselves. Cormorants and shags

POWDERING *A bittern rubs its head on its breast, gathering powder-down to clean eel slime off its feathers. It then combs itself, scratching off the powder and slime with its pectinated claw. It then oils and preens, perhaps repeating the whole process more than once.*

SUNNING *A blackbird spreads its wings and tail in the sunshine – possibly as an aid to keeping down the numbers of feather parasites. It may also be a cooling device, helping the bird to lose heat through exposing sparsely feathered areas to the air and breeze.*

DUSTING *House sparrows make scrapes in the ground, then work dust into their feathers. Other birds, including gamebirds, owls, hoopoes, certain hawks and nightjars, wrens and skylarks, also enjoy dust baths. The habit probably helps to combat feather parasites.*

perch on rocks and 'hang out' their wings to dry.

OILING After its bath, the bird oils its plumage, applying a secretion from its preen gland. Oiling waterproofs plumage and maintains its heat-insulating properties; it is particularly important to water birds and very small land birds.

SUNNING Birds sun themselves by lying out in the sun with tail and one or both wings spread.

It is thought that this may help to make parasites move about so the bird can pick them off more easily; and that the sun's ultra-violet light may convert the preen oil into vitamin A which can be ingested when the bird preens.

POWDERING Some birds, such as gamebirds, never voluntarily bathe in water; and others, including some pigeons, do not oil themselves.

DIRECT ANTING *The starling gathers a billful of ants and rubs them on its flight feathers, spreading formic acid and any other body fluids of the ants, together with its own saliva. Chaffinches and meadow pipits use a single ant at a time.*

INDIRECT ANTING *A jay allows worker ants to run all over its plumage, deliberately arousing them so that they aggressively squirt out their formic acid. The jay leans back on its tail, with wings spread out in front of it; the blackbird, song thrush and mistle thrush half squat among the ants with wings out; and the carrion crow and rook lie down, spread-eagled, to wallow among the ants.*

Instead they powder themselves using powder-down – specially modified body feathers, which grow continuously and disintegrate into a fine 'talc' of minute, dusty particles that permeate the plumage when the birds preen.

DUSTING Gamebirds, such as pheasants and grouse, dust themselves in dry, fine earth, grit or sand. They scrape hollows in the ground and work the dust up among the feathers, shaking it all out before preening.

ANTING In this bizarre habit, birds use formic-acid-producing worker ants. Some ornithologists believe that birds ant for the sensuous pleasure of having their skins stimulated by formic acid – but it has a practical purpose: formic acid is an insecticide strong enough to kill feather mites.

MERGING WITH FERNS *Foraging for weeds and insects on the woodland floor, the female pheasant is camouflaged from her natural enemies, such as foxes and stoats. Her dark upper plumage remains sombre even in bright light, and her intricate markings blend with the ferns and dead leaves among which she moves. Her paler underside reduces the effect of tell-tale shadow. When surprised, the bird runs for shelter and crouches down until the danger has passed.*

BEACH CAMOUFLAGE *The ringed plover, sitting on its nest on an open beach, has no cover to protect it from attack by predators such as foxes, or to shelter it from egg-thieving crows. For this bird, concealment is the only defence. Black markings on its face and breast break up the outline; and when the bird stands, its pale underparts eliminate shape-revealing shadow. It stays motionless when it senses danger.*

Camouflage – an effective defence

A natural disguise is frequently the best defence for birds that nest and feed individually or in small numbers, and many birds escape their enemies by being camouflaged in their natural habitat. In species such as the nightjar, both sexes have specially coloured or patterned plumage; in others only the more vulnerable sex is camouflaged. When the male takes no part in incubation – such as with the black grouse – it is usually the female that has so-called cryptic plumage. Ducks, which take sole charge of sitting on the eggs, are camouflaged all year round, but drakes acquire an inconspicuous plumage only when they are unable to fly because they have moulted their flight feathers. One of the simplest types of camouflage disrupts

MIMICKING LOGS *At dusk the nightjar is on the wing hunting for insects, which it catches in flight. But during the hours of daylight it is usually resting on the ground, in heathland or on the edge of a wood, often with little natural cover to hide it and its nest from enemies. However, the bird can remain inconspicuous even in these surroundings, camouflaged by plumage markings, which make it look like the fallen logs among which it often settles.*

HIDDEN IN THE REEDS *The bittern's plumage matches the reeds among which it lives. When alarmed, it stretches up to show the long, dark stripes on its neck, which are patterned like reeds, and holds its bill vertical. In this position it freezes motionless; or if there is a breeze it sways with the reeds.*

the normal effects of light and shade. The upper parts have dark plumage and the underside light – the opposite of what happens when light falls onto an object, creating a light upper surface and a dark shadow beneath. This is often seen in shore and estuary birds.

Other birds' plumage matches their usual background in tone, colour and pattern; this is especially striking where white winter plumage develops to match the snow. Special patterns on plumage – such as the face and breast markings of ringed plovers – help to break up a bird's outline so it merges with pebbles on the beach. Protective plumages, combined with a bird's ability to 'freeze' when danger is near, reduce the chances of being detected by predators.

FEIGNING INJURY *Foxes or hedgehogs looking for eggs or chicks can be distracted if they get too near to the nest of a little ringed plover. The parent bird will draw off the predator by running away from the nest, then squatting on the ground, flapping a wing awkwardly as though it were broken. The hunter, sensing an easy kill, follows, leaving eggs or young unharmed. Once it has lured the attacker away, the plover makes its escape.*

INTIMIDATING THE ENEMY *A young tawny owl will frighten off a squirrel or pine marten by fluffing up its plumage, spreading wide its wings and staring defiantly with large, shining eyes.*

Methods of defence

For flocking birds, sheer numbers provide protection against the hunter. Flocks of starlings and waders become compact in flight, making it difficult for birds of prey to pick on an isolated bird – and predators seldom fly at a bunched flock. Flocks also manoeuvre in tight formation, making the predator's task of catching a bird harder still. Some birds, such as Sandwich terns,

make use of the aggressiveness of such species as black-headed gulls. They form a colony within the colony, relying on the bolder birds to drive away crows or foxes. Flocks of starlings may 'mob' a predator by moving towards and round it. A few larger species, such as crows, will do the same singly or in pairs, swooping over a heron on the ground, calling loudly.

PROTECTING THE NEST *The avocet defends its nest on sandy flats or mud-flats against crows and black-headed gulls in search of eggs. When confronted at close quarters, it will resort to intimidation, rising up over the nest, cocking its tail, spreading its wings to show their striking black and white markings and calling out defiantly. Avocets have even been known to display like this to 'warn off' cows, horses and human intruders.*

MOBBING THE ATTACKER *A small group of lapwings nesting together will often choose attack as their best method of defence. When one spots a carrion crow flying overhead on the lookout for unattended nests to raid, it gives the 'mobbing' call. The lapwings set off in angry pursuit, calling loudly and flying around and at the predator. The commotion often alerts other birds, which join in and help repel the intruder.*

A perched sparrowhawk may be mobbed by small birds, especially tits, finches and thrushes. They fly towards it and away again, repeatedly giving loud 'scolding' calls and flicking it with wings and tails. When chased, individual birds will twist and turn in the air and dive for cover as soon as possible. Water birds dive underwater. Ducks scuttle along the surface, diving suddenly and emerging to move off in a new, unexpected direction. Waders will also dive to escape attacks from the air. Finally, blackbirds and other thrushes may sometimes escape from the very jaws of a predator by having a 'fright moult'. These birds have dense, loose plumage on their backs, and can struggle free, leaving the predator with only a mouthful of feathers.

BIRD-TABLE FARE *Most kitchen scraps are suitable food for birds. Meat bones and fat are always popular, as are stale biscuits, cake, bread and cheese. Thrushes are very partial to fruit, however rotten, and many birds will eat boiled rice, potatoes and suet.*

PUTTING OUT FOOD *A bird-table may greatly increase the number of birds visiting a garden. Tits like a fresh, halved coconut, and many birds will eat from a hanging basket.*

WATER IS VITAL *Even in the coldest weather birds continue to bathe, for it helps them to keep their feathers in prime condition; and they always need water to drink. So an all-year-round supply of water is just as important as a regular source of food.*

Attracting birds to your garden

Whether you live in the town or the country, you can easily turn your garden into a private bird sanctuary; and by making sure there is a plentiful supply of food and water, as well as places for birds to nest and roost, you can attract a variety of different species. If you plant the right flowers and shrubs, you can expect to see not only familiar garden birds such as robins, wrens, dunnocks, tits and sparrows, but also less common species such as flycatchers and goldcrests. In spring and autumn, migrant birds may use your garden as a resting place on their long and often dangerous journeys.

The more variety you can bring into the design of your garden, the better birds will like it. An open lawn will attract birds foraging for

WINTER BERRIES *Berry-bearing shrubs provide a rich source of food in winter when there is little else to eat. Blackbirds and other thrushes, finches, tits and starlings, feed on a variety of berries, including holly, rowan, barberry, hawthorn and cotoneaster. These plants may also attract migrants such as redwings, fieldfares and if you are lucky, waxwings.*

NESTING BOXES *Many of the trees and shrubs which provide food for birds also offer places to nest. Few gardens are wild enough to offer many natural nest sites, so compensate for this by putting up nest-boxes.*

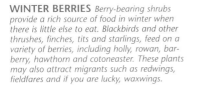

HYGIENE *Scrub bird-tables and clean feeders regularly – and clean out nest-boxes after the breeding season is over. Always use cleaners that will not be harmful to the birds. It is also a good idea to move them about to avoid a build-up of waste below, which can lead to bacterial infection.*

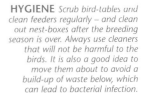

PROVIDING SEEDS *Allowing the right plants to grow – even weeds such as thistles – attracts birds that feed on their seeds and fruit, and on the insects they harbour.*

worms and grubs; a pool and a small rockery will provide a rich supply of food for insect-eating birds. If your garden is large enough, trees offer shelter for roosting and nesting birds, as well as food. Even dead trees are very attractive to birds, for insects breed in the rotting bark, and there are plenty of holes and crevices where birds can make their nests.

One way of making sure that the smaller birds have their share of food is by making bird-food cake, and pressing portions of it into crevices in trees and other places which large birds cannot easily reach. Make the cake by mixing together ingredients such as seed, crumbs, currants, rice and even a few meat scraps. Then cover the mixture with melted fat and allow it to set.

INDEX

Page numbers in bold type refer to the main entry.

Wild Britain: Birds is based on material in *Reader's Digest Guide to Britain's Wildlife, Plants & Flowers; Nature Lover's Library: Field Guide to the Birds of Britain* and *Book of British Birds* published by The Reader's Digest Association Limited, London.

First Edition Copyright © 2007
The Reader's Digest Association Limited,
11 Westferry Circus, Canary Wharf,
London E14 4HE
www.readersdigest.co.uk

Origination by Colour Systems Limited, London
Printed in China

We are committed to both the quality of our products and the service we provide to our customers. We value your comments, so please feel free to contact us on **08705 113366**, or via our website at **www.readersdigest.co.uk**

If you have any comments about the content of our books, email us at **gbeditorial@readersdigest.co.uk**

Book code 400-317 UP0000-1
ISBN 978 0 276 44212 4
Oracle code 250010895S.00.24

Acknowledgments

COVER f www.photodisc.com, Siede Preis; **b** Doug Steley/ Amaly Images. 2–3 Nature Picture Library©Nial Benvie
MAPS Jenny Doodge
ILLUSTRATIONS Stephen Adams 36-42; Norman Arlott 222-223, 234-265, 288-289, 312-315; Peter Barrett 208-209, 212-213, 277-286, 290-291; Trevor Boyer 88-91, 138-155, 172-197, 202-207; John Busby 6-17; John Francis 80-87, 128-137, 155, 164-169, 171; Robert Gillmor 94-97; Tim Hayward 69-79, 92-93, 122-127, 156-157, 163, 198-201; Mick Loates 344-345; Sean Milne 34-35; Robert Morton 31-33, 43-68, 158-162, 210-211, 214-220, 224-227, 303-311; D.W. Ovenden 228-233, 287; Ken Wood 98-121, 266-278, 292-302. Pages 316-342: Norman G. Barber, Kathleen Flack, Eric Fraser, Robert Gillmor, Hermann Heinzel, Rosemary Parslow, Philip North Taylor, Sydney Woods

EDITOR Lisa Thomas
ART EDITOR Austin Taylor
SUB-EDITOR Helen Spence
EDITORIAL CONSULTANT Jonathan Elphick
PROOFREADER Barry Gage
INDEXER Marie Lorimer

Reader's Digest General Books

EDITORIAL DIRECTOR Julian Browne
ART DIRECTOR Anne-Marie Bulat
MANAGING EDITOR Alastair Holmes
HEAD OF BOOK DEVELOPMENT Sarah Bloxham
PICTURE RESOURCE MANAGER
Sarah Stewart-Richardson
PRE-PRESS ACCOUNT MANAGER Penelope Grose
SENIOR PRODUCTION CONTROLLER
Deborah Trott
PRODUCT PRODUCTION MANAGER
Claudette Bramble